1994

# Researching health care

'At every level of clinical practice today, from the delivery of a baby to the care of an octogenarian, the use and evaluation of therapy is beset by controversy, dissension and doubt.'

Alvan Feinstein

Health care delivery is undergoing intense scrutiny and pressure for change: people have high expectations and want value for money. Research can do much to evaluate the effectiveness of health care, but deeply rooted disciplinary preconceptions – about what should be done and how, and about what is scientific – have hampered relevant research. *Researching Health Care* brings together an international team of health researchers from the fields of clinical care, clinical epidemiology, biostatistics, sociology, health economics and health policy.

The problem of research method is central to the evaluation of health care, and the contributors therefore focus on the three most important methods in use at present: experimental methods, surveys and other quantitative methods, and qualitative methods. The strengths and limitations of each method are spelled out, and the contributors show how some methods are more appropriate for evaluating the technical aspects of medicine, others for social and community issues. They argue that complex health care problems can be adequately addressed only by an equally broad range of research study designs, as well as by a willingness to co-operate with others in a multi-disciplinary approach.

These essays represent an important starting-point for anyone planning to do health research and will be immensely helpful in the proper evaluation of research grant proposals and the effective targeting of research projects. The book will be essential reading for all health care policy researchers and planners as well as for students and lecturers in social policy, social work and sociology.

**Jeanne Daly** is a Research Fellow in the Sociology Department at La Trobe University, Melbourne, where **Evan Willis** is a Senior Lecturer. They are both members of the Health Sociology Research Group, also at La Trobe. **Ian McDonald** is a practising cardiologist, Director of the Cardiac Investigation Unit, St Vincent's Hospital, Fitzroy, Melbourne, and member of the Australian Health Technology Advisory Committee.

# Researching health care
## Designs, dilemmas, disciplines

Edited by
Jeanne Daly, Ian McDonald and
Evan Willis

Tavistock/Routledge
London and New York

First published in 1992
by Routledge
11 New Fetter Lane, London EC4P 4EE

Simultaneously published in the USA and Canada
by Routledge
a division of Routledge, Chapman and Hall Inc.
29 West 35th Street, New York, NY 10001

Typeset in Times by LaserScript, Mitcham, Surrey
Printed in Great Britain by
Biddles Ltd, Guildford and King's Lynn

*British Library Cataloguing in Publication Data*
A catalogue record for this book is available from the British Library.

*Library of Congress Cataloging in Publication Data*

Researching health care: designs, dilemmas, disciplines/edited by
  Jeanne Daly, Ian McDonald, and Evan Willis.
  p. cm.
  Includes bibliographical references and index.
  1. Medical care – Research – Methodology – Congresses.
  2. Medical care – Research – Evaluation – Congresses. I. Daly, Jeanne.
  II. McDonald, Ian G. III. Willis, Evan
  [DNLM: 1. Research Design. W 20.5 R4348]
  RA407.A2R47 1992
  362.1'072 – dc20
  DNLM/DLC
  for Library of Congress                                      91-36911
                                                                    CIP

ISBN 0–415–07077–5
     0–415–07078–3 (pbk)

# Contents

# Illustrations

## FIGURES

## TABLES

# Contributors

**Jeanne Daly** is a Senior Research Fellow in the Department of Sociology, La Trobe University, Melbourne. Her academic background is in the physical, environmental and social sciences and her research interest is in the use of technology in clinical care.

**Robert Dingwall** is Professor of Social Studies at the University of Nottingham. His research interests lie in the field of research method, comparative sociology of professions and socio-legal aspects of health care.

**David Hailey** is Head of the Health Technology Unit at the Australian Institute of Health. He has chaired the National Health Technology Advisory Panel of the Commonwealth Department of Community Services and Health and has had responsibility for the regulation of pathology laboratories and pharmaceuticals.

**Jack Hirsh** is Director of the Hamilton and Civic Hospitals Research Center and Professor of Medicine at McMaster University, Hamilton, Ontario. His research interests include the study of thromboembolism and the application of clinical epidemiology to clinical practice.

**Michael Jelinek** is Deputy Director of the Cardiac Investigation Unit of St Vincent's Hospital, Melbourne. He is a practising cardiologist and a member of several scientific advisory committees of the National Heart Foundation of Australia. His research interests include ischaemic heart disease and clinical epidemiology.

**Ian McDonald** is Director of the Cardiac Investigation Unit of St Vincent's Hospital, Melbourne, Professorial Associate of the University of Melbourne and a member of the Australian Health Technology Advisory Committee. His research interests are in technology assessment and clinical epidemiology.

**John McKinlay** is Vice President and Director of the New England Research Institute in Boston. He is also Director of the Center for Health and Advanced Policy Studies, Professor of Sociology and Research Professor of Medicine at Boston University. His research interests include cardiovascular risk, the frail elderly and the political economy of health.

**Jake Najman** is Reader in Medical Sociology at the University of Queensland, St Lucia, where he holds a joint appointment in the Department of Anthropology and Sociology and the Department of Social and Preventive Medicine. His research interests include social epidemiology, research methods and policy-oriented research.

**David Newell** is Deputy Director of the National Health and Medical Research Council Clinical Trials Centre at the University of Sydney. He is Emeritus Professor in the Department of Medical Statistics at the University of Newcastle upon Tyne, where he was previously Director of the Health Care Research Unit.

**Jeff Richardson** is Professor of Economics in the Public Sector Management Institute at Monash University, Melbourne. He is Director of the National Centre for Health Program Evaluation and President of the Australian Economists' Group. His research interests are in the diffusion of medical technology, the geographic distribution of medical practitioners and cost-utility analysis.

**David Silverman** is Professor of Sociology at Goldsmiths' College, University of London. He has written on qualitative methods in sociology and his research interest in the field of health care is in doctor-patient communication, most recently as it occurs in HIV clinics.

**Evan Willis** is a Senior Lecturer and member of the Health Sociology Research Group in the Department of Sociology, La Trobe University, Melbourne. His research interests include the relations between health occupations, occupational health and safety and the social relations of medical technology.

**Christel Woodward** is Professor in the Department of Epidemiology and Biostatistics at McMaster University, Hamilton, Ontario. With a background in education and clinical psychology, her research interests include health-care research methods, program evaluation, survey research and medical epidemiology.

# Acknowledgements

Funding for the symposium at which the papers in this collection were delivered was provided by the Australian Institute of Health, the Research and Development Grants Advisory Committee of the Australian Department of Community Services and Health, and the Victorian Health Promotion Foundation. We are grateful to them for this support.

# Introduction
## The problem as we saw it

*Jeanne Daly and Ian McDonald*

Health care budgets are under pressure, and this has led to the search for strategies to ensure that the health care dollar is spent where it will be most effective. The problem is that we know too little about the effectiveness of health care – how well a procedure works in practice, whether it meets the criteria of humane care and whether the benefits are equitably distributed. A more fundamental problem is that we do not even know how to evaluate effectiveness. Thus, as Alvan Feinstein (1983a) has argued: 'At every level of clinical practice today, from the delivery of a baby to the care of an octogenarian, the use and evaluation of therapy is beset by controversy, dissension and doubt.' An important area of doubt concerns the most appropriate research method for the study of health care.

The debate is, in part, a technical one about the respective scientific merits of different approaches to research. Most health care research to date has placed heavy emphasis on randomised controlled studies and on quantitative data analysis. The debate, however, is also about what kinds of evidence researchers and health care workers find convincing. There is some doubt about how effective controlled studies are as a means of changing health care practice. There is even evidence that practitioners can keep a tenacious hold on procedures likely to do more harm than good – radical mastectomy and adenotonsillectomy are perhaps the best known examples. Even when an impeccable scientific trial has demonstrated a procedure to be ineffective except in a minority of patients – for example, electronic fetal monitoring – its use can flourish (Lumley, 1987). The tendency is then to deal with the lack of impact of studies by calling for 'stronger' methods of evaluation 'in order to enhance their reliability as guides to clinical action' (Institute of Medicine, 1985: 196). This ignores the possibility that change is resisted not because physicians are irrational but because they have professional or financial motives for not changing (see Waitzkin, 1979, for an analysis of the use of coronary care units). These, the social aspects of practice, are commonly ignored in technical studies in the incorrect belief that they will yield to rational persuasion based on evidence of effectiveness.

The need for methodological rigour is beyond dispute. But what is rigour? Our argument is that the problem of ineffective evaluation cannot be reduced simply to one of 'weak' methods; inherent in this search for the 'strong' method there is indeed an important issue of methodological bias. Adherence to methods because they are seen as 'strong' may lead to the wrong problems being addressed – because the right problems are not susceptible to analysis by the favoured method. On the other hand, the right problem may be addressed but by the wrong method – one which distorts the problem in order to make it conform to the requirements of a 'strong' method. Worst of all, important health care questions may be ignored because the problem appears too difficult to study within the constraints of a specific set of methodological assumptions. Evaluation which addresses the wrong problems or addresses the right problems badly must run the risk of failing to persuade.

The problem of research method is thus of central importance to the evaluation of health care, yet little has been done to resolve this controversy at the level of critical analysis. Indeed, a serious problem is that there is very seldom a common forum for debating issues of method, and practitioners from various disciplines have little contact and little opportunity for learning about other approaches to research. In order to initiate the debate on research method in health care a symposium of Australian and international researchers was brought together at the end of 1989. The aim was to debate the issue and to seek agreement on when and where specific methods of analysis are best applied. Our aim is to contribute to the development of methodological guidelines for the effective evaluation of health care.

## THE PROBLEM

### Disciplines and method

Even under ideal circumstances evaluating the effectiveness of health care is not easy, but it is made substantially more difficult when there is a lack of agreement concerning appropriate research methods. The problems which need to be addressed by researchers may be generated by clinical or community concerns, or by the policy needs of governments or funding bodies. There is a range of research study designs stretching from the controlled experiment, through surveys with quantitative data analysis, to qualitative analysis of data obtained by unstructured methods of data collection. What we need is to know where in the range a particular study is best located. The reason why such a versatile approach to research is seldom used is often because of the limitations set by rigid disciplinary boundaries.

The problems encountered in health care are the focus of research for a range of disciplines – medicine, epidemiology, economics and the social and behavioural sciences. Each discipline brings to the evaluation of health care its own traditional methods of study – experimental or observational in design with analysis by quantitative or qualitative means. Within each of these disciplines there may be a narrow commitment to one particular approach. Experimental design and quantitative methods of analysis comprise the dominant research method in health care. The medical literature reveals that most medical studies concern the description and mechanism of disease and controlled studies or randomised trials. There is almost no analysis of how well procedures are applied in clinical care, in the day-to-day management of patients. Indeed, questions have been raised about the limits of the randomised controlled trial in assessing the procedures of clinical practice (Feinstein, 1983b). It is in other fields – sociology, ecology, education and program evaluation – that there has been a recognition that excessive emphasis on quantitative data derived from an experimental design can place severe limitations on what is researched (Cronbach, 1982: 29).

Most researchers are trained in one or more methods of analysis which they naturally recognise as rigorous and scientific. Quite reasonably, they tend to perceive as questions for research only those which are amenable to analysis by the methods in which they are trained. But if rigid adherence to a particular method causes them to ignore important questions, this is scarcely scientific behaviour.

Experimentally based methods of analysis successfully measure the outcome of technical interventions like surgery in terms of one important outcome, usually a decrease in mortality, but there are endpoints which are recognised as being important in the everyday practice of medicine but which are more difficult to quantify – such as the reassurance of anxious patients by a negative test result (Dollery, 1978: 18). In cost–benefit analyses it is common to relegate to the 'intangibles' category what may be the most important aspect of treatment for patients – how they and their families subjectively experience it. Despite being difficult to quantify, such outcomes are too important to be ignored.

There are very few quantitative methods to date which address the problem that patient perceptions and expectations are highly individual, difficult to ascertain in a valid fashion and may even, for an individual patient, vary markedly over time (Schwartz and Griffin, 1986). Aware of the need to address such subtle and elusive questions in health care, researchers apply methods which distort the very phenomena they seek to understand. Thus the synthesis of patient data to generate a quality-of-life scale may have the advantage of simplicity but the disadvantage is that the scales may fail to capture in a valid fashion the complex and various ways in which patients experience health and illness and may thus lack credibility with practising clinicians. Even more difficult to account for are community concerns over health care and the well-articulated interests of consumer or pressure groups.

On the other hand, when community groups generate their own research their methods are seen as idiosyncratic and often cause concern to the more experimentally inclined practitioner: there is often an insufficient attention to methodological justification, and readers cannot distinguish between research which *is* or that which only *appears* to be impressionistic and biased. Even with research which explicitly justifies the methods used on the issue of bias, there is the problem of generalisability – knowing whether a study done on a small population also applies to other, larger groups. It should, however, be added that questions of bias and generalisability are at issue with any method of analysis, and it is a widespread problem that all health care research pays insufficient attention to the justification of a study in these terms. In quantitative data analysis, statistically generated guarantees of accuracy often give assurances which a closer examination of the data does not justify.

Any discipline may adhere in a blinkered fashion to a very narrow range of research methods. Contributing to misunderstanding about method, and to prejudice, is limited contact between disciplines. One discipline commonly fails to understand and hence cannot apply the methods of another. There may even be ignorance that different methods of analysis exist. The qualitative methods are particularly prone to this problem: recently a Swedish report on medical technology assessment relegated 'complex social issues concerning societal values' about technology to the sidelines because 'there are today no established criteria to rely on for identifying, or assessing, the social consequences related to developing and utilising medical technology.' (Brorsson and Wall, 1985: 115). Ignorance of the well-established methods of other disciplines will also mean ignorance of important and relevant findings from the research of that discipline, and multidisciplinary research may be particularly difficult to appreciate.

## Health policy, funding bodies and methods

Government authorities all over the world require randomised trials of effectiveness and safety before new drugs are used. Quantitative methods tend also to dominate the decision-making process when health insurance reimbursements are sought for other procedures, particularly expensive new technologies. Thus governments favour 'hard' evidence to justify exerting control over health care practice for financial or other reasons. The most powerfully persuasive tool in health care at present is taken to be cost-effectiveness analysis; this method has enjoyed an exponential rise in popularity. As a means of structuring a complex problem, cost-effectiveness analysis is useful but it requires effectiveness to be expressed as a number. This has exacerbated the pressure for quantitation in evaluating effectiveness.

Here again, disciplinary problems are evident. Clearly from the perspective of the economists, accustomed as they are to expressing economic phenomena as cost estimates, health care evaluators should be able to produce the same simple numerical value for the effectiveness of a health care procedure. From the perspective of the health care researcher, however, the problem is that numerical indices may inherently lack validity and may in fact distort the analysis of health care, thus providing a misleading basis for policy. Such differences cannot be resolved by ignoring the methodological problems involved.

Not surprisingly the problem of methodological priorities also influences the way in which granting committees and funding bodies set their priorities and assess applications for funding. A practical illustration is that applications are commonly required to be submitted in a form designed with hypothesis-testing in mind and suitable for experimentally based biomedical research or clinical trials. Such methods are not appropriate for research which aims to understand and interpret action for the purpose of generating theory. This affects matters as fundamental to health care as lay perceptions of illness and the ways in which doctors and patients interact. The design of such studies often requires unstructured interviewing and qualitative methods of data analysis, and the samples are necessarily small – requirements likely to provoke ill-informed questions about methodological rigour.

We would argue that when a given problem is studied, different approaches to research will ask different questions, collect different data and use different frames of analysis. Indeed, methods of analysis can be based on varying philosophies of knowledge, and the criteria for judging what counts as rigorous within one method cannot be transferred to another with fundamentally different epistemological assumptions. It follows that, unless funding bodies are familiar with the full range of study designs applicable to health care, prejudice against certain methods will lead to a systematic neglect of important issues. Funding bodies which lack the necessary criteria for judging research using non-experimental methods of research run the risk of ignoring much-needed analysis of social and community issues in health care, and the necessary eclectic and inter-disciplinary approach to research will be inhibited.

## Questions and methods

Effective health care research cannot be reduced to a question of using a 'strong' method. According to Hammersley and Atkinson (1983: x), methods 'must be selected according to purposes.' Health care issues should be identified from problems encountered in clinical practice or by community concerns. These, in turn, determine the questions to be re-searched. The logical and scientific approach is to choose that study design which is capable of providing the most comprehensive and valid answers in the face of inevitable constraints. The most obvious constraint is how much is already known about a particular area; that is, whether it has been sufficiently well researched to allow the generation of specific hypotheses or whether a more pressing concern is to generate a broad-based under-standing and interpretation of actions. Then there are ethical problems such as randomisation of treatment allocation to patients in clinical trials, and practical difficulties such as obtaining co-operation from practising physicians and working within the limitations of available funding.

In short, our belief is that the broad range of questions that arise from complex health care problems can only adequately be addressed by an equally broad range of research study designs. Those who undertake evalu-ation and research in health care must therefore cultivate methodological flexibility. The methods and theoretical approaches used by other disci-plines cannot be easily acquired, so health care research demands both an understanding of the capabilities and limitations of a wide range of study designs as well as a willingness to co-operate with others in a multi-disciplinary approach.

## THE METHODS

In reality, there are as many research designs as there are combinations of questions and constraining external circumstances. Furthermore, more than one approach may be used in a single study. However, for the purposes of this publication, we have selected the following study designs, commonly used in health care research – the experimental approach, observational methods with quantitative data analysis, and qualitative research methods. What follows is a brief exposition of the structure, applications, strengths and weaknesses of each.

**Experimental method**

The research method with most credibility within medicine is the random-ised controlled trial which is commonly used to assess the effectiveness of therapy. The therapy is administered to a selected population of patients on a random basis so that its effect on an intervention group and a control group can be compared. Careful definition of patient selection and controlled conditions of treatment aim to minimise bias and the influence of confounding variables. Statistical analysis is used to choose the required sample size and to place limits on the risk of chance error. Most commonly there is one specific outcome, specified in quantitative terms, and this is usually mortality.

The strength of the method rests on its claims to internal validity achieved by devising statistical control over systematic (bias) error and random (chance) error. However, the rigorous demands of trial designs can be difficult to achieve. The randomised trial is of undoubted value in assessing the effectiveness of a drug or any other therapeutic intervention. The clinical circumstances surrounding the administration of a drug are relatively simple so that the necessary controls can be instituted. In a clinical trial of a surgical intervention, confounding variables are more difficult to control and the results are correspondingly difficult to interpret. Clinical trials have found only a limited application in the clinical assess-ment of diagnostic tests which are used in a complex clinical milieu where diagnostic results interact with other clinical information in a manner which is not possible or desirable to control.

Even in a context where controls are technically feasible, it is not easy to exclude subtle biases of patient selection such as that of physicians selectively referring or withholding patients, say from a trial of coronary graft surgery. Problems with the definition of outcomes, such as death in cancer trials, may distort results. The most important problem is that which affects all experimental approaches: whether the internally valid results are also externally valid, that is the extent to which findings can be generalised beyond the experimental context to patient management in general.

Finally there are practical problems. If there is a worthwhile treatment effect, or if one begins to emerge in the course of a trial, referral to the trial may become unethical. Trials, especially the multicentre variety, are ex-pensive, difficult to mount and supervise, and the time taken to obtain results is a serious problem when confronting a rapidly moving target like a new medical technology.

With their high internal reliability, trials remain the classic method of research for applying hypothesis testing to the assessment of health care interventions. The method does not purport to study processes with numerous interacting variables and has limited applicability to the clinical context of patient management. The narrow scope of trials can be widened for use in the clinical context by using a variety of quasi-experimental designs. These use control groups without randomised allocation such as in the case control and cohort analytic studies popular in epidemiological research, as well as historical controls and time series. In the process of becoming more applicable to existing clinical conditions, some statistical control is sacrificed, but quasi-experiments provide an important experimental means of testing hypotheses about established clinical procedures where randomisation is ethically impossible.

## Observational methods with quantitative data analysis

These methods, characterised by surveys, express data in quantitative forms for the purposes of categorisation and comparison. The aims may be description, explanation, prediction or a combination of these and the data may be obtained by questionnaire or from existing records. It is the study protocol which sets out the precise definition of the range of concepts used, provides criteria for classifying each concept and develops appropriate scales for quantification. As a result, subjective but important aspects of clinical care such as the experience of breathlessness or pain may be defined, graded and made available for quantitative analysis. Data is collected from samples which can be randomly selected to ensure generalisability to a wider population. There may be a large number of variables, and statistical techniques are then applied to analyse the contribution of each variable to the outcome by controlling the others.

Observation with quantitative analysis obviously has wide application in the study of health care. Studies range in scale from simple fact-gathering exercises to international registers which can be used to obtain comparative data on the utilisation of health care and its effect on mortality. It is possible to follow trends over time. Despite the fact that surveys lack the control which the experimental approach has over internal validity, the broad range of contexts and questions to which they can reliably be applied makes surveys the most widely used research instrument in health care.

The obvious strengths of quantitative surveys are their versatility and practicality for generating new or utilising existing data for analysis. They provide an indispensable means of providing a structured overview of a process or system by generating both explanations or further hypotheses. Their major weakness is the lack of control necessary to distinguish covariation from cause and effect. A more subtle but potentially important problem is that the processes of categorisation and quantification necessarily impose the researcher's assumptions and concepts onto the field of study. The process of quantification may thus distort complex social phenomena which it purports to study. Surveys, like experiments, are by their nature stripped of the context of social interaction, and they have been accused of engendering a view of society as 'an aggregation of disparate individuals' who have no social interaction with each other (Bryman, 1988: 39).

## Qualitative research methods

Qualitative method is indispensable for the study of those aspects of health care which depend upon the social interactions between individuals or groups. Its contribution is made primarily in the study of two important aspects of health care: a) how patients and health care workers interpret their experience of health care and the significance which this has for the way in which the health care system functions and b) the cultural, historical and political circumstances which influence the nature of health care and its delivery.

If *quantitative* methods require a researcher to enter a setting and apply a pre-structured research instrument for the collection of data, *qualitative* sociological analysis requires researchers to approach their task within a broad but explicit theoretical framework about social structures and functions. In order to avoid the bias of basing an analysis on the assumptions and perspectives of one, usually a dominant, social group, researchers are required to immerse themselves in the social setting being researched, to listen and ask questions until they understand how each social group makes sense of its experience. A wide range of unstructured material may serve as data – for example, tape-recorded conversations, observations, current and historical records and other communications.

There are theoretical rules for the rigorous analysis of unstructured data. These may vary in practice from developing explicit codes for categorising interview transcripts (which may be tested statistically for interobserver variability) to using data directly to generate explanatory models which will account for the observed behaviour. Changes in behaviour over time can also be the focus of analysis. Thus social research may be unique in being able to analyse historical variations in the definition of disease without any preconceived notion of one particular version being more 'correct' than another. In this way we can analyse the manner in which a specific social context influences what is seen as disease.

As each social setting is unique, the researcher must respond to these differences, and the research method essentially emerges with the data. Yet the distinguishing mark of a good qualitative analysis is that it accounts successfully for the way in which individuals interact with their social context. The ultimate criterion of accuracy is the ability of the theory to fit existing knowledge in a coherent manner and to explain and predict phenomena in a convincing fashion – the ultimate test of any scientific theory. While this provides the basis for judging both the bias and the generalisability of the study, problems remain. Because of the extensive nature of the data collected, most qualitative studies are based on small samples. This makes it difficult to generalise the results of a single study and apply them to larger groups. With large groups the survey can provide a more trustworthy analysis. Qualitative methods are not generally comparable with experimental methods when what is required is the testing of rival hypotheses.

Since a qualitative method is specific to its social setting it is a difficult method to reduce to a set of explicit instructions. In this way, learning to do qualitative analysis has parallels with learning the 'art' of medicine. The variety of theoretical approaches within sociology, each of which can provide the basis for a qualitative study, can be very confusing to practitioners trained in the more unified approach of the natural sciences and may, indeed, yield different answers.

## OBJECTIVES

The aims of this collection are to focus attention on the problem of choice of research study design and to clarify what researchers see as the basic assumptions on which their research is based and where their methods of research are most effectively applied to the problems of health care. Difficulties and differences of interpretation related to institutional requirements, training or even professional ideology will not be easily resolved. We propose to initiate the necessary dialogue among disciplines. To achieve consensus would be a vain hope, so the emphasis will be on debate and on a search for common ground.

Section 2 starts with the problem of evaluating health care from the perspective of the policy maker, set out by David Hailey from the Australian Institute of Health. Next we have the perspective of the health care researcher to whom the policy maker has increasingly turned for policy advice, the health economist; Jeff Richardson from the Public Section Management Institute of Monash University, Melbourne, assesses the contribution of cost–utility analysis as a means of evaluating health care.

Section 3 deals with the randomised controlled trial as epitomising the experimental approach. David Newell, from the Clinical Trials Centre of the Australian National Health and Medical Research Council, sets out what he sees as the role of trials in research. Jack Hirsh from the Hamilton

Civic Hospitals Research Center of McMaster University, Canada, presents the approach of the researcher addressing clinical problems using trial designs; and Michael Jelinek, a cardiologist in Melbourne, addresses the problem of being a user of information from trials in the course of clinical practice.

Section 4 deals with observational methods with quantitative data analysis. Chris Woodward, from the Department of Clinical Epidemiology and Biostatistics, McMaster University, Canada, shows how quasi-experiments and non-experimental quantitative designs research extend into areas where the randomised controlled trial cannot be used. John McKinlay from Boston University and the New England Research Institute applies the survey to the analysis of older people. Jake Najman from the Department of Anthropology and Sociology assesses the applicability of the survey to a study of pregnancy.

Section 5 turns to qualitative research method with Robert Dingwall from the Department of Social Work, University of Nottingham, giving a review of what qualitative methods achieve. David Silverman from the Department of Sociology, University of London, gives an account of applying qualitative methods to the study of cardiological practice and of AIDS. Lastly, the editors, from the University of Melbourne and La Trobe University, Melbourne, present a case study of cardiological practice.

## REFERENCES

Brorsson, B. and Wall, S., 1985, *Assessment of Medical Technology: problems and methods*, Stockholm's Swedish Medical Research Council.

Bryman, A., 1988, *Quantity and Quality in Social Research*, London: Unwin Hyman.

Cronbach, L.J., 1982, *Designing Evaluations of Educational and Social Programs*, San Francisco: Jossey-Bass Publishers.

Dollery, C., 1978, *The End of an Age of Optimism: medical science in retrospect and prospect*, London: Nuffield Provincial Hospitals Trust.

Feinstein, A.R., 1983a, 'An additional basic science for clinical medicine: I. The constraining fundamental paradigms', *Annals of Internal Medicine*, 99, 3: 393–7.

—— 1983b, 'An additional basic science for clinical medicine: II. The limitations of randomized trials', *Annals of Internal Medicine*, 99, 4: 544–50.

Hammersley, M. and Atkinson, P., 1983, *Ethnography: principles in practice*, London: Tavistock Publications.

Institute of Medicine, 1985, *Assessing Medical Technologies*, Washington, DC: National Academy Press.

Lumley, J., 1987, 'Assessing technology in a teaching hospital: three case studies', in Daly, J., Green, K., and Willis, E. (eds), *Technologies in Health Care: Policies and Politics*, Canberra: Australian Institute of Health.

# Part I
# Issues of policy

# 1 The perspective of the policy maker on health care research and evaluation

*David Hailey*

This contribution is given from the perspective of the Australian Institute of Health, an agency which informs the policy process rather than formulating policy itself. Probably the best customers for the various evaluation and statistical development activities at the Institute are policy areas in government. Policy areas outside health authorities are also important but government agencies tend to dominate consideration because of their closeness to decisions that will eventually affect the funding of health care programs.

Although most of this publication is concerned with the details of evaluation methodology, it is worth setting part of the scene by commenting on the nature of the policy process and the climate in which those responsible for formulating policy have to operate. After all, much of the purpose for attempting the difficult and costly process of health care evaluation is to influence the decisions taken by governments and others. To succeed in this dubious task it is as well to have some appreciation of the nature of the target.

## CHARACTERISTICS OF POLICY AREAS

Pressing concerns for the policy makers in health authorities include the immediate directions of the Minister and the wishes of the government of the day, limited budgets for an apparently ever-expanding set of responsibilities, the relationship to coordinating departments and the short time scale in which decisions often have to be taken and results judged. Policy areas will often be under pressure to come up with something definite relatively quickly.

Other realities are that the policy maker will have to take on board a very broad perspective of the requirements in the health portfolio (considerably beyond the range envisaged by the typical researcher), and will need to respond to pressures, not only from the political arena, but also from professional groups. Typically, providers will be seeking access to government funds while health authorities will be defending their budgets.

Resulting action after a policy decision is taken may be difficult to reverse or adjust – for example, alteration to levels of reimbursement may be cumbersome to achieve. Another characteristic seems to be a relatively rapid turnover of policy staff, perhaps associated with an increasing trend towards use of generalists. There may be capacity only for limited review and analysis and while control of health care programs may be significant there are limitations as to what can be achieved by a health authority. These features contribute to the caution shown in some policy making areas.

In recent years cost containment has been a dominant theme, often at the expense of any major consideration of benefit from provision of health care programs. Frequently the constraints on the policy maker are such that a new initiative may be acceptable only if some alternative program can be reduced or given up. While policy makers may need to respond quickly they may also, in the interests of budgets or other government commitments, need to delay introduction of new health programs. There can be an interesting tension between the need for immediate advice and a bureaucratic preference for delay.

The policy maker will need to consider if the new health initiative will replace old methods or supplement them, or if it will have a significant effect on infrastructure. If so, will it be the responsibility of the area serviced by the health authority or can it be passed over to another level of government or to health insurance funds? In Australia, the split in responsibilities between Commonwealth and states adds to the complexity.

## EVALUATION AND THE POLICY PROCESS

Evaluation may often be seen by the policy maker as something of a wild card. Potentially, evaluation can help by providing data that can contribute to better-informed decision-making. Difficulties are that the evaluation data may not be easily assimilated into policy decisions, and in some cases may be regarded as embarrassing if they point to a need for significant change.

Evaluation is only one input to the policy making process. There are dangers for those who assess health care if it is not appreciated that the most elegant and detailed analysis may have no impact on the policy process and any subsequent action by government if the timing is wrong, the results are not presented in a way that is intelligible to policy makers or the recommendations are unrealistic in political terms.

The recent experience in Australia of introduction of Magnetic Resonance Imaging (MRI) services provides an illustration. Future policy on this expensive technology will be informed by the results of the

Australian assessment program and by relevant data from overseas, but other impacts on the policy process will include pressures from coordinating departments, states, professional bodies, consumer organisations, manufacturing industry and various vested interest groups.

At present we are dealing with perhaps the fourth generation of persons in the relevant policy area since the MRI program started. Such turnover does not help in establishing some sort of understanding of the methods, strengths and constraints of evaluation.

I have noted elsewhere (Hailey, 1985) that in a climate where governments want results of assessments quickly, perhaps within 12 months and in appropriately brief form, it is difficult to encourage an appreciation of the need for detailed evaluation. The 'quick and nasty' approach can easily become the norm and carry greater weight with the policy maker than more detailed studies. Excellent proposals for evaluations will not necessarily attract support, and clinical studies of several years' duration do not sit easily with the imperatives implicit in the policy making process.

## SOME ATTITUDES TO EVALUATION

Comments made at the recent evaluation meeting organised by the Public Health Association (PHA) and the National Health and Medical Research Council (NHMRC) (PHA, 1989) provide some interesting insights into the perspectives of policy makers, though some of the views expressed may not be very comforting for researchers or evaluators.

The point was made that policy making in the health area has a relationship to the political process, which will include party politics. It is also closely related to power plays within the bureaucracy or involving it. It was suggested that one view of evaluation is that it helps the health authority to push away the problem – this is the idea of deferring the evil day when hard decisions might need to be made about support of a particular health care program. NHMRC was not seen as very relevant to the short term needs of the Commonwealth Department of Community Services and Health.

Consultants were seen as useful, as being able to generate quick opinions which departmental officers could choose to use or not, as required – with no one else involved. (A counter view expressed was that often too little briefing and definition of tasks were provided to consultants and that insufficient funds were made available to them.) Perhaps more worrying, lack of control of evaluators was seen as a concern.

With these sort of attitudes, it may be difficult for researchers to judge the success of their work in terms of the health authority's view. From the policy maker's perspective, success through evaluation was seen in terms of providing new information, informing the policy process (including synthesis of available data), confirming the position previously adopted, and perhaps to bury a particular topic so that it could be filed and forgotten. It is very easy for government to file and forget things, and the view that the 'government knows' if the material is on file somewhere is not particularly helpful. The fact that the health authorities hold data does not mean that such information is necessarily relevant to the current decision-making process.

It was emphasised again at the PHA meeting that although research and evaluation can give useful input, policy formulation is a much broader process including, for example, relationships between the Commonwealth and state governments. I believe that, while this is true, at times there may be a tendency for policy areas to shelter behind this rationale to an unreasonable extent.

## NEED FOR COMMUNICATION AND MUTUAL EDUCATION

Overall there seems to be a communication problem – a lack of contact between the policy areas and evaluators and, in turn, sometimes between the evaluation areas and professional groups. The policy area in a health authority to some extent has to be regarded by the evaluator as a 'black box', given the various additional inputs to the policy process both from within and outside departments. The concern of evaluators must be that the 'black box' does not develop into a black hole with data from research going in, but no relevant feedback being provided.

At the PHA meeting, Professor Gavin Mooney mentioned some of the barriers to evaluation influencing choice, if such choice exists. These include the management decision environment touched on already, the aloofness of professionals – Mooney talked in terms of the medical profession, but aloofness and reluctance to communicate with other disciplines are not peculiar to that group – the fact that health care is a highly political football, a suspicion of economists (and other evaluators) and a lack of advocacy.

The dilemma between desire for rapid input and the realities of lengthy evaluation periods emerges in all areas of health care, but is perhaps particularly apparent with the current interest in preventative measures and health promotion activities. Often the evaluation problems in these areas will be related to the need for long term protocols, countered by the wish of policy makers and governments to see a return on expenditure.

As noted by Penny Hawe, there are a series of problems in evaluating program effectiveness, including premature evaluation – looking for program effects before the program is functioning properly – evaluation without sufficient resources and results being ignored (Hawe, 1989). She also points out that process evaluation, impact evaluation and outcome evaluation have to be done in sequence to make sense. I see this providing a problem. There may be impatience on the part of policy areas with the process side of evaluation – that is, the necessary assurance that the program is working correctly before seeking measures of impact and outcome.

The needs of policy areas may include clear, realistic recommendations, a description of a health program from more than one aspect (considering perspectives other than those of its proponents) and overall appraisal of costs and benefits. There is still a problem for policy areas in considering benefits from health care programs. First, benefits are less easy to quantify than costs; second, they may have less impact on immediate policy pressures; and third, they may not be reflected in the budgets of those that pay for the programs. Finally, they may take a long time to emerge. There is also the familiar problem of the moving target, especially with some of the recent technologies and uncertainties regarding measurement of cost utilities.

Is all this a counsel for despair? I do not think so. There seems to me to be far greater acceptance of the need for evaluation of health care than was the case a few years ago. Some additional resources for evaluation are starting to emerge from governments. There is some appreciation that the assessment process can help and may be necessary for effective operation of health care programs.

Some of the more negative views of evaluation that seem common in policy areas may in the longer term be self-defeating, running the risk of leading to inefficient or unworkable health care programs. It seems to me that evaluation has to make data and analysis explicit, being itself open to challenge and subject to change.

I would see a need for evaluators to continue their efforts to communicate with policy areas, to describe health care programs clearly so that they are comprehensible to the policy advisers, and to provide analysis in intelligible terms on a short enough time scale. There is a major need for methods that are quick enough to inform the decision-making process adequately, in addition to longer term research.

In turn, policy areas need to develop approaches to be able to take on board results of longer term studies. What we need is evaluation which is better able to deal with the concerns and realities of the policy process and establish the essential place of assessment in consideration of health care.

## REFERENCES

Hailey, D.M., 1985, 'Health care technology assessment', in National Health and Medical Research Council (NHMRC), *Resources for Health Care Evaluation*, Canberra: NHMRC, 112–28.

Hawe, P., 1989, 'The last thing you should look at is cost effectiveness', in PHA, *National Health Care Evaluation Workshop*, Canberra: PHA.

Public Health Association of Australia (PHA), 1989, *National Health Care Evaluation Workshop*, Canberra: PHA.

# 2 Cost-utility analyses in health care
## Present status and future issues

*Jeff Richardson*

## INTRODUCTION

Most goods and services are evaluated by the market and decisions about the desirability and level of production are based upon demand and the cost of production. As a result, 'micro-economic' analysis has been primarily concerned with the analysis of markets: how they operate, when they fail and the consequences of various types of intervention. Explicit project evaluation was a late arrival in economics. In its modern form it dates back to 1936 when a US law directed the army to investigate the costs and benefits of river and harbour projects for which there was no market. It took ten years for cost–benefit analysis to evolve into its present form. By the 1950s it was recognised that benefits could not always be measured in dollars. Once again it was the US military that took the initiative. With the development of cost-effectiveness analysis, projects could be ranked using the criterion of cost per unit of effectiveness. For the military, projects would be preferred which had, for example, a lower cost per death inflicted (on the enemy!) or, in 'macro' analysis, cost per mega death. Similar problems of evaluation arise in the health sector, and the techniques developed by the military have even adopted – with, of course, some modification to the unit of effectiveness.

Four types of economic evaluation can be distinguished, the defining characteristic in each case being the way in which output is measured (see Table 1). With cost–benefit analysis (CBA), benefits are converted into dollars and directly compared with costs. Subject to budgetary and distributional considerations an unambiguous decision may be made. Benefits do or do not exceed costs and, consequently, the project should or should not proceed. The other three techniques listed in Table 1 do not have this important property. Rather they are only capable of ranking projects in order of their desirability.

When cost–benefit analysis was applied to the health sector, the value of

*Table 1* Alternative economic analyses for health and health care evaluation

| Type of analysis | Benefits included | Defining characteristics |
|---|---|---|
| 1 Cost benefit | only benefits which can be valued in $ are included often excludes 'intangibles' | benefits measured in dollars only one project needs to be considered |
| 2 Cost minimisation | relevant outcomes identical | more than one project: projects are ranked no assessment of 'value' of outcome |
| 3 Cost-effectiveness analysis | only one 'dimension' of outcome is relevant e.g. life years; cases detected | as for Cost minimisation different 'levels' of outcome are possible |
| 4 Cost utility | outcome is multidimensional: quality of life is quantitatively important | quality of life is measured life years are weighted to obtain 'Quality Adjusted Life Years' projects are ranked |

*Source*: Richardson and Hall, forthcoming

life was measured either as the value of future earnings (the 'human capital approach') or by the willingness to pay, as revealed through court awards or, more commonly, by willingness to pay for an incremental decrease in the probability of death.

Because of the obvious shortcomings of both of these approaches, most of the recent studies involving human life have used cost–effectiveness analysis (CEA). With this, projects are ranked by comparing cost per unit of output, where this is determined by the nature of the projects. In health studies, output has sometimes been measured by the number of morbid days or episodes of illness. On occasions, an intermediate measure has been used such as the number of cases of a disease detected by a diagnostic test. More commonly, however, output has been equated with the number of life years saved. Thus a redistribution of funds to projects with a low cost per life year will increase the total number of life years that may be saved.[1]

The major weakness of CEA is that it treats all years of life equally. It is now widely accepted that life years must be treated as having different values when the quality of life differs. The alternatives being analysed may have different side effects and a longer life may be traded off against comfort and functional ability. Both CBA and CEA refer to these quality of life factors as 'intangibles', to be noted but not quantified. With the development of cost–utility analysis (CUA) in the last twenty years, techniques have evolved which permit the quantification of these intangibles and their inclusion in the analysis by the calculation and comparison of costs per Quality Adjusted Life Year (QALY).

While there is little doubt that it represents a major advance in economic evaluation, there are still major practical problems with the application of CUA and a surprisingly large number of unresolved and in some cases almost unaddressed conceptual issues. In this chapter, following a description of the major measurement techniques, there is a review of the chief methodological issues in CUA. The most fundamental, yet most neglected, methodological issue is the question of what precisely is measured or should be measured. This issue is described next. Finally, it is concluded that, despite a formidable list of developmental issues which need to be resolved, there are very compelling reasons why CUA should be used as an input into decision-making even in its present, imperfect state.

## UTILITY MEASUREMENT[2]

It has been recognised for a long time that evaluation studies should include the measurement of health outcome, and so a very large number of health status measures have been developed.[3] However, the usefulness of these instruments has been variable. Many have had poor if any evidence of validity or reliability and the purpose for which they were developed has varied. While many of the instruments may have contributed in a general sense to the 'evaluation of health outcome', they have often been unsuited to the specific question addressed in economic evaluation, namely, whether or not they indicate a treatment which should be chosen in preference to some other treatment for the same or for some other disease.

The latter question is explicitly addressed by cost–utility analysis. Projects or options are ordered according to the cost per QALY attributable to the project. All else equal, the most desirable options are taken to be those which result in the cheapest QALY. That is, QALYs are the criterion of value in the sense that more are better and, all else equal, projects with more QALYs should be preferred. Despite the recognition of numerous practical problems there appears to be a fairly widespread acceptance of the steps involved in the calculation of QALYs. They are estimated as expected life years times an index of 'utility', where this is measured on a 0–1 scale and is taken as quantifying that aspect of the quality of life upon which decisions should be made.[4]

Five techniques have been used to measure utility directly. These involve the use of category rating or a Rating Scale (RS), the Standard Gamble (SG), the Time Trade Off (TTO), the Equivalence Technique (ET) and the ratio scale or Magnitude Estimation (ME). (A detailed description of each of these is given in the Appendix to this paper.[5]) Each technique involves the presentation of a health state description to interviewees and the eliciting of their preferences for this state relative to some reference states, usually full health and death. The utility revealed by these techniques is taken as having an interval property. Thus, for example, the difference between utility values of 0.2 and 0.4 is treated as being quantitatively equivalent to the difference between 0.6 and 0.8. The interval property is required for the valid summation of utilities.

A second, indirect, approach to measurement requires the prior establishment of a 'multi-attribute' utility scale which may be applied to any health state. Three commonly used scales have been devised by Rosser and Kind (1978), Torrance (1982), Kaplan and Bush (1982) and Kaplan *et al.* (1976). With each of these, a health state is broken down into different 'attributes' or 'dimensions' such as 'physical functioning', 'socio-emotional function' and 'health problem'. Each attribute has a separate scale with scores initially determined from interviews using one of the techniques listed above. A particular health state may then be measured and scored on each scale and the scores combined with a predetermined formula.

Using both the multi-attribute and the holistic approach to measurement a large number of health states have been assessed and 'league tables' published showing the utility of different states (see Table 2). It is widely accepted that 'CUA can no longer be considered as being in the experimental stage but is now at the point where it merits serious consideration by health care decision makers' (Drummond *et al.*, 1987). At least one regional authority in the UK has explicitly employed it as an aid to decision-making (Gudex, 1986).

## Problems with utility measurement

While not necessarily disagreeing with the conclusion above, I should point out that there are still a number of very fundamental conceptual and practical issues which are unresolved. Perhaps the most surprising feature of the literature is the limited attention that has been given to some of the theoretical questions and the minuscule amount of empirical research done to resolve or clarify practical difficulties. Table 3 lists the chief issues noted in the literature and classifies them (sometimes a little arbitrarily) as dealing with theory, measurement or interview techniques.

*Table 2* Some utilities for health states

| Health States | Utility |
|---|---|
| Healthy (reference state) | 1.00 |
| Life with menopausal symptoms (judgement) | 0.99 |
| Side effects of hypertension treatment (judgement) | 0.95–0.99 |
| Mild angina (judgement) | 0.90 |
| Kidney transplant (TTO, Hamilton, patients with transplants) | 0.84 |
| Moderate angina (judgement) | 0.70 |
| Some physical and role limitation with occasional pain (TTO) | 0.67 |
| Hospital dialysis (TTO, Hamilton, dialysis patients) | 0.59 |
| Hospital dialysis (TTO, St John's, dialysis patients) | 0.57 |
| Hospital dialysis (TTO, general public) | 0.56 |
| Severe angina (judgement) | 0.50 |
| Anxious/depressed and lonely much of the time (TTO) | 0.45 |
| Being blind or deaf or dumb (TTO) | 0.39 |
| Hospital confinement (TTO) | 0.33 |
| Mechanical aids to walk and learning disabled (TTO) | 0.31 |
| Dead (reference state) | 0.00 |
| Quadriplegic, blind and depressed (TTO) | <0.00 |
| Confined to bed with severe pain (ratio) | <0.00 |
| Unconscious (ratio) | <0.00 |

*Source*: Torrance, 1987

*Table 3* Issues in the measurement of utility and CUA

| Issue | Authors | Comments |
|---|---|---|
| **A  Theoretical basis** | | |
| 1 Is the theoretical basis of the SG acceptable: is it a 'gold standard'? | Torrance and Feeny, 1989 Schoemaker, 1982 Hershey, *et al.*, 1982 | See comments in this paper. The Von Neuman-Morgenstern axioms are often contradicted. The axioms have been defended as being normative, not positive. |

*156, 079*

*Table 3* (cont'd)

| Issue | Authors | Comments |
|---|---|---|
| 2 Does SG produce a consistent result? | Hershey and Schoemaker, 1985<br>Llewellyn-Thomas, *et al.*, 1984 | Achieving equivalence in the SG by varying probabilities gives a different result from varying quantities. |
| 3 What is the theoretical basis of the TTO technique? | Torrance, 1986<br>Mehrez and Gafni, 1989 | Initially proposed as an approximation to the SG revealing 'value' not 'utility'. Mehrez and Gafni argue that the TTO identifies points on an indifference curve between quality and quantity. |
| 4 What is the relationship between the RS, TTO and SG? | Torrance, 1976 | Cites psychometric research to suggest a power function relation between them. |
| 5 Should only the patient's utility be considered? | Loomes and McKenzie, 1989<br>Carr-Hill, 1989 | Loomes and Mckenzie argue that a wider group, namely those chiefly affected, should be included. |
| 6 Should health costs of a normal life be considered as one of the costs of saving a life? | Weinstein and Stason, 1977 | In principle, yes; in practice this may not make a great difference. |
| 7 How should medical risk and uncertainty be included? | Gafni and Torrance, 1984<br>Mehrez and Gafni, 1989<br>Hellinger, 1989 | Mehrez and Gafni argue that this necessitates the use of the SG.<br>Gafni and Torrance argue risk is the sum of gambling, quantity and time preference effects. Hellinger's empirical results suggest no pure-risk behaviour but context-specific behaviour. |

*Table 3* (cont'd)

| Issue | Authors | Comments |
|---|---|---|
| 8 Is total cost/QALY the appropriate ratio for choice? | Linard, forthcoming<br>Birch and Donaldson, 1987 | Numerator should have budgetary costs only if budgets are limited. Indirect benefits cannot therefore be in the denominator: they cannot be combined with QALYs in the denominator. Decisions should refer to marginal changes where possible. |
| 9 Which indirect (production) benefits should be included? | Richardson, 1991 | The value of total future production gains is often subtracted from direct program costs. This involves double counting of benefits. |
| 10 Is it possible to aggregate utility across individuals? | Torrance and Feeny, 1989<br>Torrance, 1986<br>Carr-Hill, 1989 | Generally agreed this must be and is done in practice. Limited enquiry into the assumptions which permit this and little discussion of the relation between assumptions and underlying value systems. |
| 11 How should QALYs be distributed? | Richardson, 1991<br>Loomes and McKenzie, 1989<br>Wright, 1986 | QALYs may be valued differently at different ages or subject to some other distributional criteria. |
| 12 Which discount rate should be applied for future values? | Torrance and Feeny, 1989<br>Richardson, *et al.*, 1990<br>Evans, forthcoming<br>Lipscomb, 1989 | Dispute between the use of the Social Opportunity Cost and the Social Rate of Time Preference. |

*Table 3* (cont'd)

| Issue | Authors | Comments |
|---|---|---|
| **B** *Accuracy of measurement* | | |
| 13 Are utility measures reliable? | Torrance, 1976, 1982<br>Churchill, *et al.*, 1984<br>Buxton, *et al.*, 1986 | Internal, and test, re-test reliability are 'satisfactory'. However, correlation between tests is not high. |
| 14 Are utility measures valid? | Torrance, 1986<br>Churchill, *et al.*, 1984<br>Evans, *et al.*, 1985, 1987 | Validity is often defined using the SG as the gold standard. |
| 15 Do different utility measures give the same result? | Torrance, 1976<br>Read, *et al.*, 1984<br>Buxton, *et al.*, 1986<br>Richardson, *et al.*, 1990 | Patient and clinician's evaluations correspond. Comparison suggests: TTO < SG. RS systematically differs. Orders of magnitude of TTO and SG very similar, but statistically significant differences exist. |
| 16 Do MAU measures give the same results as direct measurement? | Buxton, *et al.*, 1986<br>Richardson, *et al.*, 1990 | Rosser scale must be transformed. Similar order of magnitude of results. Present MAU scales appear unable to measure disutility of psycho-social distress. No comparisons of QWB and MAU scales. |
| 17 Can results from one scale be transformed to obtain results compatible with another? | Torrance, 1976<br>Richardson, *et al.*, 1990 | Torrance improves compatibility of RS and TTO using a power function. Richardson, *et al.* cannot replicate result. |
| 18 Can utility results be applied to individuals or only to populations? | Loomes and McKenzie, 1989<br>Torrance and Feeny, 1989 | Standard deviation of individual measures is high. For the mean value from populations it is not. |
| 19 Will utility vary with SES? | Sackett and Torrance, 1978 | This single study found only a weak relationship. |

*Table 3* (cont'd)

| Issue | Authors | Comments |
|---|---|---|
| 20 Is the utility of a health state constant through time? | Sackett and Torrance, 1978<br>Mehrez and Gafni, 1989<br>Loomes and McKenzie, 1989<br>Richardson, *et al.*, 1990 | Daily utility falls with duration of condition. Utility may vary with prognosis; stage of life; idiosyncratic time preferences. Rate may differ when future generations' welfare is affected. Suggests the need to measure an entire health scenario until death or return of full health; not an annual index of health state utility. |

### C Interviewing techniques

| Issue | Authors | Comments |
|---|---|---|
| 21 Who should be interviewed?<br>- patients<br>- cross section of population<br>- health professionals | Torrance, 1986<br>Loomes and McKenzie, 1989<br>Epstein, *et al.*, 1989<br>Carr-Hill, 1989 | Patients often give higher utilities than non-patients for a given health state. Claimed that patients and professionals have a greater understanding of the health state. The counterclaim is that societal values including those (i.e. of non patients) are desired, not those of patients. |
| 22 Are patient responses the same as those of non-patients? | Epstein, *et al.*, 1989 | High correlation for overall health, functional, social and emotional status. |
| 23 How adequate are health state descriptions? | Boyd, *et al.*, 1982 | General agreement that good descriptions are a critical factor in accurate measurement but level of detail in practice varies greatly. Sequence and method of presenting descriptions alters results. |

*Table 3* (cont'd)

| Issue | Authors | Comments |
|---|---|---|
| 24 Do utilities depend upon the 'context' of the health state? | Brooks, 1986<br>Hellinger, 1989<br>Sutherland, *et al.*, 1983 | Results differ significantly with context which casts doubt upon conventional theory. |
| 25 Will utilities vary with the reference points used for a scale? | Hershey, *et al.*, 1982<br>Sutherland, *et al.*, 1983<br>Llewellyn-Thomas, *et al.*, 1984 | Yes |
| 26 Are utilities sensitive to the 'framing' of descriptions and labels? | Brooks, 1988<br>Hershey, *et al.*, 1982, 1985<br>Sutherland, *et al.*, 1983<br>Wilson, *et al.*, 1987<br>Sackett and Torrance, 1978 | Outcomes normally found to vary with 'framing' and use of labels. 'Positive' language increases utility values. |
| 27 Will stated preference (in an interview) correspond with revealed preferences? | Brooks, 1986<br>Carr-Hill, 1989 | No reliable results but those from transport economics support the validity of stated preferences, correctly obtained. |

*Source*: Richardson, 1991b

In the first category there has been considerable discussion of the SG. The technique is derived from the theory of utility under conditions of risk. The theory, which is based upon the axioms of rational choice proposed by Von Neumann and Morgenstern (1947), has been the subject of a vigorous and voluminous debate in the general economics literature. Despite the resulting doubt about the empirical validity of the axioms, most economists still appear to regard the SG as the 'gold standard' for measurement. The issue is discussed further below. There has been little consideration of the theoretical basis of the other techniques for direct utility measurement, as these appear to be regarded as substitutes for the SG.

In practice, CUA has included only the QALY gains by the patients receiving a treatment, and costs have been limited to those directly attributable to the program. In principle, these do not include all costs and benefits. Others will benefit from the recovery of a patient, especially in the case of invalidity or psychological illnesses which impinge upon family and friends. Although the current practice is to treat each QALY as being of equal value, there may be a general agreement that life is more important at some stages of the life cycle than at others.

If people live longer as a result of an intervention, they will incur other medical costs as they contract other illnesses. More generally they will impose other costs on society which are currently ignored by CUA. Depending upon future productivity, savings and contribution to taxation, the benefits they confer may or may not exceed the costs they impose either upon society as a whole or upon particular groups in the society. There has been very little discussion of how distributional issues should be included, or if they should be included, in CUA.

A particular inconsistency arises in the treatment of 'indirect' benefits – the increased value of production which occurs when individuals live longer because of a medical intervention. At present, these are often subtracted from the cost of the medical intervention to obtain a net societal cost. (This has not, generally, been done in UK studies.) The procedure has strong distributional implications. Interventions which save the lives of the young will be 'cheaper' – they will result in a smaller net loss of resources – than those which save the lives of the elderly, as the former group is still economically productive. More fundamentally, the procedure involves the double counting of benefits. A large part of an individual's future production will be matched by the individual's consumption which is necessary for the continuation of a normal life. That is, the true benefit to society is the additional life and this additional life presumes normal consumption. The residual value of production, not absorbed by this consumption, may legitimately be regarded as a net benefit to society. However, present techniques both include the value of life (in the QALY) and subtract the full value of production from the costs.

The issues in utility measurement relating to the accuracy of measurement must be resolved through empirical research – and, as noted above, there has been very little of this. There have been few studies to establish the reliability of the techniques and an equally small number to determine whether or not different techniques produce similar results. There do not appear to be any comparisons between the use of the Equivalence Technique or the direct application of ratio scaling (Magnitude Estimation) with any of the other techniques. Torrance (1976) suggests that power function transformations may improve the relationship between the Rating Scale and Time Trade Off. The function reported by Torrance could not be reproduced by Richardson *et al.* (1990) and it did not improve the correlation between the results of the RS and TTO.

An important measurement issue which has received some attention recently is whether or not a single index of utility is applicable to a health state over a period of time. QALYs are calculated by multiplying life years by an index of utility. The question is whether or not the value of the index varies with the stage of a person's life and with medical prognosis. More generally, the functional relationship between a person's utility and time may be incompatible with a single yearly index. An additional problem is that future benefits – QALYs – are normally discounted in CUA studies in an orderly, exponential way using an estimate of the social rate of time preference. However, individuals may not behave in this way when evaluating future benefits.

Health states are unlikely to remain unchanged until death. The usual approach to this problem is to evaluate each of the health states which will be encountered and then to total the discounted QALYs experienced in each health state on the assumption that the health states are independent. If the assumptions discussed above are invalid, then this procedure is also invalid. Mehrez and Gafni (1989) have suggested that, for this reason, the usual composite approach to the calculation of QALYs should be replaced by a holistic measure of the utility of an entire multi-period scenario. They suggest that the resultant utility be converted into Healthy Year Equivalents (HYEs). The suggested change in title – HYE to replace QALY – would emphasise the new methodological basis for the calculation. Richardson *et al.* (1990) have investigated this issue empirically. They found that the holistic and composite approaches to a multi-state scenario give very different results, thereby supporting Mehrez and Gafni's suggestion.

If the last argument is correct and it is necessary to evaluate holistic health state scenarios which continue for a number of years, then cost–utility analysis could face what Richardson *et al.* (1990) describe as an 'intractable dilemma' (theoretically, not practically). Future health benefits must be discounted, and there is a debate over the appropriate rate at which this should be done. There are very strong arguments for using the social opportunity cost. However, holistic measurement necessarily allows individuals to discount the future at their own subjective rate of time preference.[6] This is likely to be different from the social opportunity cost. If the latter is accepted at the correct rate, holistic measurement will also give an incorrect answer.[7]

Finally, there has been a fairly substantial investigation of the importance of the interview. This draws upon extensive literature on the subject outside the context of CUA. As elsewhere, it has been found that results are sensitive to the way in which health states are described and the way in which scales are presented. Two additional questions are relevant. The first is the choice of subject for interview. Some have argued for the use of patients or health professionals who have experienced or observed the health state and can appreciate and evaluate it more empirically. Others have argued that a random cross-section of the society should be interviewed as it is society's resources that are allocated to health programs. A further view is that if CUA is to reflect consumer sovereignty, interviewees should be potential patients as it is the values of this group that would count if individual decision-making were possible.

The second question is whether stated preferences in the context of an interview correspond with the preferences individuals reveal when faced with a real choice. There has been no evaluation of this difficult issue in the CUA literature. However, results from transport economics suggest that 'stated preferences' closely correspond to 'revealed preferences' when interviewing is carried out in an appropriate way.

## The unit of output[8]

Much of the appeal of CUA must be attributable to the fact that it uses as its unit of output the QALY. Few would dispute that the adjustment of life years for quality represents a methodological advance, albeit not the final one. While the choice of the title was a successful marketing device for CUA, it obscures the fact that quality has no precise meaning and that different techniques used in the literature may be measuring a different concept of quality or may not be measuring quality in any meaningful sense. One approach to this issue has been simply to define quality as 'utility'. The real unit of output is then the 'utility adjusted life year' which may or may not be as intuitively appealing as the quality adjusted life year. A second approach is to determine whether 'utility', as measured, is correlated with other measures believed to reflect 'quality' (Churchill *et al.*, 1984; Evans *et al.*, 1985, 1987). This approach, of course, begs the difficult issue of what should be measured.

There are two relevant questions: the first is what the different techniques actually measure; the second is what do we want to be measured? The first of these questions can be further subdivided: a) Abstracting from practical problems associated with comprehension and wording, what will a technique measure? and b) Do practical problems alter the answer to *a*? Question *b* is empirical, and it is the first issue that is considered here.

The outcomes of both the TTO and the ET are relatively easy to understand. The TTO gives, by definition, the number of healthy years which are equivalent to a stated period in the health state, S, being measured. The unit of outcome – the healthy year equivalent – is a 'basic concept' in the sense that it requires no further explanation to be understood. It has both an interval and a ratio property. That is, there is a clear meaning to the statement that (all else equal) six healthy year equivalents are double three healthy year equivalents. Similarly, there is a clear, comprehensible, meaning to the outcome of the ET. By definition, $x$ people in one health state are equivalent to $y$ people in another – possibly full health. If the number of years in these states is specified then the meaning is very similar to the meaning of the Time Trade Off. The unit of measurement becomes the life year and when the comparison state is full health, the unit is the healthy year equivalent.

Although commonly used in psychometrics for the quantification of subjective magnitudes, neither the RS nor ME technique results in an outcome which is, itself, a comprehensible, behavioural unit. It is probably for this reason that these scales have produced very dissimilar results from the TTO and SG. The RS gives a distance along a calibrated linear scale which a subject believes indicates, in some sense, the value or worth of a health state relative to the reference points on the scale. This outcome is in centimetres along a scale or a fraction of a linear distance. Neither of these are meaningful behavioural units and they must be translated. The question that the rating scale leaves unanswered concerns the functional relationship between the units of the scale and welfare, utility, the acceptable trade-off with healthy years or the relationship with any comprehensible unit. Similarly with ME, subjects are asked 'How many times worse is one state than another?' As there is no universally accepted scale for health states, the meaning of the question is obscure. Presumably subjects must translate the question into an equivalent TTO or RS question to produce an answer. Alternatively, subjects may give a purely subjective 'feeling' response, the meaning of which can vary from person to person. As different individuals are likely to use different heuristics to answer the question, it is difficult to place a clear meaning on the final scale and its units.

Finally, the SG purports to measure utility – or more precisely, 'Von Neumann–Morgenstern, or N–M utility. Once again, this does not produce a unit which is a 'basic concept'. The result of the SG is, literally, the probability, $p$, which makes an individual indifferent between a certain and a probabilistic choice. The parameter $p$ has little intrinsic meaning (or face validity) as it is the result of a singularly unrealistic situation in which the individual (in the usual gamble) faces instant death as part of one option. The probability necessarily reflects risk attitude towards instant death. It can only be equated with N–M utility if it is assumed that the Von Neumann–Morgenstern axioms are valid. Further, it appears to be difficult to describe what N–M utility is, except in terms of the process of its creation. Lane (1987) gives one approach to this definition when he states that 'utilities are easy to interpret because they are defined, directly, in terms of a specific trade off between the consequence and the probabilistic choice between two reference consequences' (Lane, 1987: 591). Similarly N–M utility could be defined as an outcome of a mapping function which incorporates the Von Neumann–Morgenstern axioms of rational choice.

However, both approaches explain how N–M utility is derived rather than explain what it is in terms of 'basic' or behaviourally meaningful concepts.

This shortcoming is compounded by the fact that the axioms which define N–M utility have been found to be theoretically wanting and empirically unreliable to such an extent that in any given context they cannot be assumed to be applicable unless independently verified (for a review of the empirical evidence see Schoemaker, 1982; and for a discussion of the theory, see Pope, 1990). One common rejoinder to this evidence is that the axioms are the best available. However, this presupposes that behavioural analysis must be based upon axioms – a view not universally accepted outside modern micro-economics and medieval metaphysics. At best, this argument provides a defence of the expected utility hypothesis and the Von Neumann–Morgenstern axioms in the context of a positive, predictive analysis where the accuracy of the predictions may be verified. In the context of utility measurement the axioms are an end in themselves – the defining properties of an otherwise undefinable outcome.

An alternative defence of the Standard Gamble and its underlying assumptions offered by Torrance and Feeny is that Von Neumann–Morgenstern utility is normative – it indicates what individuals should do even if the outcome does not correspond with their own choice. Thus, Torrance and Feeny (1989) argue that

> the theory and measurement methods were developed by Von Neumann–Morgenstern (1944) as a normative (prescriptive) model for individual decision making under uncertainty . . . The model was a normative one. That is, they prescribed how a rational individual *ought* to make decisions when faced with uncertain outcomes.
>
> (Torrance and Feeny, 1989: 2,4)

The historical interpretation of Von Neumann–Morgenstern is open to doubt (Richardson, 1991b). More important, there are serious difficulties with the approach. As noted, the Von Neumann–Morgenstern axioms and their interpretation have been subject to serious theoretical criticisms. For example, the axioms ignore both regret and anticipation by individuals and, as acknowledged by Von Neumann and Morgenstern (1947) (but subsequently misunderstood), the axioms do not allow for the utility or disutility of risk taking *per se* (see Pope, 1990). If there are factors operating which affect utility but are ignored by the axioms then there is little justification for applying rules based upon the axioms. They will not necessarily maximise well-being in any external sense. More fundamentally, if N–M utility can only be defined and understood in terms of its axioms then the usual justification for their use involves a logical tautology. The usual argument is that the axioms indicate behaviour which maximises utility. But in this case maximising utility means nothing more than adopting behaviour which is consistent with the axioms.

The conclusion drawn from this discussion is that the use of N–M utility in CUA cannot be justified by an appeal to its theoretical basis and it cannot be supported by its intrinsic appeal as a unit of measurement.

In the absence of compelling theoretical reasons for the use of the N–M utility-based measurement, there is an issue of the appropriate criteria with which to evaluate output measures. As the chosen measure is to be used for economic evaluation the first requirement is that more units are considered to be better than less, and that, all else equal, projects are to be preferred when there is a lower cost per unit. Further, the selected units should have the interval property discussed earlier. A second requirement is that the unit is sensitive to variation in the attributes of a health state. Finally, it is suggested here that the unit should have a clear and unambiguous meaning. This permits decision makers to appreciate what is being obtained in exchange for their expenditures. More important, as political and distributive objectives are likely to influence decisions, the trade-off between these objectives and maximum output, as defined by the unit, can be made with a full appreciation of the nature of the trade-off.

These criteria would be met by QALYs if they were what they purported to be in some clear and meaningful sense. But QALYs, as determined by the current 'gold standard' of measurement, are in fact 'utility adjusted life years', and the meaning of these is unclear. The alternative measure which is already widely used is the QALY as measured by the Time Trade Off or indirectly by the Equivalence Technique. As both of these are based upon equivalences and do not involve any adjustment as a result of the measurement of 'quality', the nomenclature of Mehrez and Gafni (1989) – the Healthy Year Equivalent (HYE) – is more descriptive of the unit (although Mehrez and Gafni had a different purpose for introducing the term). As previously noted, the concept of an HYE is clear and appealing. There would be universal agreement that, all else equal, more HYEs would represent better outcome. When all else is not equal, the concept of an HYE is sufficiently simple that the implications of an adjustment for particular circumstances or a trade-off against some other objective could be readily grasped.

At least three objections could be raised against the proposal to adopt the HYE as a unit of outcome when this is obtained directly by the TTO or ET. First, there is no theoretical basis for either of these measures, unlike the Standard Gamble. Second, healthy years are an unrealistic concept as continuous, full health is a relatively unusual state. Third, the TTO and ET involve measurement under conditions of certainty whereas all health states involve risk and uncertainty.

The first of these issues is easily dismissed. If there is widespread agreement that a unit fulfils its social objective then there is no need for further, theoretical support. This is only required when the unit cannot be evaluated and comprehended in itself. Analogously, although centimetres, litres, kilograms and dollars have particular measurement properties, the unit in each case does not need to be derived from a theory. It is simply defined and the relevant question becomes whether or not there is a superior unit for fulfilling its function. In the present context, the issue is whether or not HYEs satisfy the criteria for a unit of economic evaluation.

The second issue is that 'healthy years' – by implication years of no ill health – are unusual. As people age, their physical well-being deteriorates to a greater or lesser extent. Normal health involves a succession of minor and occasional major illnesses. This suggests that the unit of measurement should be the 'normal' rather than the 'healthy' year. The *a priori* arguments for each of these appear to be inconclusive. The health state chosen as the unit of measurement should be easily understood by the person interviewed. It should also be understood by those interpreting the results. 'Normal' health is more realistic but it is not necessarily the more easily visualised by subjects. The unreality of the healthy year is not a defect if it is understood as a unit of measurement, not as an option. Further, a 'normal year' may have different meanings to different subjects unless defined in the interview. Unless all interviews adopt a common description of this, cross-study comparisons may be invalidated.

Third, the discussion leaves unresolved the question of how real world risk and uncertainty should be incorporated into evaluation when it is believed that they are likely to have a significant impact upon the preferences for a health state. One possibility which does not appear to have been employed is to include in the health state descriptions of either the TTO or the ET a statement of the risks involved. The practicality of this option would depend upon the complexity of the resulting description and upon the subject's capacity to understand it in the context of a limited interview.

Finally, there has been no attempt made so far to discriminate between the ET and the TTO. No studies appear to have been carried out to compare empirical results or to evaluate the relative complexity of the procedures. Both may be used to obtain an equivalence between life years and different health states, but the perspectives in the judgement may be quite different. The ET asks interviewers to carry out a detached judgement on the welfare of anonymous individuals. The TTO often, but not always, asks interviewees to imagine that they are in the health state described. There is a difference in the value basis of these approaches. The first involves a societal judgement. An attractive feature is that it is not unlike the Rawlsian 'veil of ignorance'. The interviewee does not know whether he or she is ever likely to be in either of the health states. As noted earlier, Torrance (1986) has also argued for the use of a random cross-section of the community as interviewees because it is generally community resources which will be used to fund projects. The argument is not, however, compelling. The use of community resources does not necessarily imply community-imposed values. A state health system may provide access and funding but permit, where practicable, an individual choice of services.

When the TTO is personalised and used to obtain values from potential patients it replicates in some important respects the values underlying ordinary economic evaluation. In this, the preferences which determine choice are the preferences of those who, in light of their own assessment of the costs and benefits, voluntarily consume goods and services. The great appeal of this system of 'consumer sovereignty' is that it is based upon a concept of liberty and non-coercion. However, consumer sovereignty also implies that the importance of individual preferences will be weighted by the individual's purchasing power – by income and wealth. By contrast, the application of the TTO (or any of the techniques described here) gives an equal weight to each person. This probably adds to the acceptability of the technique as there appears to be a widespread acceptance of egalitarian values in respect to the provision of major medical services.

These properties are not a sufficient basis for the final selection of a measurement technique as there are still unsettled issues concerning their application and use. In particular, the way in which discounting should be carried out with the different techniques is unresolved. Abstracting from these considerations, the discussion here suggests that the properties of the TTO may well make it the technique which could achieve the most widespread acceptability as the 'gold standard' in measurement.

## CONCLUSION

In a recent article on QALYs, Carr-Hill (1989) concludes by 'doubting the utility of a global index given the wide variety of assumptions involved'. The contrary view usually put forward by advocates of CUA, including the present author, is that CUA should not be evaluated against abstract standards of theoretical perfection but against the alternative methodologies that are available for economic evaluation. At present there are no alternative, sensible methodologies which take into account the strength of a person's preference for a health state.

It remains true that the list of unresolved questions reported in this chapter is formidable, but these problems should be kept in perspective. Although their resolution will improve and refine the methodology and provide a more satisfactory theoretical basis for measurement, in many cases this is unlikely to result in a substantial quantitative difference to the measurement, especially when this is compared with the alternative of not adjusting life years. The available studies show differences between the major techniques but a surprising similarity in the orders of magnitude of the results produced. Other issues, such as the distribution of benefits and the choice of a discount rate, are not unique to CUA or to the economic evaluation of health care. They are issues which must be faced in any evaluative methodology.

It may be a beguiling argument that the combination of such disparate attributes as life years and the preference for life years cannot be sensibly achieved. However, it is not uncommon for useful indices to be constructed which include very dissimilar items. The best example in economics is, perhaps, the Gross Domestic Product (GDP). This combines such disparate items as cigarettes, automobiles, air travel, education and the output from government bureaucracies. The practical problems in measuring GDP are immense and the plethora of conventions, heuristics and inconsistencies might well make it appear a chimera. The reason why the GDP is, in fact, an invaluable index is that there is an acceptable and sensible unit which, in principle, can measure the value of the disparate items and that, formidable as the measurement problems may be, they are not sufficiently important, quantitatively, to debase the index.

Perhaps a more fundamental defence of the assumptions underlying CUA is that most of them are implicit in any decisions which are made in practice. One of the major strengths of CUA is that the assumptions behind a decision are explicit; they may be located and changed.

It has been argued here that, despite the unsatisfactory state of the theory, some of the techniques presently in use have acceptable properties for the comparison of health states when they are judged – as they should be – by easily comprehended and generally acceptable criteria. On the evidence available, they result in reliable and sensible values. Many of the practical problems also have no definitive solutions at present. But there should be little question that even in its present state CUA represents a major methodological improvement over the previous analytical framework. Approximate adjustment for an individual's preferences for different health states represents a significant advance over evaluation with no adjustment. Measurement and modelling are seldom ideal, but this should not inhibit the use of second-best solutions.

## APPENDIX: UTILITY MEASUREMENT TECHNIQUES

### Rating scales

A typical rating scale consists of a line with clearly defined endpoints. The most preferred health state is placed at one end of the line and the least preferred at the other. The remaining health states are placed between these two, in order of their preference, such that the intervals between the placements correspond to the differences in preference as perceived by the subject. Variations include category scaling in which a specified number of categories are used.

### Standard Gamble

The subject is offered two alternatives. Alternative 1 is a treatment with two possible outcomes: either the patient is returned to normal health and lives for an additional $t$ years (probability $p$), or the patient dies immediately (probability $1-p$). Alternative 2 has the certain outcome of chronic state $i$ for life ($t$ years). Probability $p$ is varied until the respondent is indifferent between the two alternatives, at which point the required preference value for state $i$ is $p$.

### Time trade-off

Two alternatives are offered – alternative 1: state $i$ for time $t$ (life expectancy with the chronic condition) followed by death; alternative 2: healthy for time $x$. Time $x$ is varied until the respondent is indifferent between the two alternatives, at which point the required preference value for state $i$ is given by $h_i = x/t$.

### Equivalence technique

The subject is asked the following kind of question: 'If there are $x$ people in adverse health situation A and $y$ people in adverse health situation B, and if you can only help (cure) one group, which group would you choose?' One of the numbers $x$ or $y$ can then be varied until the subject finds the two groups equivalent in terms of needing or deserving help. The undesirability (disutility) of condition B is $x/y$ times as great as that of condition A.

### Ratio scale (magnitude estimation) technique

The subjects are asked to provide the ratio of undesirability of pairs of health states – for example, is one state two or three times worse than the other state? If state B is judged to be *x* times worse than state A, the undesirability (disutility) of state B is *x* times that of state A. A series of questions allows all states to be located on the undesirability scale.

Descriptions in this Appendix are taken from a more detailed description in Torrance (1986). Also see Brooks (1986).

## NOTES

1  The major CEA studies in the literature are reviewed by Drummond *et al.* (1987).
2  The most comprehensive statement on utility measurement is Torrance (1986).
3  Some of the most well-known measures are the Sickness Impact Profile (SIP) (Bergner *et al.*, 1976), the Spitzer QL index (Spitzer *et al.*, 1981), the Quality of Wellbeing (Kaplan *et al.*, 1976) and the Nottingham Health Profile (Hunt *et al.*, 1986). For review of the major scales see Hall and Masters (1986) and for a classification of them see Labelle *et al.*, (1989).
4  For a discussion of these steps see Gudex and Kind (1988) or Furlong *et al.* (1989).
5  Descriptions may also be found in Torrance (1986) and Brooks (1986).
6  Certain measurement techniques cannot avoid the use of inter-temporal scenarios. The Time Trade Off is one example.
7  The problem is partially overcome by the use of the shadow price of capital in combination with the social rate of time preference for consumption benefits. This is commonly accepted as an appropriate approach (Evans, forthcoming). However, this does not reconcile the approaches. The use of the shadow price will give a cost per QALY which is a function of the undiscounted values of the QALYs, capital expenditures and both the social opportunity cost and rate of time prefer- ence. The adoption of the social opportunity cost as the discount rate gives a result which is not a function of the rate of time preferences.
8  For a more detailed discussion of the issues in this section, see Richardson (1991a).

## REFERENCES

Bergner, M., Gilson, B., Bobbit, R., and Carter, W., 1976, 'The Sickness Impact Profile: Conceptual formulation and methodology for the development of a health status measure', *International Journal of Health Services*, 6, 3: 393–415.

Birch, S. and Donaldson C., 1987, 'Applications of Cost Benefit Analysis to Health Care: Departures from Welfare Economic Theory', *Journal of Health Economics*, 6, 3: 221–6.

Boyd, N.F., Sutherland, H.J., Ciampi, A. Tibshirani, R., Till, J.E., and Harwood, A. 1982, 'A Comparison of Methods of Assessing Value Quality in Laryngeal Cancer', in Deber, R.B. and Thompson, G.G. (eds) *Cancer in Health Care: Decision Making and Effectiveness*, Toronto: University of Toronto, Department of Health Administration.

Brooks, R.G., 1986, *Scaling in Health Status Measurement; Outline Guide and Commentary*, Lund: The Swedish Institute of Health Economics.

Buxton, M., Ashby, J., and O'Hanlon, M., 1986, 'Valuation of Health States Using the Time Trade-off Approach', HERG Discussion Paper No. 2, Uxbridge: Brunel University, Health Economics Research Group.

Carr-Hill, R.A., 1989, 'Assumptions of the QALY Procedure', *Social Science and Medicine*, 29, 3: 469–77.

Churchill, D.N., Torrance, G.W., and Taylor, D.W., 1984, 'Quality of Life in End Stage Renal Disease: Reliability, Validity and Use of the Time Tradeoff Method', paper presented to the 1984 National Meeting of AAP/ASCI/AFRC (Washington, DC) May 3–6, 1984.

Drummond, M.F., Stoddart, G.L., and Torrance, G.W., 1987, *Methods for the Economic Evaluation of Health Care Programs*, Oxford: Oxford Medical Publications.

Epstein, A.M., Hall, J.A., Tognetti, J., Son, L.H., and Conent, L., 1989, 'Using Proxies to Evaluate Quality of Life', *Medical Care*, 27, 3: 91–8.

Evans, D.B., forthcoming, 'The Discount Rate for Use in Public Sector Projects', in Scotton, R.B. and Goss, J. (eds), *Economic Evaluation of Health Services*, Canberra: Australian Institute of Health.

Evans, R.W., Manninen, D.L., Garrison, L.T., Heart, L.G., Blagg, C.R., Gutman, R.A., Hull, A.R., and Laurie, E.G., 1985, 'The Quality of Life of Patients with End Stage Renal Disease', *New England Journal of Medicine*, 312: 533–9.

—— 1987, 'The Quality of Life of Kidney and Heart Transplant Recipients', *Transplant Proceedings*, 17: 1579–82.

Furlong, W., Feeny, D., Torrance, G.W., Barr, R., and Housman, J., 1989, *Guide to Design and Development of Health State Utility Instrumentation*, Hamilton, Ontario: McMaster University, Centre for Health Economics and Policy Analysis Working Paper.

Gafni, A. and Torrance, G.W., 1984, 'Risk Attitude and Time Preference in Health', *Management Science*, 30, 4: 440–51.

Gudex, C., 1986, 'QALYs and Their Use by the Health Service', Discussion Paper 20, York: University of York, Centre for Health Economics.

Gudex, C. and Kind, P., 1988, 'The QALY Toolkit', Discussion Paper 38, Health Economics Consortium, York: University of York, Centre for Health Economics.

Hall, J. and Masters, G., 1986, 'Measuring Outcomes of Health Services: A Review of Some Available Measures', *Community Health Studies*, 10, 2: 147–55.

Hellinger, F.J., 1989, 'Expected Utility Theory and Risky Choices with Health Outcomes', *Medical Care*, 27, 3: 273–9.

Hershey, J.C. and Schoemaker, P.J.H., 1985, 'Probability Versus Certainty Equivalence Methods in Utility Measurement; Are They Equivalent', *Management Science*, 31, 10: 1213–29.

Hershey, J.C., Kunreuther, H.C., and Schoemaker, P.J.H., 1982, 'Sources of Bias in Assessment Procedures for Utility Functions', *Management Science* 28, 8: 936–54.

Hunt, S.M., McEwen, J. and McKenna, S.P., 1986, *Measuring Health Status*, London: Croom Helm.

Kaplan, R.M. and Bush, J.W., 1982, 'Health Related Quality of Life Measurement for Evaluation Research and Policy Analysis', *Health Psychology*, 1: 61–8.

Kaplan, M., Bush, J., and Berry, C., 1976, 'Health States: Types of Validity and the Index of Well Being', *Health Services Research*, 11, 4: 478–507.

Labelle, R., Feeney D., and Torrance, G., 1989, 'Conceptual Foundations of Health Status and Quality of Life Utility Measures', unpublished paper, Hamilton, Ontario: McMaster University, Department of Clinical Epidemiology and Biostatistics.

Lane, D.A., 1987, 'Utility, Decision, and Quality of Life', *Journal of Chronic Diseases*, 40, 6: 585–91.

Linard, K., forthcoming, 'Decision Contexts and Decision Rules for Economic Evaluation of Health Services', in Scotton, R.B. and Goss, J. (eds), *Economic Evaluation of Health Services*, Canberra: Australian Institute of Health.

Lipscomb, J., 1989, 'Time Preference for Cost Effectiveness Analysis of Medical Care', *Inquiry*, 27, 3: 233–53.

Llewellyn-Thomas, H., Sutherland. H.J., Tibshirani, R., Ciampi, A., Till, J.E., and Boyd, N.F., 1984, 'Describing Health States: Methodological Issues in Obtaining Values for Health States', *Medical Care*, 22, 6: 543–52.

Loomes, G. and McKenzie, L., 1989, 'The Use of QALYs in Health Care Decision Making', *Social Science and Medicine*, 28, 4: 299–308.

Mehrez, A. and Gafni, A., 1989, 'Evaluating Health Related Quality of Life; Interpretation for the Time Trade Off Technique', working paper, Hamilton Ontario: McMaster University, Centre for Health Economics and Policy Analysis.

Von Neuman, J. and Morgenstern, O., 1947, *The Theory of Gains and Economic Behaviour*, Princeton, N.J.: Princeton University Press.

Pope, R.E., 1990, 'Additional Perspectives on Modelling Health Insurance Decisions', in Selby-Smith, C. (ed.), *Economics and Health: Proceedings of the Eleventh Conference of Health Economists*, Melbourne: Monash University, Public Sector Management Institute.

Read, J.L., Quinn, R.J., Burwick, D.M., Fineberg, H.B., and Weinstein, M.C., 1984, 'Preferences for Health Outcomes: Comparison of Assessment Methods', *Medical Decision Making*, 4, 3: 315–29.

Richardson, J., 1991a, 'What Should We Measure in Health Program Evaluation', in Selby-Smith, C. (ed.), *Economics and Health: Proceedings of the Twelfth Conference of Health Economists*, Melbourne: Monash University, Public Sector Management Institute.

Richardson, J., 1991b, 'Economic Assessment of Health Care Theory and Practice', *The Australian Economic Review*, first quarter: 4–21.

Richardson, J. and Hall, J., forthcoming, 'The Assessment of Benefits in Health Care Evaluation', in Scotton, R.B. and Goss, J. (eds), *Economic Evaluation of Health Services*, Canberra: Australian Institute of Health.

Richardson, J., Hall J., and Salkeld, S., 1990, 'Cost Utility Analysis; The Compatability of Measurement Techniques and the Measurement of Utility Through Time' in Selby-Smith, C. (ed.), *Economics and Health: Proceedings of the Eleventh Conference of Health Economists*, Melbourne: Monash University, Public Sector Management Institute.

Rosser, R. and Kind, P., 1978, 'A Scale of Valuations of States of Illness: Is There a Social Consensus?' *International Journal of Epidemiology*, 7, 4: 347–58.

Sackett, D.L. and Torrance, G.W., 1978, 'The Utility of Different Health States as Perceived by the General Public', *Journal of Chronic Diseases*, 31: 697–704.

Schoemaker, P.J.H., 1982, 'The Expected Utility Model: Its Variants, Purposes, Evidence and Limitations', *Journal of Economic Literature*, 20: 529–63.

Spitzer, W.O., Dobson, A.J., Hall, J., Chesterman, E., Levi, J., Shepherd, R., Battista, R.N., and Catchlove, B.R., 1981, 'Measuring the Quality of Life of

Cancer Patients; A Concise QL Index for Use by Physicians', *Journal of Chronic Diseases*, 34: 585–97.

Sutherland, H.J., Dunn, V., and Boyd, N.F., 1983, 'Measurement of Values for States of Health with Linear Analog Scales', *Medical Decision Making*, 3, 4: 477–87.

Torrance, G.W., 1976, 'Social Preferences for Health States: An Empirical Evaluation of Three Measurement Techniques', *Socio-Economic Planning Sciences*, 10, 3: 129–36.

—— 1982, 'Multiattribute Utility Theory as a Method of Measuring Preferences for Health', in Kane, R.L. and Kane A. (eds), *Values and Long Term Care*, Lexington, MA: DC Heath.

—— 1986, 'Measurement of Health-State Utilities for Economic Appraisal: A Review', *Journal of Health Economics*, 5: 1–30.

—— 1987, 'Utility Approach to Measuring Health-Related Quality of Life', *Journal of Chronic Diseases*, 40, 6: 593–600.

Torrance, G.W. and Feeny, D., 1989, 'Utilities and Quality Adjusted Life Years', *International Journal of Technology Assessment in Health Care*, 5, 4: 559–75.

Weinstein, M.C. and Stason, W.B., 1977, 'Foundations of Cost-Effectiveness Analysis for Health and Medical Practices', *New England Journal of Medicine*, 296, 13: 716–21.

Wilson, D.K., Kaplan, R.M., and Schneiderman, L.J., 1987, 'Framing of Decisions and Selections of Alternatives in Health Care', *Social Behaviour*, 2: 57–9.

Wright, S.J., 1986, 'Age, Sex and Health: A Summary of Findings from the York Health Evaluation Survey', Discussion Paper 15, York: University of York, Centre for Health Economics.

# Part II
# The randomised controlled trial

# 3 Randomised controlled trials in health care research

*David J. Newell*

## INTRODUCTION

Social scientists Webb *et al.* (1966) state

> First, and most satisfactory, is experimental design. It is a sad truth that randomised experimental design is possible for only a portion of the settings in which social scientists make measurements and seek interpretable comparisons. The number of opportunities for its use may not be staggering, but where possible experimental design should by all means be exploited. Many more opportunities exist than are used.
>
> (Webb *et al.*, 1966: 6)

This quotation establishes two of the four essential points to be made in this paper:

1 Designed experiments are sometimes both possible and useful in policy issues.
2 On other topics, observational studies must suffice if scientific research is to contribute to policy decisions.
3 Multidisciplinary studies can combine the approaches of the randomised controlled trial and the 'qualitative' study.
4 Research pitfalls identified in one area (e.g. randomised controlled trials) can be relevant in others (e.g. observational studies).

## BRIEF THEORY OF RANDOMISED CONTROLLED TRIALS

A randomised controlled trial (here to compare *two* 'treatments' but easily generalisable to more than two) typically selects a group of patients/clients, randomly allocates each of those individuals to one or other of the treatments, makes measurements after (and frequently also before) the treatment is administered, and compares the results by a statistical analysis. At every step of this apparently simple structure, pitfalls abound. Some of these are described below; to make the points more relevant to this context, reference will be made to one or other of two health care randomised controlled trials, each with policy implications.

1   Should patients requiring surgery for hernia or haemorrhoids be treated by 'day-case surgery', returning home from the hospital on the same day as the operation, or should they be retained in hospital for post-operative recovery, typically (in UK in 1976) for five days (Russell *et al.*, 1977)?
2   Should frail elderly people be cared for in a nursing home or retained in a long-stay hospital ward (Bond *et al.*, 1989b)?

## OUTLINE PROTOCOL

This section of the chapter is a brief discussion of topics arising under the headings of a typical trial protocol. These include: background and specific objectives (hypothesis); patient/client selection criteria; treatment definition; criteria of evaluation; study design; ethical considerations; randomisation; required size of study; conduct and administration; analysis; and interpretation and policy decisions.

### Background and specific objectives

As in all scientific research, the scientific background allows us to stand on the shoulders of those who came before us, and thus see a little further. The majority of randomised controlled trials relate to drug treatments, and until recently have had little relation to major policy decisions. Recent trials of expensive drugs, perhaps continuing for many years in prophylaxis, have policy implications in relation to medical benefits and cost effectiveness. Many of the lessons learned in drug trials can be applied to trials of health care methods in the broader sense. Background information in such trials will include the number of patients/clients who might be affected by the outcome of the trial: this may be a measure of the incidence of an acute condition, the prevalence of a chronic condition, or the client base of a particular service on a local or national basis. Broad-brush estimates of the cost of the alternative services as part of the background information may help a funding body to decide whether a trial is worth undertaking, but the detailed costing will usually be part of the trial itself.

The specific objectives of the trial are a more concise definition of those hypotheses concerning treatment efficacy and safety which are to be examined by the trial.

**Patient/client selection criteria**

The *population* to be included in the trial must be carefully defined, essentially in terms of a diagnosis for inclusion and of specified exclusions. The 'diagnosis' in policy-related trials may often be partly defined by service considerations, such as 'patients with inguinal hernia or haemorrhoids who have been referred to a surgeon', 'frail old people in geriatric hospital' or 'children with enuresis taken to the GP' (general practitioner). The exclusions may be for medical, social, legal or administrative reasons, such as 'being pregnant', 'living alone', 'being below the age of legal consent' or 'living outside the designated hospital area'. Exclusions should not be too restrictive, as strictly speaking the results of the trial are applicable only to the population from which the patients/clients were selected. In practice, if a treatment is shown to be effective, some extrapolation to a somewhat wider group will be made, but this can be hazardous, as in the extrapolation of 'allergic rhinitis' to 'upper respiratory infection', which led to the widespread ineffective use of antihistamines in the treatment of the common cold.

**Treatment definition**

The *treatments* in a policy-related study may be pharmaceutical preparations, but for a publicly funded study will often be regimes with more than one facet. Thus in the study of day-case surgery for hernias and haemorrhoids, the operative treatment was the same for all cases, but the 'treatments' consisted of: a) surgical operation near the beginning of the day's list, normal post-operative nursing during the day, discharge home that evening to family care with domestic district-nurse nursing and GP supervision, or b) 'traditional' hospital post-operative stay (five days for hernias, six for haemorrhoids) with less attention from GP, district nurse or family required on discharge home.

The 'treatments' were more difficult to define in the study of institutional care for frail elderly people. The 'experimental mode' consisted of the three NHS experimental nursing homes in Britain, and the 'control mode' of the related long-stay wards in general hospitals, under the leadership of a medical consultant, variously a geriatrician or a general physician with responsibility for the care of elderly people. But even during the study (1984–8) the move towards transferring suitable 'continuing care' patients from the long-stay wards to community care (whether permanently or intermittently) began to be introduced, more particularly at one of the three 'control' hospitals.

The new nursing homes were even more complex to define as 'a treatment'. The experimental mode comprised the three demonstration NHS nursing homes which are small, community-based, self-contained units serving defined catchment areas. Existing buildings were adapted to provide single rooms for the majority of residents. They are nurse-managed, with general practitioners providing medical care. With 24, 25 and 30 places, they are located in three widely dispersed health authorities in England. But these descriptions of architecture and local management are far from sufficient to describe those characteristics of the homes which impact on the desirable outcomes of care. In moving from the *structure* to the *process* of care, we must call on the various techniques and measuring devices developed by sociologists and others. Our team consisted of people with basic training in statistics, sociology, medicine, nursing, health economics, computing and anthropology. The actions of nursing home and hospital staff, their interactions with patients and other staff, were observed by a nurse–researcher in an ethnographic multiple-case study, to provide analytical descriptions and comparisons of modes of care given in the experimental NHS nursing homes and the conventional continuing care wards. Note that in a service setting with several autonomous institutions, it is seldom possible, as in a simple drug trial, to specify in advance the detailed process of care. Within the broad perimeters defined by the architectural and staffing structures, the content depended quite considerably on local cultural, political and organisational qualities of the health authorities, and on the staff attitudes towards the care of frail elderly people.

## Criteria of evaluation

The *criteria* used to evaluate trials are very trial-specific, and textbook accounts generally suggest that there should be one major criterion of success of a new treatment, such as a reduction in mortality. In policy-related trials, this is unlikely to be achievable, and may not be desirable. In the study of day-case surgery (a clinical, social and economic evaluation), criteria relating to each of the three disciplines were necessary. First, no difference was expected in the direct effect of surgery, but post-operative recovery might well depend on the location of care. On the social side the implications outside of the hospital are considerable. Do patients prefer to be at home? Do carers cope with a recently operated patient? Are home nurses, who are more accustomed to caring for elderly or maternity cases, happy to treat post-operative bleeding? Is the GP prepared to care for the surgeon's patient? The economic questions are complex. Within the hospital, what are the savings arising from early discharge: saved bed-days? If so, at average or marginal cost, at financial or opportunity cost? If the result is that only more seriously ill patients remain in the surgical ward, does this imply additional staffing costs? Outside the hospital (an area often ignored by surgeons in decision-making) what are the costs of providing nursing and GP care for these patients? In the UK, an interesting economic anomaly is that the additional GP care involves no cost to the NHS – since GPs receive a salary for accepting responsibility for the primary medical care of a defined list of patients – but that an opportunity cost is incurred because the GP could have been doing something else with the time. Finally, at the domestic level, we must look at the costs to the patients themselves, if the two regimes produce different times off work; and to their carers, who no longer have to visit the hospital, but have to provide additional care including food, fuel, laundry and possibly analgesics and dressings. Hospital bills were not then relevant in the UK context, but may well be in other countries and at other times. In this particular study, the clinical and social outcomes were sufficiently similar that the essential criterion of success was economic. In general, a much more difficult policy decision would involve trade-offs between clinical disbenefits and reduced costs. In such cases, better decisions can be made if the trade-offs are made explicit.

In the study of nursing homes, very careful consideration is necessary in defining outcomes. Survival and personal well-being (quality of life) are 'final outcomes', but parts of the process of care are often regarded as 'intermediate outcomes' – such as type and level of activity of the residents. The Australian Commonwealth/State Working Party on Nursing Home Standards (1987) included as 'outcomes' accessibility of medical care, social independence, residents' freedom of choice, variety of experience, safety, etc., many of which could be classified as part of the 'process' leading to personal well-being and survival 'outcomes'. An illustration of the difficulties of interpretation of intermediate outcomes appeared in another study, where morbidity was regarded initially as an important criterion. One group of nursing homes had a comparatively high rate of fracture of the femur. But the comparison was with another group who kept their elderly patients bedfast. Freedom to move about can imply freedom to fall and fracture a leg. The judgement between these two is certainly not value free. However, opinion is still forming about the most important intermediate outcomes. Grimley Evans (1984) has proposed autonomy as the global aim of all services for the elderly. As a single criterion, the QALY (quality adjusted life year) has been proposed (see, e.g., Williams, 1985). This measure is a combination of the expected life years gained from consumption of a health care procedure and some judgement about the quality of those additional years. However, the assessment of quality of the added years of life for a frail elderly person did not seem to us to be sufficiently well developed for the QALY to be a useful outcome measure for the nursing home study (Donaldson *et al.*, 1988). Instead we aim to compare survival in the two modes of care, and assess separately personal well-being, using a variety of established rating scales and indices.

## Study design

We have found the concepts of 'Pragmatic' and 'Explanatory' Trials (Schwartz *et al.*, 1980) very helpful (Bond *et al.*, 1989a). Without going into detail here, I will say that the pragmatic trial which allows some deviation from the 'treatment' is more realistic, particularly in the world of independent health authorities and individuals. An essential element of the pragmatic trial is that the analysis must be based on 'intention to treat'. As qualitative studies may often concentrate on those actually receiving the specified treatment, an illustration of the pitfalls of not analysing on the basis of intention to treat could be helpful.

It was believed at one time that keeping premature babies at low temperatures in the immediate post-natal period was beneficial. In a randomised controlled trial of low-temperature (85° F) incubators compared with those at standard temperatures (98° F), an initial analysis was conducted based on the compliers (those babies who were *maintained* at those temperatures). This suggested that the low temperature was saving lives. But it excluded babies who were unable to control their temperatures, through general debilitation or infection – the very babies most likely to die. When the babies were properly analysed in the temperature group to which they were allocated, the results rejected the low temperature incubator (Jolly *et al.*, 1962). Failure to identify the necessity of 'intention to treat' analysis could have led to many premature babies dying in the cold.

Returning to our first example, it is clear that a pragmatic trial, with 'intention to treat' analysis, dictated that we retained in the day-case surgery group those patients *allocated* to be sent home on the day of operation but who had to stay in hospital, either because of a medical complication or some unexpected occurrence at home. This mimics the real-life future situation if day-case surgery for these operations were introduced uniformly: sometimes the patient would have to stay in hospital, and arrangements would have to be sufficiently flexible to allow this. Similarly, in the nursing home study, some patients allocated to traditional long-stay ward care were transferred elsewhere during the study, and some in the new nursing homes needed acute transfer to hospital for a while. Even if the latter died in hospital, the death is correctly assigned to the nursing home type of care. (Note that such deaths would *not* appear in the official death rate in the home.)

In drug trials, it is often possible to ensure that neither the patient nor the assessing investigator is aware which treatment the patient is receiving (a 'double-blind' trial). This is rarely possible in health care trials, so careful attention must be paid to avoiding bias in the assessment of outcome.

## Ethical considerations

Under most legislations, *ethical considerations* must be carefully discussed and documented before patients are admitted to a randomised controlled trial. The investigator should believe that there is no general advantage of one of the two treatments. If investigators do not so believe, their personal and professional ethical standards should disbar them from undertaking the trial, as they would be knowingly allocating some patients to a treatment they believed to be inferior. (There are special considerations when one of the treatments is in limited supply.) Similarly, if the investigator is convinced that for a particular patient one of the trial treatments has real advantages over the other, that patient should not be admitted to the trial. When the investigator has decided the patient is suitable for the trial, the patient must then be given the opportunity to choose whether to participate ('informed consent').

## Randomisation

An essential element in the randomised controlled trial is *randomisation*. The object of the study is 'to compare like with like'. Judgemental allocation to one treatment or the other almost inevitably leads to bias. A method which randomly allocates patients (without cheating) to one or the other treatment avoids these potential biases. Thus if the Heads of Homes in the nursing homes study had been allowed to choose their patients from the available pool of elderly patients in the hospital long-stay wards, they might easily have chosen those without an overt psychiatric underlay to their physical condition, or those they judged would be more co-operative in the home. Either of these conditions is likely to be related in some way to an outcome variable. Selection bias arising from different catchment areas – very well known in educational research – would invalidate the study if, for example, the nursing home accepted only patients whose homes were nearby, but controls were taken from the wider area served by the geriatric wards. To avoid this, a patient is only admitted to the trial if the investigator decides that either of the treatments would be suitable: the patient is then randomly allocated to one or the other. In this instance, stratification by area is necessary, ensuring that equal numbers of cases and controls are selected in each of the three nursing home areas. When one of the treatments is standard (as in the long-stay wards) an option is to use the randomised consent design (Zelen, 1979). In two of the nursing home areas, each patient referred to the study was interviewed by the field worker, who sought consent to the data collection. Following randomisation, the consultant sought patient consent only from those allocated to the new nursing homes. The remainder, who would normally have been treated in the long-stay ward, were so treated – they had nothing special to which to consent.

## Size of study

The required *size of a study* has both scientific and ethical components. Clearly a trial with very few patients is unlikely to identify a difference between treatments unless the difference is very large; that is, the new treatment is very effective (or disastrously worse) compared with the control. A decision on the required size of a trial depends on three numbers: the significance level (often taken as five per cent, but smaller if the results are to be inspected a number of times during the trial); the critical difference between treatments which is of such clinical importance that it should not be missed (e.g. a twenty per cent reduction in mortality); and the probability of missing such a difference (say ten per cent). The first and third of these are often referred to as the probabilities of errors of the first and second kinds.

Useful tables for the size of a trial have recently been published by Machin and Campbell (1987), while Pocock (1983) gives in his excellent book on clinical trials an understandable account of 'the realistic assessment of trial size'.

The ethical aspect of sample size is that if a trial is of insufficient size to detect (for the benefit of future patients) a better treatment, it can hardly be ethical to include a patient in the trial, particularly as this will often involve discomfort, disturbance or some small element of risk to the patient.

## Conduct and administration

The *conduct and administration* of a trial require endless attention to detail if the trial is to be completed in a reasonable time and have an unambiguous interpretation. Details must be worked out specifically for each trial to ensure that selection criteria are adhered to, treatments are given as specified, criteria (of both satisfactory outcomes and undesirable side effects) are applied and measured consistently throughout, ethical guidelines are observed across changes in personnel in the currency of the trial, randomisation remains unbiased and adequate numbers are recruited to the study. (In the day-case surgery study, when the number of haemorrhoid patients admitted fell below the planned rate of accrual, it was necessary to organise a 'pile-drive' amongst local GPs.) These administrative procedures, while undramatic, are absolutely essential, and must be planned for in the funding of the study.

## Analysis

*Statistical methods* impinge three times in a well-conducted trial: in the planning stages; to monitor progress; and to analyse the results. While the details of calculations of the analysis have no place here, certain general ideas are brought to attention.

Significance levels strictly apply if a single criterion is assessed once at the end of the trial. If the data are to be reviewed during the trial (sequential or group-sequential analyses), special considerations apply. Similarly, if multiple measures of outcome are available, a few pre-planned evaluations can be made validly, but difficulties arise if the authors hunt for a sub-group of patients in whom the response appears to be better (e.g. the new treatment is highly effective in males aged 25 to 34, with a history of measles and intravenous drug use, born within 20km of the teaching hospital in one specified city). If the particular combination of attributes makes any sort of biological sense, this may be used to suggest future studies, but the result from the current study is 'hypothesis forming' rather than 'hypothesis testing'. Pocock (1983) gives a useful account of solutions to these difficulties.

## Interpretation and policy decisions

The *interpretation* is theoretically straightforward if the protocol has been strictly adhered to: one of the drugs in the specified dosage produces a (significantly) better response on the specified criterion; or neither drug is better by more than the specified difference which is of clinical importance.

In the multidisciplinary, policy-oriented study with a number of measures of outcome, interpretation is often more difficult. Some comments on the impact of trials on policy decisions are given below.

## QUALITATIVE RESEARCH AND RANDOMISED CONTROLLED TRIALS

### The role of qualitative research in randomised control trials

Both of the illustrative trials in this paper have had a sociological input and have employed some qualitative research methods. This interplay between qualitative and quantitative methods extends the scope of these particular studies, and may also be almost essential in other informative research of health policy issues.

Although the day-case surgery study was essentially a randomised controlled trial, and thus based on the quantitative paradigm, it included very little quantitation in its analysis. The clinician's observations of complications were qualitative, and the questionnaire and interview techniques for obtaining patients' and nurses' opinions, preferences and personal costs were semi-structured or open ended. On the economic side, no preconceived value scale was set, and a number of alternatives were considered in assessing opportunity costs.

In the more recent nursing home study, the sociological input was even stronger, modelling itself on the wide literature of the last twenty years. One comment of Donabedian (1980: 81) stands out: 'the most direct route to an assessment of the quality of care is an examination of that care'. In addition to the randomised controlled trial itself, six other linked studies took place in the three nursing homes and six long-stay wards (two in each area):

1  a multiple-case study of the modes of care provided in the nine locations, to provide analytical descriptions and comparisons of the care given, using participant observation;
2  two surveys before and towards the end of the trial, of all continuing care institutions used by elderly people in the relevant areas. These provide a general description and note any changes in the provision of other institutional services which may have affected the nine trial sites;
3  a financial study of relative capital and revenue costs;
4  a nursing staff survey to describe the characteristics and explore the views of the nurses;
5  a survey of relatives visiting patients/residents, to obtain views on physical and social environments;
6  a survey of volunteer workers for their views on the environments and reasons for undertaking voluntary work.

This multiplicity of data sources indicates both the strengths and the weaknesses of the qualitative approach. The sources enabled the team to describe separately aspects of the structure, the process and intermediate outcomes of care, all of which impinge on the final outcomes of survival and personal well-being in the randomised controlled trial. When the various sources support each other, conclusions are strengthened. When and if they diverge, this very divergence leads to sociological insights into the concepts of care.

Although the pragmatic approach in the trial can lead to the conclusion 'provide this package of services and produce better survival or personal well-being', the qualitative method attempts to unwrap the package. If benefits are obtained in the nursing homes, is this because single rooms are provided, because nurses rather than doctors are administratively in charge, because GPs rather than consultants provide medical care, because nursing staff were on first name terms, because patients did not wake so early, because patients had greater autonomy, etc.? These facets are not all independent, but in future nursing homes it might be possible to provide some but not all of them without seriously affecting outcome. The trained and experienced 'qualitative' research worker is more likely to be able to unravel the web than the unidisciplinary investigator more accustomed to quantitative measures.

### Lessons from randomised controlled trials which could inform qualitative research

The ideal interplay between qualitative and quantitative methods occurs when individuals from the caring professions, the numerical sciences and the social sciences work together as a team with parity of esteem. In this way, the qualitative researcher learns some aspects of the discipline of the quantitative, and vice versa. While retaining the professional skills of their basic discipline, each learns elements from the other's armamentarium, becoming what is termed a 'generic health care research worker'. In this context, it is useful to isolate just one element from the randomised controlled trial to see what lessons it has for the qualitative researcher. Let us look then at the pragmatic trial, with its implication of 'intention to treat' analysis. This concept has not been grasped by many qualitative researchers. Thus they might be prepared to take a collection of people at home who had returned from hospital on the same day as their operation, to gather views on the efficacy of the procedure. Very interesting interviewees they would have been, ranging from the man who walked home at 3 p.m. after his hernia operation because he could not be bothered to wait for the ambulance due at 5 p.m., to another patient whose recurrent bleeding following return home after a haemorrhoid operation led to severe stress on patient and relatives and required considerable intervention from the district nurse and general practitioner, who eventually arranged for the patient to be readmitted to hospital. But that 'sample' would be biased, perhaps seriously, because it had excluded all those who had been 'allocated' to day-case surgery but had been retained for one or several nights in hospital because of post-operative complications.

A similar problem of selection bias arises in the nursing home study, where those whose medical or psychiatric state has led to transfer out of the home, are therefore unavailable to any researcher who interviews only residents present in the nursing home. Awareness of the 'intention to treat' mode of analysis reduces our risk of biased interpretation from this particular cause. A further aspect of this problem is the selective bias of death. During the study, about seventy per cent of the randomised patients died. Interviews with those with fairly long experience of the experimental or control mode of care were accordingly those with the 'not-so-frail' frail elderly residents.

The account of the cold treatment of premature babies shows that ignoring the 'intention to treat' concept is not a mere matter of statistical nicety or attention to irrelevant detail, but is a genuine life-or-death issue, which in that particular case could have led to the unjustified endorsement of 'cold' incubator treatment and innumerable unnecessary deaths of premature infants.

The hazards of using 'convenience samples' can be seen from past experience in quantitative research. Before controlled clinical trials of a wide variety of medical treatments were introduced, many which have now been shown to be valueless had previously been enthusiastically and authoritatively recommended on the basis of samples from which the failures had 'conveniently' been excluded. A further hazard of convenience samples in the absence of a randomised trial is that those in one facility (the nursing homes), being selected as 'suitable' for that facility, would almost inevitably fare better than the remainder who were left in the traditional long-stay wards. Even if adjustments for the usual demographic characteristics were made, this bias would almost certainly persist.

## Lessons from qualitative research which could inform randomised controlled trials

It has been said that a statistician *qua* statistician never has hypotheses, but merely tests them. To those who regard a statistician as one who merely manipulates the numbers, this criticism may ring true. However, applied statisticians working in a health care team attempt to understand their field of application and will always listen to an expert who wishes to collaborate. In any case, most statisticians nowadays go beyond hypothesis testing to indicate the range of possible population effects which are compatible with the data.

Hence in the unscrambling of a multifaceted package like a nursing home for frail elderly people, the skills of the qualitative analyst present almost the only scientific way forward. A government may claim that the nation's accounts could not 'afford' the whole package, and would wonder if some of the more expensive elements could be eliminated without seriously compromising the final outcomes. A qualitative assessment might possibly propose a 'cheaper' package, or decide that all of the more expensive elements are essential: this would be much more valuable than a purely political decision uninformed by science.

A broader description of the approach is given by Mullen and Iverson (1982), supporting Weiss (1972):

> Such cases demand an approach which aims to develop a coherent and appropriate near-to-complete description of the relevant systems prior to the intervention of a new programme, of the nature of the intervention, and of the new system which then develops in which intervention is a dynamic constituent.

(Mullen and Iverson, 1982: 14)

From this emerge testable new health care options.

## THE ROLE OF CONTROLLED TRIALS IN POLICY DECISION-MAKING

Policy decisions seldom follow immediately from a randomised controlled trial in health care. Funding sponsors of research may (from another pocket) be responsible for the implementation of some of the results. Nevertheless, they will seldom be willing in advance to specify the weightings which they (or their successors) will allocate to specific clinical, social or economic outcomes. In the area of health care, too, the word 'decisions' relating to policy is seldom as firm as it sounds. As Garroway and Prescott (1977) point out,

> if a limited number of outcome variables is used, the results of the trial will enable health administrators to see the broad consequences of implementing one of the health care options. The better option for one area might not necessarily be preferred elsewhere because of different local priorities, one area being perhaps strongly influenced by the social effects and another placing a higher priority on cost.

(Garroway and Prescott, 1977: 132)

In reporting on the nursing homes study, we recognise that the end result in policy terms depends in part on the relevance and acceptability of the findings to at least four groups of stakeholders: the government department that sought and bought the study; the scientific communities which advise that department and are also generally interested in evaluation research and the care of elderly persons; other policy makers nationally and locally; and providers of care and their professional organisations. Since the application of research cannot be independent of the 'political' differences of these various stakeholders, a multidiscipline, multimethod project runs the risk of criticism for not remaining within the scientific paradigms of the different stakeholders and their advisers.

Finally, we can consider the 'policy' results of the day-case surgery study. The study suggested that day-case surgery for hernia repair and one-day stays for haemorrhoids impose no additional clinical, social and financial costs on the patient. We emphasised, however, that the economic benefits to the NHS depend almost entirely on the use which would be made of the resources thereby released. (The freed bed-days could be wasted, used to close a small ward at the hospital, or used to avoid the construction of a new small ward.) Unless the resources are put to good use, we concluded, it is not worth incurring the 'political costs' associated with the introduction of any new policy.

The Minister of Health, Dr David Owen (1976), commenting on a pre-publication report of our study, cut through all this 'opportunity cost' qualification and stated

> The consequences of treating hernias on a day-care basis suggested savings of about 30 pounds (sterling) per case in 1973 prices. Since there are about 90,000 hernia operations every year, the savings in current prices from the general adoption of such a policy could be as much as 4.5 million pounds without any reduction in the quality of clinical care.
>
> (Owen, 1976: 1,008)

It is a matter of history that soon after the Lancet published Dr Owen's paper, he was appointed Foreign Secretary.

Nevertheless, the duration of stay for haemorrhoids operations decreased and the proportion of hernias treated by day-case surgery increased considerably over the following ten years or more. Not a distinct 'policy decision', but a strong lead to a changed climate of opinion amongst the professionals who made the decisions.

## SUMMARY

Randomised controlled trials can be conducted in health care research, with patients truly randomly allocated to one 'treatment' (regime, institution) or another. Both quantitative and qualitative methods have a role to play in the design, analysis and interpretation of such studies. Two specific studies are given for illustration: day-case versus traditional hospital stay for surgery for hernias and haemorrhoids, and new nursing homes versus traditional hospital long-stay wards for the care of frail elderly people. The relevance of these and other studies to policy decisions is discussed.

# ACKNOWLEDGEMENT

I wish to thank my colleagues at the Health Care Research Unit, University of Newcastle upon Tyne, and the UK Department of Health for support since 1970 to develop the ideas outlined in this paper.

# REFERENCES

Bond, J., Atkinson, A., Gregson, B.A. and Newell, D.J., 1989a, 'Pragmatic and Explanatory Trials in the Evaluation of the Experimental National Health Service Nursing Homes', *Age Ageing*, 18: 89–95.

Bond, J., Gregson, B.A., Atkinson, A. and Newell, D.J., 1989b, 'The Implementation of a Multicentred Randomised Controlled Trial in the Evaluation of the Experimental National Health Service Nursing Homes', *Age Ageing*, 18: 96–102.

Commonwealth/State Working Party on Nursing Home Standards, 1987, *Living in a Nursing Home*, Canberra: Australian Government Printing Service.

Donabedian, A., 1980, *The Definition of Quality and Approaches to its Assessment*, Ann Arbor: Health Administration Press.

Donaldson, C., Atkinson, A., Bond, J. and Wright, K., 1988, 'QALYs and long-term care for elderly people in UK: Scales for assessment of quality of life', *Age Ageing*, 17: 379–87.

Garroway, M. and Prescott, R., 1977, 'Limitations of the Controlled Trial in Health Care', *Health Bulletin*, 35: 131–4.

Grimley Evans, J., 1984, 'Prevention of age-associated loss of autonomy: epidemiological approaches', *Journal of Chronic Diseases*, 37: 353–63.

Jolly, H., Molyneux, P. and Newell, D.J., 1962, 'A controlled study of the effect of temperature on premature babies', *Journal of Paediatrics*, 60: 889–94.

Machin, D. and Campbell, M.J., 1987, *Statistical tables for the design of Clinical Trials*. Oxford: Blackwell.

Mullen, P.D. and Iverson, D., 1982, 'Qualitative Methods for Evaluative Research in Health Education Programs', *Health Education Quarterly*, 13: 11–17.

Owen, D., 1976, 'Clinical Freedom and Professional Freedom', *Lancet*, i: 1006–9.

Pocock, S.J., 1983, *Clinical Trials: a practical approach*, Chichester: Wiley.

Russell, I.T., Fell, M., Devlin, H.B., Glass, N.J. and Newell, D.J., 1977, 'Day-case Surgery for Hernias and Haemorrhoids – A Clinical, Social and Economic Evaluation', *Lancet*, i: 844–7.

Schwartz, D., Flamant, R. and Lellouch, J., 1980, *Clinical Trials*, London: Academic Press.

Webb, E.J., Campbell, D.T, Schwarz, R.D. and Sechrest, L., 1966, *Unobtrusive Measures: Nonreactive Research in the Social Sciences*, Chicago: Rand McNally.

Weiss, C.H., (ed.), 1972, *Evaluating Action Programs*, Boston: Allyn and Bacon.

Williams, A., 1985, 'Economics of Coronary Artery By-pass Grafting', *British Medical Journal*, 291: 326–9.

Zelen, M., 1979, 'A new design for randomised clinical trials', *New England Journal of Medicine*, 300: 1243–5.

# 4   The impact of clinical research on clinical practice

*Jack Hirsh*

Clinical research can be defined in various ways. For the purpose of this discussion I will define clinical research as the investigation of a clinically relevant problem, the solution of which will improve clinical practice. Defined this way, clinical research is driven by a pressing clinical problem and stimulated by the desire to solve the problem. Two additional critical ingredients (apart from the clinical problem of interest) are required to perform clinical research successfully (Figure 1). The first and most important is a plausible rationale for the hypothesis to be tested (e.g. the scientific basis for selecting an intervention or for selecting a new diagnostic test to replace an existing test). In general, the more that is known about the biological process under investigation, the greater the likelihood that the clinical experiment will be successful. The second requirement is the sensible application of methodological principles of design, measurement and analysis, which is the basis of the clinical epidemiological component of clinical research. The application of these methodological principles ensures that the findings obtained are valid – specifically, that a positive finding has not occurred as a result of bias, or that a negative finding has not occurred as a result of bias, inadequate sample size, or the use of imprecise or nonresponsive outcome measures.

The discussion in this chapter is structured to present examples of clinical problems related to diagnosis, prevention and treatment of thrombosis and then to consider the impact that the results of these studies have had on clinical practice.

## DIAGNOSTIC STUDIES

The methodological requirements for evaluation of a diagnostic test have been reviewed in many excellent texts (Sackett *et al.*, 1985; Fletcher *et al.*, 1988). The most important requirements are as follows. The experimental test should be compared with a reference method (the so-called 'gold

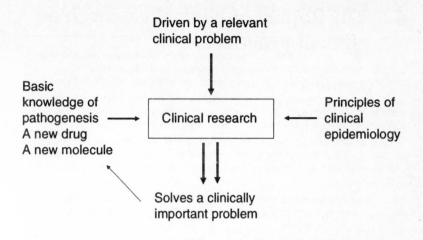

*Figure 1* The ingredients needed to perform clinical research successfully

standard'). Both diagnostic approaches (the experimental and the control) should be performed on a broad spectrum of consecutive patients suspected of having the disorder of interest and with conditions that may be confused clinically with the disorder of interest. This requirement is necessary to ensure that the results are generalisable. The results of both tests should be interpreted independently of each other by observers who are unaware of the patient's clinical status. This precaution is necessary to avoid bias in the interpretation of the diagnostic test. In addition, the sample size should be sufficiently large to provide reasonably narrow confidence intervals on the observed parameters of efficacy, which are: sensitivity, specificity, positive and negative predictive values and accuracy (Table 4) (Figure 2).

### Diagnosis of venous thrombosis

Twenty years ago patients with clinically suspected venous thrombosis were diagnosed on clinical features alone even though there was evidence in the literature that clinical diagnosis is nonspecific and that it was well known that the treatment of venous thrombosis is expensive, requires hospitalisation and is potentially dangerous. Well-designed studies in the 1970s and 1980s using venography (an invasive radiology procedure) as the reference standard confirmed the earlier observations that approximately fifty per cent of patients with clinically suspected venous thrombosis do not have venous thrombosis (Hirsh *et al.*, 1986; Forbes and

*Table 4* Essential design features for studies evaluating the efficacy of a
diagnostic test

---

The test should be evaluated in consecutive patients, all of whom undergo both
the diagnostic test and the reference test to determine the four indices of
efficacy: sensitivity, specificity, and positive and negative predictive values.

The evaluation of the diagnostic test should be performed in a broad spectrum of
patients with and without the disease in question. Failure to include a broad
spectrum of patients may result in a falsely high estimate of efficacy.

Diagnostic suspicion bias should be avoided by entering consecutive patients
into the study and by interpreting the results of the diagnostic tests and reference
tests independently and without knowledge of each other or of the patient's
clinical findings.

The clinical validity of negative test findings should be evaluated by long-term
clinical follow-up to determine the safety of withholding treatment in patients
with a negative test result.

---

*Source*: Hull *et al.*, 1987

Lowe, 1987; Haeger, 1969; Browse, 1978; Stamatakis *et al.*, 1978;
Fishman, 1962; McLachlin *et al.*, 1962; Hull *et al.*, 1981a; Hull *et al.*,
1981b). The results of these studies have had a marked impact on clinical
practice. Clinicians began to accept the need for objective testing (slowly at
first) to confirm a clinical suspicion of venous thrombosis, and today it
would be unacceptable to make definitive management decisions solely on

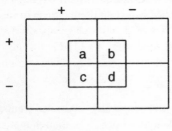

*Figure 2* Observed parameters of efficacy

the basis of clinical suspicion of venous thrombosis. A number of circumstances led to the acceptance by clinicians of the need for objective tests to confirm the clinical suspicion of venous thrombosis. The first was the remarkable consistency of the observation from a number of different centres in a number of different countries that clinical diagnosis is nonspecific (as above; also Huisman *et al.*, 1986; Wheeler *et al.*, 1975). The second was the demonstration that it is safe to leave patients who have negative objective tests untreated provided that their venogram or noninvasive test (the impedance plethysmogram) is normal (Hull *et al.*, 1981a and b; Huisman *et al.*, 1986; Wheeler *et al.*, 1975; Hull *et al.*, 1985b; Peters *et al.*, 1982). The third reason for acceptance was that reliable objective tests – initially venography, then impedance plethysmography and most recently B-mode imaging (Lensing *et al.*, 1989) – are readily available to the clinician.

The first two diagnostic tests (venography and impedance plethysmography) have been shown to be useful in a clinical setting (Huisman *et al.*, 1986; Wheeler *et al.*, 1975; Hull *et al.*, 1985b) while the most recent test, B-mode imaging, has been shown to be accurate when compared with venography (Lensing *et al.*, 1989). Thus, after twenty years of clinical research, the impact on clinical practice of clinical research into the diagnosis of venous thrombosis has been profound.

The situation is different, however, for the diagnosis of pulmonary embolism (PE), in which diagnostic confusion still exists despite consistent findings from two recent studies (Hull *et al.*, 1983, 1985a). This confusion exists because a number of competing but unreliable diagnostic procedures were introduced and accepted into clinical practice before they were evaluated and shown to be accurate. Consequently, it has been more difficult to reverse an entrenched practice based on publications in reputable journals and the strong opinions of experts than it was to introduce an approach into a clinical setting in which there were no competing objective tests. The problem has been compounded because the diagnostic process for PE is more complex and may require tests that are not readily available in many hospitals.

Traditionally, the diagnosis of PE was ruled in or out on the basis of clinical manifestations, the chest x-ray and the electrocardiograph (Hull *et al.*, 1983, 1985a; Robin, 1977; National Cooperative Trial, 1974). This approach was shown to be insensitive and nonspecific. Arterial blood gas analysis was then added to the diagnostic process and accepted (Hull *et al.*, 1983, 1985a; Robin, 1977). It is now clear that the arterial blood gas analysis does not have the sensitivity or specificity to be clinically useful for diagnosis (as above; also National Cooperative Trial, 1974). Finally an imaging test, the perfusion lung scan, was introduced, and for over a decade the diagnosis of PE was based on the result of this scan. The nonspecificity of the perfusion scan was then demonstrated in a number of well-designed studies (as above; also McNeil, 1980; Biello *et al.*, 1979). The diagnostic approach was changed, then changed once again so that the diagnosis of PE was made when the perfusion defect was large; further studies then demonstrated that the use of this diagnostic outcome was associated with a thirty per cent frequency of a falsely positive diagnosis (McNeil, 1980; Biello *et al.*, 1979). Finally a new technology, the ventilation scan, was introduced and various patterns of ventilation and perfusion scans were used to either rule in or rule out the diagnosis of PE. Once again this approach turned out to be inaccurate and the diagnostic process had to be revised yet again (Hull *et al.*, 1983, 1985a). It is not surprising, therefore, that the clinician is confused.

Why did these repeated errors in the diagnostic approach occur? They occurred because tests were introduced into practice either on the basis of studies which were deficient in the necessary design features (arterial blood gases) or on the basis of intuitive physiological principles (the perfusion scan and then the combination of the perfusion ventilation scan). Even after well-designed studies were performed which refuted the clinically accepted approaches, clinical practice has been slow to change. However, practice is changing now and would not have changed at all if methodologically rigorous studies had not been performed.

A number of messages emerge from these examples. The first is that results of well-designed clinical studies of diagnostic testing can affect clinical practice particularly if more than one study is performed and the results of these studies are consistent. The second message is that there is a strong tendency to introduce tests into clinical practice before they are evaluated using appropriate methodology. This temptation should be resisted because it is not only potentially dangerous to the patient, but it is wasteful financially and is difficult to change even when the approach is proven to be incorrect.

## PREVENTION OF VENOUS THROMBOSIS

The methodological requirements for performing intervention studies of either prophylaxis or treatment are also well defined. Whenever possible the study should be randomised and double blind to avoid bias. The outcome should be clinically relevant, reproducible and valid, and the sample size should be large enough to ensure that there is a reasonable chance of detecting true differences which are clinically important.

The initial studies of prophylaxis of venous thrombosis did not include these methodological standards and led to false conclusions about the efficacy of various prophylactic agents. For example, in an early study of aspirin prophylaxis, the study was randomised but unblinded, and clinical diagnosis was used as the outcome measure of venous thrombosis (Harris *et al.*, 1974). Aspirin was reported to be effective in preventing venous thrombosis, but since aspirin is an analgesic and pain is a common clinical symptom of venous thrombosis, the observed effectiveness of aspirin could have been spurious since the drug might have relieved pain without preventing the underlying thrombosis with its associated risks of pulmonary embolism. Subsequent studies using reliable outcome measures have demonstrated that aspirin is ineffective as a prophylactic agent for venous thrombosis (Clagett and Reisch, 1988). Despite this evidence, in a recent survey of orthopaedic surgeons carried out in the USA, aspirin was the most common method of prophylaxis used in patients who had total hip replacement (Paiement *et al.*, 1987). Why did this occur? The reasons are multiple. Aspirin is inexpensive, easy to administer and relatively safe (even though it is not effective). The initial publication appeared in a very reputable journal (Harris *et al.*, 1974) and was followed by a second publication from the same group in the same journal using a reliable outcome measure which confirmed the initial finding (Harris *et al.*, 1977). Subsequent studies by the same and other investigators using reliable outcome measures for thrombosis and results of a meta-analysis indicate aspirin is relatively ineffective and much less effective than a variety of other readily available prophylactic methods (Clagett and Reisch, 1988; Harris *et al.*, 1985; Morris and Mitchell, 1977; Stamatakis *et al.*, 1979).

The interpretation of prophylactic studies of venous thrombosis has not been straightforward because substitute outcome measures are usually used. Post-operative venous thrombosis, the condition against which prophylaxis is directed, is important because it may lead to fatal PE (a very uncommon event) and the post-phlebitic syndrome. The outcome measures used in most studies have been clinically silent calf vein thrombosis which, while relatively common, is clinically unimportant unless the thrombosis extends into the large veins of the thigh (popliteal and more proximal veins).

Pooled analyses of studies evaluating the effects of different methods of prophylaxis on post-operative venous thrombosis in general surgical patients (Clagett and Reisch, 1988) and in patients undergoing hip surgery (Hirsh and Levine, 1989) indicate that impressive reductions in post-operative venous thrombosis occur with several different forms of prophylaxis (see Table 5).

Despite the convincing evidence that prophylaxis is effective, surveys performed in England (Morris, 1980), Sweden (Bergqvist, 1980), and the United States (Conti and Daschbach, 1982) reported that most surgeons do

*Table 5* Relative risk reduction

|         | Control | HEP | DEX | IPC | GC  | Aspirin |
|---------|---------|-----|-----|-----|-----|---------|
| ALL DVT | 25.1    | 65* | 36* | 51* | 62* | 12      |
| P DVT   | 6.9     | 78* |     |     |     |         |
| PE      | 1.6     | 57* | 57* |     |     |         |
|         | 0.87    | 70* | 82* |     |     |         |

\* Statistically significant.
*Source*: The effectiveness of different forms of prophylaxis on the incidence of post-operative thrombosis following general surgery. Own analysis of pooled data from randomised trials.

not use effective prophylaxis even in very high risk patients (Clagett and Reisch, 1988; Paiement *et al.*, 1987).

The reasons for the failure to use prophylaxis are complex and include the perception by surgeons (despite evidence to the contrary) that venous thromboembolism is not an important complication of surgery (Bell and Zuidema, 1979; Hayes and Baker, 1985; Strandness, 1986), the rarity of major or fatal PE in any individual surgeon's practice, the fear that pharmacological prophylaxis with anticoagulants produces serious bleeding (Pachter and Riles, 1977; Van Ooijen, 1986), the inconvenience of certain physical methods, and misconceptions about costs (Salzman and Davies, 1980; Oster *et al.*, 1987).

## REASONS FOR NOT USING PROPHYLAXIS

The clinically important thromboembolic outcomes are proximal vein thrombosis and fatal PE. Proximal vein thrombosis occurs in four to eight per cent of high-risk patients undergoing general surgical procedures and in twenty per cent of patients undergoing hip and major knee surgery (Clagett and Reisch, 1988; Hirsh and Levine, 1989). Proximal vein thrombosis is important clinically because more than fifty per cent of these patients develop post-thrombotic complications (the post-thrombotic syndrome) over a five-to-ten-year period. The incidence of fatal PE is low, between 0.5 and 1 per cent after major or general surgery (Clagett and Reisch, 1988) and approximately two per cent after hip surgery (Paiement *et al.*, 1987), but even this low risk would justify the use of effective prophylaxis unless the benefit is offset by side effects or unacceptable costs.

A number of inexpensive prophylactic agents are effective in reducing venous thrombosis following general surgery (Clagett and Reisch, 1988). Low dose heparin (LDH) and dextran have been shown to reduce the incidence of both proximal vein thrombosis and fatal PE between 70 per cent and 82 per cent. For LDH there is no increase in major haemorrhage, but there is an increase in wound haematoma which are not life threatening (Clagett and Reisch, 1988). Similarly, adjusted dose heparin (ADH), oral anticoagulants, dextran and, more recently, low molecular weight heparin (LMWH) are effective in hip surgery (Paiement *et al.*, 1987).

From the absolute risk reduction (Clagett and Reisch, 1988) with low dose heparin it can be calculated that twenty high-risk general surgical patients would have to be given prophylaxis to avert one episode of proximal vein thrombosis and two hundred patients would have to receive prophylaxis to avert one death. These benefits would be achieved without increasing the risk of major bleeding, but at a cost of approximately ten wound haematoma for each fatal PE averted. Given the far greater importance of proximal vein thrombosis or fatal PE than wound haematoma, prophylaxis with LDH is clearly indicated in high-risk general surgical patients. Other forms of prophylaxis such as external pneumatic compression are as effective as LDH in preventing total post-operative thrombi, but the studies have been too small to assess their effects on proximal vein thrombosis or fatal PE. Nevertheless, these physical methods are free of bleeding risks and would be particularly attractive for use in patients with a high risk of bleeding.

The case for prophylaxis is even greater for patients undergoing elective hip replacement since the incidences of proximal vein thrombosis and fatal PE are even higher than in high-risk general surgery (Paiement *et al.*, 1987). Two approaches, LMWH and ADH, have been shown to reduce the risk of total DVT (deep-vein thrombosis) and proximal DVT by seventy per cent without increasing the risk of major bleeding. With either of these forms of prophylaxis only eight patients would have to receive prophylaxis to avert one episode of proximal vein thrombosis and only about seventy patients would have to receive prophylaxis to avert one death from PE.

Although the results of surveys taken in the last decade are disappointing, the consistent message in published literature (Clagett and Reisch, 1988; Paiement *et al.*, 1987), the recommendations by various international organisations and by consensus conferences (Hirsh, 1986) and the development of new, safe and effective prophylactic approaches such as LMWH give cause for optimism that prophylaxis will be used much more widely in the future.

## THROMBOLYTIC THERAPY IN MYOCARDIAL INFARCTION

The history of thrombolytic therapy for patients with acute myocardial infarction (AMI) dates back three decades (Fletcher *et al.*, 1959). For the first two decades, there was little enthusiasm for thrombolytic therapy because the studies were either negative or inconsistent. In the last decade, we have witnessed a wave of enthusiasm for the use of thrombolytic therapy in AMI, and this approach is recommended strongly by cardiologists and internists around the world. Why the marked change in attitude? The early studies were designed without a clear understanding of the pathogenesis of AMI and without a knowledge of optimal dosage of the thrombolytic drugs used, and were too small to have the power to demonstrate clinically important and biologically realistic differences (Yusuf *et al.*, 1985; Cairns *et al.*, 1989). Thus, many patients in most of the early studies commenced treatment at least twelve hours after the onset of ischaemic pain when thrombolytic therapy may be only marginally effective. Streptokinase (SK) was given in relatively low concentrations over a period of 12 to 48 hours and studies lacked the power to reliably detect true differences in mortality of 25 to 30 per cent. The major reasons responsible for the renewed interest in thrombolytic therapy for the treatment of AMI are:

1  the investigation of patients with AMI by coronary angiography and the demonstration that the coronary artery supplying the region of infarction has an occlusive thrombosis in ninety per cent of patients who are investigated within one or two hours of clinical presentation (DeWood *et al.*, 1980). This provided the biological rationale for thrombolytic therapy;
2  the demonstration that SK infused into the coronary artery lysed approximately seventy per cent of the thrombi and by so doing reduced mortality (Kennedy *et al.*, 1983);
3  the demonstration that high-dose SK or tissue plasminogen activator (tPA) infused intravenously produced coronary thrombolysis in the majority of patients (Chesebro *et al.*, 1987; Verstraete *et al.*, 1985a); and
4  the demonstration that intravenous SK (ISIS-2, 1988; Gruppo Italiano, 1986), rtPA (Wilcox *et al.*, 1988; Verstraete *et al.*, 1985b) and APSAC (AIMS Study, 1988) reduced mortality in patients with myocardial infarction.

The appealing biological rationale plus the consistency of results from a number of large, well-designed studies using different thrombolytic agents provided such compelling evidence that the change in clinical practice has been rapid and widespread.

## ASPIRIN IN THE PREVENTION OF COMPLICATIONS OF ATHEROSCLEROSIS

Aspirin has been known for fifty years to impair haemostasis, was shown to inhibit platelet function over twenty years ago, and its mechanism of inhibition of platelet function was defined over ten years ago (Roth and Majerus, 1975). The early randomised trials with aspirin for the secondary prevention of reinfarction and death in patients with myocardial infarction showed small trends in favour of aspirin but lacked the power to demonstrate clinically important differences (Antiplatelet Trialists' Collaboration, 1988). Enthusiasm for aspirin in the secondary prevention of myocardial infarction was dampened by the preconception that coronary thrombosis would not be prevented by an agent (aspirin) which did not inhibit platelet aggregation induced by the three major platelet-aggregating agonists – namely, thrombin, collagen and adenosine diphosphate (Cairns *et al.*, 1985). These preconceptions of the mechanism of arterial thrombosis and rethrombosis were not entirely correct because aspirin, an agent which inhibits but one of many pathways of platelet aggregation, has proven to be effective in reducing the risk of arterial thrombosis (Antiplatelet Trialists' Collaboration, 1988). Thus, aspirin is effective in reducing the incidence of AMI and death in unstable angina (Antiplatelet Trialists' Collaboration, 1988; Cairns *et al.*, 1985; Lewis *et al.*, 1983); in preventing death and reinfarction in patients with AMI (Antiplatelet Trialists' Collaboration, 1988; ISIS-2, 1988); in preventing stroke in patients with atherosclerosis (Antiplatelet Trialists' Collaboration, 1988; UK-TIA Study Group, 1988); and in preventing early occlusion of aorta coronary by-pass grafts (Goldman *et al.*, 1987).

There are two lessons to be learned from the aspirin story. The first is that our preconceptions of biology are not always correct and may be modified by the findings from well-designed clinical trials. The second is that when event rates are relatively low in the control group (as they were in the initial trials of aspirin in AMI) and the disorder is a common cause of death (as it is for myocardial infarction), then even relatively large studies may be too small to detect true differences which are clinically important. This latter problem led to the concept of using a technique of pooled analysis (Antiplatelet Trialists' Collaboration, 1988) which, despite some limitations, provides a more reliable estimate of efficacy than single studies which lack the power to reliably demonstrate clinically important differences.

# REFERENCES

AIMS Trial Study Group, 1988, 'Effect of intravenous APSAC on mortality after acute myocardial infarction: Preliminary report of a placebo-controlled clinical trial', *Lancet* 1: 545–9.

Antiplatelet Trialists' Collaboration, 1988, 'Secondary prevention of vascular disease by prolonged antiplatelet treatment', *British Medical Journal*, 296: 320.

Bell, W.R. and Zuidema, G.D., 1979, 'Low-dose heparin-concern and perspectives', *Surgery*, 85: 469–71.

Bergqvist, D., 1980, 'Prevention of postoperative deep vein thrombosis in Sweden: Results of a survey', *World Journal of Surgery*, 4: 489–95.

Biello, D.R., Mattar, A.G., McKnight, R.C. and Siegel, B.A., 1979, 'Ventilation-perfusion studies in suspected pulmonary embolism', *American Journal of Radiology*, 133: 1033–7.

Browse, N., 1978, 'Diagnosis of deep vein thrombosis', *British Medical Bulletin*, 34: 163–7.

Cairns, J.A., Gent, M., Singer, J., Finnie, K.J., Froggatt, G.M., Holder, D.A., Jablousky, G., Kostuk, W.J., Mehendez, L.J., Myers, M.G., Sackett, D.L., Sealey, B.J. and Tanser, P.H., 1985, 'Aspirin, sulfinpyrazone, or both in unstable angina', *New England Journal of Medicine*, 313: 1369–75.

Cairns, J.A., Collins, R., Fuster, V. and Passamani, E.R., 1989, 'Coronary thrombolysis', *Chest*, 95, 2: 73S–87S.

Chesebro, J.H., Knatterud, G., Roberts, R., Borer, J., Collen, L.S., Dalen, J.E., Dodge, H.T., Francis, C.K., Hillis, D., Ludbrook, P., Markis, J.E., Mueller, H., Passamani, E.R., Powers, E.R., Rao, A.K., Robertson, T., Ross, A., Ryan, T.J., Sobel, B.E., Willerson, J., Williams, B.D., Zaret, B.L. and Braunwald, E., 1987, 'Thrombolysis in myocardial infarction (TIMI) trial, phase 1: A comparison between intravenous plasminogen activator and intravenous streptokinase', *Circulation*, 76: 142–54.

Clagett, G.P. and Reisch, J.S., 1988, 'Prevention of venous thromboembolism in general surgical patients: Results of meta-analysis', *Annals of Surgery*, 208: 227–40.

Conti, S. and Daschbach, M., 1982, 'Venous thromboembolism prophylaxis', *Archives of Surgery*, 117: 1036–40.

DeWood, M.A., Spores, J., Notske, R., Mouser, L.T., Burroughs, R., Goulden, M.S. and Lang, H.T., 1980, 'Prevalence of total coronary occlusion during the early hours of transmural myocardial infarction', *New England Journal of Medicine*, 303: 897–902.

Fishman, L.G., 1962, 'Erroneous diagnosis of thrombophlebitis of the lower extremities', *Khirugiya*, 38: 58–62.

Fletcher, A.P., Sherry, S. and Alkjaersig, N., 1959, 'The maintenance of a sustained thrombolytic state in man: II. Clinical observations on patients with myocardial infarction and other thromboembolic disorders', *Journal of Clinical Investigation*, 38: 1111–19.

Fletcher, R.H., Fletcher, S.W. and Wagner, E.H., 1988, 'Diagnosis', in Fletcher, R.H., Fletcher, S.W. and Wagner, E.H. (eds), *Clinical Epidemiology: The Essentials*, Chapter 3, Baltimore: Williams & Wilkins.

Forbes, C.D. and Lowe, G.D.O., 1987, 'Clinical Diagnosis', in J. Hirsh (ed.), *Venous Thrombosis and Pulmonary Embolism: Diagnostic Methods*, New York: Churchill Livingstone.

Goldman, S., Copeland, J., Moritz, T. and Henderson, W., 1987, 'Effect of anti-platelet therapy on early graft patency after coronary artery bypass grafting', VA Cooperative Study #207 (abstract), *Journal of the American College of Cardiology*, 9: 125A.

Gruppo Italiano per lo studio della Streptokinase Nell infarcto Micardico (GISSI), 1986, 'Effectiveness of intravenous thrombolytic treatment in acute myocardial infarction', *Lancet*, 1: 397–402.

Haeger, K., 1969, 'Problems of acute deep vein thrombosis: The interpretation of signs and symptoms', *Angiology*, 20: 219–22.

Harris, W.H., Salzman, E.W., Athanasoulis, C., Waltman, A.C. Baum, S. and De Santis, R.W., 1974, 'Comparison of warfarin, low-molecular-weight dextran, aspirin, and subcutaneous heparin prevention of venous thromboembolism following total hip replacement', *Journal of Bone and Joint Surgery*, 56: 1552.

—— 1977, 'Aspirin prophylaxis of venous thromboembolism after total hip replacement', *New England Journal of Medicine*, 297: 1246.

—— 1985, 'Prophylaxis of deep-vein thrombosis after total hip replacement: Dextran and external pneumatic compression compared with 1.2 or 0.3 gram of aspirin daily', *Journal of Bone and Joint Surgery*, 67A: 57.

Hayes, A.C. and Baker, W.H., 1985, 'Heparin prophylaxis trials of venous thrombosis: a critical review', *Seminars on Thrombosis and Hemostasis*, 2: 222–6.

Hirsh, J., 1986, 'Prevention of venous thrombosis and pulmonary embolism', National Institutes of Health Consensus Development Conference Statement, 6, 2: 1–8.

Hirsh, J. and Levine, M.N., 1989, 'Prevention of venous thrombosis in patients undergoing major orthopedic surgical procedures', *British Journal of Clinical Practice* (Supplement 65), 43, 1: 2–8.

Hirsh, J., Hull, R.D. and Raskob, G.E., 1986, 'Clinical features and diagnosis of venous thrombosis', *Journal of the American College of Cardiology*, 8, 6: 114B–127B.

Huisman, M.V., Buller, H.R., ten Cate, J.W. and Vreeken, J., 1986, 'Serial imped-ance plethysmography for suspected deep venous thrombosis in outpatients', *New England Journal of Medicine*, 314: 823–8.

Hull, R.D., Hirsh, J., Carter, C.J., Jay, R.M., Dodd, P.E., Ockelford, P.A., Coates, G., Gill, G.J., Turpie, A.G.G., Doyle, D.J., Buller, H.R. and Roskob, G.E., 1983, 'Pulmonary angiography, ventilation lung scanning and venography for clinically suspected pulmonary embolism with abnormal perfusion lung scan', *Annals of Internal Medicine*, 98, 6: 891–9.

Hull, R.D., Hirsh, J., Carter, C.J., Jay, R.M., Ockelford, P.A., Buller, H.R., Turpie, A.G.G., Powers, P.J., Kinch, D., Dodd, P., Gill, G.J., Leclerc, J.R., Gent, M., 1985a, 'Diagnostic efficacy of impedance plethysmography for clinically sus-pected deep-vein thrombosis: A randomized trial', *Annals of Internal Medicine*, 102: 21–8.

Hull, R.D., Hirsh, J., Carter, C.J., Roskob, G.E., Gill, G.J., Jay, R.M., Leclerc, J.R., Daud, M. and Coates, G., 1985b, 'Diagnostic value of ventilation-perfusion lung scanning in patients with suspected pulmonary embolism', *Chest*, 88, 6: 819–28.

Hull, R.D., Hirsh, J., Carter, C.J., Turpie, A.G.G. and Powers, P.J., 1981a, 'Clinical validity of a negative venogram in patients with clinically suspected venous thrombosis', *Circulation*, 64: 622–4.

Hull, R.D., Hirsh, J., Sackett, D.L., Taylor, D.W., Carter, C.J., Turpie, A.G.G.,

Zielinsky, A., Powers, P.J. and Gent, M., 1981b, 'Replacement of venography in suspected venous thrombosis by impedance plethysmography and 125 I-fibrinogen leg scanning', *Annals of Internal Medicine*, 94, 1: 12–15.

Hull, R.D., Secker-Walker, R.H., Hirsh, J., 1987, 'Diagnosis of deep-vein thrombosis', in Colman, R.W., Hirsh, J., Marder, V.J. and Salzman, E.W. (eds), *Hemostasis and Thrombosis: Basic Principles and Clinical Practice*, 2nd edn, Chapter 79, Philadelphia: J.B. Lippincott Co.

ISIS-2 (Second International Study of Infarct Survival) Collaborative Group, 1988, 'Randomized trial of intravenous streptokinase, oral aspirin, both or neither among 17,187 cases of suspected acute myocardial infarction', *Lancet*, 2: 329–60.

Kennedy, J.W., Ritchie, J.L., Davis, K.B. and Fritz, J.K., 1983, 'Western Washington randomized trial of intracoronary streptokinase in acute myocardial infarction', *New England Journal of Medicine*, 309: 1477–82.

Lensing, A.W.A., Prandoni, P., Brandjes, D., Huisman, P.M., Vigo, M., Tomasella, G., Krekt, J., ten Cate, J.W., Huisman, M.V. and Bullen, H.R., 1989, 'Detection of deep-vein thrombosis by real-time B-mode ultrasonography', *New England Journal of Medicine*, 320, 6: 342–5.

Lewis, H.D., Davis, J.W., Archibald, D.G., Steinke, W.E., Smitherman, T.C., Doherty, J.E., Schnaper, H.W., Le Winter, M.M., Linares, E., Pouget, J.M., Sabharwal, S.C., and Chesler, E., 1983, 'Protective effects of aspirin against acute myocardial infarction and death in men with unstable angina: Results of a Veterans Administration Cooperative Study', *New England Journal of Medicine*, 309: 396–403.

McLachlin, J., Richards, T. and Paterson, J.C., 1962, 'An evaluation of clinical signs in the diagnosis of venous thrombosis', *Archives of Surgery*, 85: 738–44.

McNeil, B.J., 1980, 'Ventilation-perfusion studies and the diagnosis of pulmonary embolism: Concise communication', *Journal of Nuclear Medicine*, 21: 319–23.

Morris, G.K., 1980, 'Prevention of venous thromboembolism: A survey of methods used by orthopedic and general surgeons', *Lancet*, 2: 572–4.

Morris, G.K. and Mitchell, J.R.A., 1977, 'Preventing venous thromboembolism in elderly patients with hip fractures. Studies of low-dose heparin, dipyridamole, aspirin, and flurbiprofen', *British Medical Journal*, 1: 535.

National Cooperative Trial, 1974, 'Urokinase-streptokinase pulmonary embolism trial. Phase 2 results', *Journal of the American Medical Association*, 229: 1606–13.

Oster, G., Tuden, R.L. and Colditz, G.A., 1987, 'A cost-effectiveness analysis of prophylaxis against deep-vein thrombosis in major orthopedic surgery', *Journal of the American Medical Association*, 257: 203–208.

Pachter, H.L. and Riles, T.S., 1977, 'Low dose heparin: Bleeding and wound complications in the surgical patient', *Annals of Surgery*, 186: 669–74.

Paiement, G.D., Wessinger, S.J. and Harris, W.H., 1987, 'Survey of prophylaxis against venous thromboembolism in adults undergoing hip surgery', *Clinical Orthopedics and Related Research*, 223: 188–93.

Peters, S.H.A., Jonker, J.J.C., deBoer, A.C., and den Ottolander, G.J., 1982, 'Home diagnosis of deep venous thrombosis with impedance plethysmography', *Thrombosis and Haemostasis*, 48, 3: 134–44.

PIOPED Investigators, 1990, 'Value of the ventilation/perfusion scan in acute pulmonary embolism: results of the prospective investigation of pulmonary embolism diagnosis (PIOPED)', *Journal of the American Medical Association*, 263: 2753–9.

Robin, E.D., 1977, 'Overdiagnosis and overtreatment of pulmonary embolism: The emperor may have no clothes', *Annals of Internal Medicine*, 87: 775–81.

Roth, G.J. and Majerus, P.W., 1975, 'The mechanism of the effect of aspirin on human platelets. I. Acetylation of a particulate fraction protein', *Journal of Clinical Investigation*, 56: 624–32.

Sackett, D.L., Haynes, R.B. and Tugwell, P., 1985, 'The interpretation of diagnostic data', in Sackett, D.L., Haynes, R.B. and Tugwell, P. (eds), *Clinical Epidemiology: A Basic Science for Clinical Medicine*, Chapter 4, Boston/Toronto: Little, Brown & Company.

Salzman, E.W. and Davies, G.C., 1980, 'Prophylaxis of venous thromboembolism: Analysis of cost effectiveness', *Annals of Surgery*, 189: 207–18.

Stamatakis, J.D., Kakkar, W., Lawrence, D. and Bentley, P.G., 1978, 'The origin of thrombi in the deep veins of the lower limbs: A venography study', *British Journal of Surgery*, 65: 449–51.

Stamatakis, J.D., Kakkar, W., Lawrence, D., Bentley, P.G., Nairm, D. and Ward, V., 1979, 'Failure of aspirin to prevent post-operative deep-vein thrombosis in patients undergoing total hip replacement', *British Medical Journal*, 1: 1031.

Strandness, D.E., 1986, 'Variations in the incidence of venous thrombosis', paper presented at the NIH Consensus Development Conference on Prevention of Venous Thrombosis and Pulmonary Embolism, Bethesda, MD.

UK-TIA Study Group, 1988, 'The UK-TIA aspirin trial: Interim results', *British Medical Journal*, 296: 316–19.

Van Ooijen, B., 1986, 'Subcutaneous heparin and postoperative wound hematomas: A prospective, double-blind, randomized study', *Archives of Surgery*, 121: 937–40.

Verstraete, M., Bernard, R., Bory, M., Brower, R.W., Collen, D., de Boug, D.P., Erbel, R., Huhmann, W., Lennanc, R.J., Lubsen, J., Mathey, D., Meyer, J., Michels, H.R., Ruesch, W., Schartl, M., Schmidt, W., Vebis, R. and Von Essen, R., 1985a, 'Randomized trial of intravenous recombinant tissue-type plasminogen activator versus intravenous streptokinase in acute myocardial infarction', *Lancet*, 1: 842–7.

Verstraete, M., Bleifeld, W., Brower, R.W., Charbonnier, B., Collen, D., de Bono, D.P., Dunning, A.J., Lennane, R.J., Lubsen, J., Mathey, D.G., Michel, P.L., Raynaud, P.H., Schofer, J., Vahanian, A., Vanhaecke, J., Van De Kley, G.A., Van De Werf, F. and Von Essen, R., 1985b, 'Double blind randomized trial of intravenous tissue-type plasminogen activator versus placebo in acute myocardial infarction', *Lancet*, 2: 965–9.

Wheeler, H.B., O'Donnell, J.A., Anderson, F.A., Penney, B.C. and Peura, R.A., 1975, 'Bedside screening for venous thrombosis using occlusive impedance phlebography', *Angiology*, 26: 199–210.

Wilcox, R.G., Van der Lippe, G., Olsson, C.G., Jensen, G., Skene, A.M. and Hampton, J.R., 1988, 'Trial of tissue plasminogen activator for mortality reduction in acute myocardial infarction: Anglo-Scandinavian Study of Early Thrombolysis (ASSET)', *Lancet*, 2: 525–30.

Yusuf, S., Collins, R., Peto, R., Furbery, C., Stampfer, M.J., Goldhaber, S.Z. and Hennekens, C.H., 1985, 'Intravenous and intracoronary fibrinolytic therapy in acute myocardial infarction: overview of results on mortality, reinfarction and side effects from 33 randomized controlled trials, *European Heart Journal*, 6: 556–85.

# 5 The clinician and the randomised controlled trial

*Michael Jelinek*

The clinician is the penultimate consumer of the results of health-related research. Whilst the clinician may engage in various forms of research, the primary role, that which defines the clinician, is that of applying knowledge to the relief of symptoms and improving life expectancy of the individual patient. In order to examine the clinician's role in evaluating medical research, a recapitulation of the clinician's background is appropriate.

The traditional medical school expects a student to have a grounding in normal body structure and function, and a knowledge of the abnormalities of structure and function which constitute diseases, before being introduced to patients and clinical practice. It is this background which is uniquely medical. More recently, limitations of this approach have been apparent and other disciplines such as psychology, sociology, and epidemiology have been added. Because the scope of these basic sciences is so vast, little is done in a six-year undergraduate course to equip a graduating clinician with the ability to evaluate the results of medical research, let alone to evaluate its methods.

One-third of medical graduates specialise. By concentrating on a limited area of clinical endeavour, it is hoped that specialists acquire a greater depth of knowledge of abnormal structure and function in specific diseases and greater clinical experience in the diagnosis and management of these states. Specialists are expected to understand the results of medical research as it applies to their specialty, and it is the specialists who instruct the generalists on the significance of new diagnostic and therapeutic techniques derived from research.

About one-third of specialists have either the good fortune or perverse interest to engage in health-related research. Such clinicians are the conduits for introducing the results of medical research into clinical practice. They usually have a doctorate in either medicine or philosophy or both and are versed in the various kinds of research methodologies. The remainder of this paper will not concern itself with this ten per cent minority group but will discuss the methods, usually not explicit, by which most clinicians handle the results of medical research.

## THE CLINICIAN AS PRAGMATIST

A clinician could be described as someone who practises clinical medicine at least fifty per cent of the time. Since most busy clinicians would consider a clinician as one working at least sixty hours per week in clinical practice, this definition may be open to challenge.

The clinical method involves an iterative process between the needs of the individual patient and the core of basic sciences. What characterises the *experienced* clinician is the more effective and efficient use of this particular process. Preventive practices, diagnostic techniques, and specific therapies are chosen which are likely to be quick, cheap and effective. Those which are not quick, cheap or effective are eventually discarded as cant. Such clinical decisions are certainly in the patient's interest provided that clinicians' concerns with income or status can be excluded.

## RESEARCH METHODS AND THE RELIEF OF SYMPTOMS

Clinicians attempt to alleviate symptoms by applying the biomedical model to the individual. Textbook descriptions list typical symptoms of disease and the mechanisms of symptom production. For a therapy to be considered at all, it should favourably affect the disease mechanism. Drug companies must show that their products actually have a physiological mechanism and that they are safe. The randomised controlled trial is often the linchpin in demonstrating that the treatment is more effective than chance in improving symptoms or affecting the disease process. In such trials, the drug and dosage are standardised, the disease is carefully defined and the data are demonstrated by objective means: the randomised, double blind, placebo-controlled, cross-over study. Since the fiasco of the internal mammary artery ligation operation for palliating angina (Cobb *et al.*, 1959), it has become necessary for surgeons to prove that their operations are more effective than chance in alleviating symptoms. In this regard, trials of coronary by-pass surgery show that this therapy is superior to drug therapy in improving the symptoms of angina (Peduzzi *et al.*, 1987). And yet there are limitations to the 'scientific' approach to relief of symptoms in practice.

The first reason for this is the limitation inherent in the concept of disease. Patients usually present doctors with symptoms. Frequently these symptoms are not caused by a recognisable or treatable pathology. The symptoms may represent anxiety, depression or untreatable social friction. Thus clinicians will frequently suspect that a patient's symptom, such as headache, is not associated with recognisable organic pathology, and will diagnose the absence of disease without the need for further testing and will attempt to reassure the patient. Sometimes this exclusion of serious disease is effective and the complaint, and the patient, leave the practice satisfied. Frequently the patient is not satisfied, and after seeking help from one or two more medical practitioners, turns for help to 'alternative medicine' with its nostrums and lack of proof. Perhaps this is an important area in which clinicians should turn back to researchers in order to refine their methods of coping. For this is really at the edge of the medical model.

Akin to this, and much more difficult in practice, is the occurrence of demonstrable pathology with atypical symptoms. Every cardiologist knows that approximately half of all middle-aged people – the sort that might present symptoms of chest pain suggesting angina – have cervical spondylitis or hiatus hernia, ten per cent may have gallstones or peptic ulcers, and two per cent may have coronary artery disease in the absence of any known clinical manifestation. How then should they respond if these diseases are found on testing? Fortunately, medical science has helped in the area of coronary artery disease with the development of exercise tests and organ imaging, especially coronary angiography. Ultimately, however, the cardiologist will decide that the chest pain is, or is not, due to coronary disease by virtue of its pattern, assisted by abnormalities seen on exercise testing and coronary angiography. A minority of patients will warrant a trial of medical or even interventional therapy in an attempt to elucidate and treat a cause of pain. In this area – duplicated in all parts of the body and in all specialties – there is no substitute for professional competence and experience.

A second limitation inherent in research and research method lies in the differing objectives of researchers and clinicians in treating symptoms. Researchers wish to prove that their therapy works better than chance. Clinicians wish to remove or improve the presenting complaint. For researchers, the placebo response is the major hurdle to jump in order to prove therapeutic efficacy. The clinician recognises the placebo effect and prescribes pills or recommends surgery with confidence in the efficacy of the treatment. Side effects are not mentioned unless they are either common or dangerous. The concept of fully informed consent, beloved of academic lawyers and consumer groups, is antithetical to full symptom relief and good patient care. The kind clinician prescribes medical or surgical therapy when the benefits of this therapy outweigh its risks – and its efficacy depends on the degree of trust of the patient in the doctor.

## RESEARCH METHODS AND THE MANAGEMENT OF DISEASE

Whilst most clinicians would agree that the relief or palliation of symptoms is the major goal of therapy in the management of most cases, the glamour in medicine, both for doctors and researchers, is the thought of prolonging a life that is satisfying to the patient. It is here that the core of medical science, research and research methods have made their greatest contribution. However, the type of knowledge that influences practice is derived from quite a variety of sources and does not depend on any one method or institution. This will be illustrated in discussing the prevention, diagnosis and treatment of coronary heart disease, the largest cause of death in our affluent society.

## SECULAR TRENDS IN DEATHS FROM CORONARY HEART DISEASE

There was a fall in age-specific death rates at all ages above 30 years old in both men and women in Australia between 1968 and 1986. Since all people eventually die, the effect of this secular trend is to sharply increase the proportion of the elderly in the population. The fall in age-specific death rates in the population is entirely explained by a 56 per cent fall in deaths certified as being cardiovascular in origin. In 1986 approximately 48 per cent of all deaths were regarded as cardiovascular in origin. Thus the major cause of increased life expectancy in the last twenty years is delaying the age at which cardiovascular death occurs rather than changing the cause of death (National Heart Foundation of Australia, 1986).

Theories abound regarding the cause of declining age-specific death rates in coronary heart disease. Community epidemiological studies have shown that although only 14 per cent of first presentations of heart disease are with a rapidly fatal cardiac disease (sudden cardiac death), 41 per cent of sudden deaths occur as the first manifestation of clinical heart disease (Kannel *et al.*, 1987). International studies have shown that the largest proportion of the fall in age-specific mortality rates is a decline in the age-specific sudden death rate which parallels a decline in the age-specific incidence of ischaemic heart disease. Although there has been an equal proportionate fall in the case fatality rate of patients hospitalised with acute myocardial infarction, since only 35 per cent of coronary heart deaths occur in hospital, the impact of hospital care on total mortality rates is proportionately decreased. Surprisingly, there has been no improvement in survival of patients with chronic established coronary heart disease (see Table 6).

The overall conclusion from the above data is that the fall in coronary heart disease death rates is two-thirds due to changing lifestyle factors and

*Table 6* Components of decline in coronary heart disease

| Source (reference) | Decline in incidence | Death rates | | |
|---|---|---|---|---|
| | | Decline in sudden death rate | Decline in hospital case fatality rate | Decline in post-hospital mortality rate |
| Oldmeadow County (Elveback, *et al.*, 1981; Elveback 1985) | + | + | + | ± |
| Boston (Goldman, *et al.*, 1982) | ? | ? | - | ? |
| H.I.P. (Weinblatt, *et al.*, 1982) | ? | ? | ? | - |
| Minnesota Heart Survey (Gillum, *et al.*, 1983; Gomez-Marin, *et al.*, 1987) | ? | + | + | + |
| Dupont (Pell and Fayerweather, 1985) | + | + | + | ? |
| Perth (Hobbs, *et al.*, 1984, Thompson *et al.*, 1988) | + | + | + | ± |
| Auckland (Beaglehole, *et al.*, 1984; Stewart, *et al.*, 1988) | ? | + | - | + |
| Worcester (Gomez-Marin, *et al.*, 1987, Goldberg, *et al.*, 1988) | + | + | + | - |
| Allegheny County (Kuller, *et al.*, 1986) | + | + | + | - |
| National Hospital Discharge Survey (Gillum 1987) | ? | ? | + | ? |
| Hunter Valley (Dobson, *et al.*, 1988) | + | + | + | ? |
| National Center for Health Statistics (Gillum, 1989) | ? | + | ? | ? |

one-third due to better medical care (Goldman and Cook, 1984). This is not a universal phenomenon and appears to occur in countries which direct their resources at lifestyle modifications, and not in countries too poor, apathetic or cynical in these areas.

## PREVENTION OF CORONARY HEART DISEASE

A consistent body of observational data shows that certain characteristics, or risk factors, are consistently found in excess in young patients with coronary heart disease. These risk factors stand out as the most powerful associations and predictors of heart disease in younger men with coronary disease: a cigarette smoking habit, high serum cholesterol and high arterial blood pressure. So consistent and quantitative are these factors in predicting coronary risk that they are generally assumed as causal for this disease. Thus, half of all cardiovascular disease occurs in the top twenty per cent of the population grouped by these risk factors (Martin *et al.*, 1986).

In order to finally prove causality, and to convince the non-medical public of the importance of these treatable risk factors, two of the larger and most costly intervention trials were embarked upon: the Multiple Risk Factor Intervention Trial (MRFIT) in the United States (Multiple Risk Factor Intervention Trial Research Group, 1982) and the World Health Organization study on primary prevention in Europe (World Health Organization European Collaborative Group, 1986). Although there were many grumbles about the actual execution of the multi-centre controlled trial, both of the studies were pursued to completion. Both studies failed to support the concept that risk factor intervention could reduce the incidence of coronary heart disease. The protagonists of controlled trials and prevention have simply ignored or explained away these results as aberrations and have used the results of smaller intervention trials to support the prevailing emphasis on multiple risk intervention.

What about single risk factor intervention? Once again, a huge body of data, at least in Western countries with a high incidence of coronary heart disease, demonstrates that the incidence and death rates from heart disease rise in quadratic fashion with increase in the number of cigarettes smoked before any manifestations of the disease are present (Hammond, 1964). Furthermore, data show that the excess death rate from heart disease associated with smoking declines rapidly with smoking cessation and is barely detectable five years after quitting the habit. The benefits of quitting are seen most starkly in comparing the death rates of patients who continued to smoke after myocardial infarction with those who quit (Daly *et al.*, 1983). These repeatedly consistent observational studies on clinical and community groups are as close to proof as is ever obtained by observational study. But the one randomised controlled trial on smoking cessation, performed on middle-aged British civil servants, failed to show any benefit from quitting smoking (Rose *et al.*, 1982). What are we to believe – the observational data supporting the causal role of smoking or the one controlled trial not supporting cause and effect?

The higher the level of arterial blood pressure, systolic or diastolic, the higher the death rate from cardiovascular disease. This has been clearly and consistently demonstrated (Martin *et al.*, 1986). In the last fifteen years there have been a number of randomised controlled trials looking at the impact of hypotensive therapy. In summary, all show a significant reduction in cardiovascular events as a result of treatment (Medical Research Council Working Party, 1985). This effect is primarily a result of the reduction in haemorrhagic strokes. The trials are inconsistent when considering deaths from coronary heart disease, and any effect in this area must be small. Clearly the case for blood pressure lowering has been proven. However, should treatment be confined to the elderly on whom the toll of strokes fall, or should middle-aged mild hypertensives be treated? The results of controlled trials do not answer these questions – perhaps the economists will have to pick up where the medical scientists finish.

The question of cholesterol reduction is much more vexed than the question of blood pressure lowering. First, currently available therapy is not as effective as blood pressure therapy in reducing the risk factor; second, the prevalence of high cholesterol is greater than that of high blood pressure and changes with changing definitions of an undesirable cholesterol level in the population; and finally, no single trial, or groupings of trials, have shown that lowering of serum cholesterol actually lowers total mortality. Once again, there is a quadratic relationship between the serum cholesterol and coronary attack or death rates. This is consistent within and between different population groups. However, despite the fact that all large lipid-lowering trials have shown a two per cent reduction in the incidence of coronary heart disease for every one per cent decline in serum cholesterol, the mortality rate in treatment and control groups is identical (Lipid Research Clinics Program, 1984). Funny things happen to actively treated people in lipid-lowering trials: they commit suicide, die in accidents and sometimes get cancer. There is no biological reason to believe that lipid reduction causes any of this, but it remains a nagging doubt in the back of the mind of every clinician and public health doctor. Should we recommend a prudent diet to the whole population? Should we screen for and treat individuals at high risk due to hyperlipidaemia? Once again the economists and not the medical scientists might have to show us the way, as the medical vested interest groups are unable to reconcile their differences in this area.

## THE DIAGNOSIS OF CORONARY HEART DISEASE

The diagnosis of coronary heart disease in life is made traditionally from the syndromes of acute myocardial infarction (heart attack), angina pectoris, and a syndrome intermediate between the two. Whilst clinical presentation alone is approximately seventy per cent accurate in making the diagnosis, errors in diagnosis may result in patients dying unnecessarily by the withholding of appropriate treatment or, conversely, by being falsely labelled with a potentially fatal cardiac condition. The role of diagnostic tests is to reduce errors in prediction of outcome but, much more importantly, to lead to treatment which improves the outcome.

The diagnostic techniques appropriate for coronary heart disease have resulted from applying technology to the heart and its coronary arteries – application of core knowledge and new technology. The techniques used are variants on the electrocardiogram and techniques used to image the heart. There is a relatively small contribution from techniques related to the biochemistry of the heart. Factors considered in introducing the techniques include their efficacy, safety and cost. Recently it has been recognised that many of these new techniques are redundant, lacking demonstrable value in improving prognostic stratification or patient outcome. Strategies for evaluation of new technologies are evolving as are these technologies themselves. Because the technology is continuously changing, it is unlikely that the controlled trial has a major place in technology evaluation now or in the future.

## THE TREATMENT OF CORONARY HEART DISEASE

As indicated earlier, improved treatment of coronary heart disease, chiefly in the phase of heart attack, has contributed to a reduction of about thirty to forty per cent in age-specific coronary disease death rates. In this area, the randomised controlled trial has been more effective than in the areas previously described, but still not decisive.

Should the acutely ill patient with suspected heart attack be transported to hospital? This is a fundamental question if we postulate a large drop in hospital mortality due to effective coronary care. Every clinician who has graduated within the last 25 years has seen effective cardiopulmonary resuscitation save lives which are enjoyed and are productive for years afterwards. Approximately five per cent of patients experiencing otherwise uncomplicated acute myocardial infarction develop ventricular fibrillation causing cardiac arrest. The results of good coronary care are almost 100 per cent effective in treating this otherwise lethal complication of myocardial infarction.

Randomised controlled trials have only confused this picture. Studies performed out of hospital have failed to show any benefit of transferring the patient with uncomplicated myocardial infarction from home to hospital (Hill *et al.*, 1978). Yet the one controlled trial of coronary care patients transferred to hospital showed a one-third reduction in hospital mortality for the patient with acute myocardial infarction managed in a coronary care unit compared with usual ward care (Hofvendahl, 1971). This latter trial is supported by many observational studies made in hospitals by cardiologists in Australia and all over the world. Why have the community trials of coronary care units clearly misled? First, they excluded the sicker patients with acute infarction at higher risk of dying, and where the benefits of coronary care were more easily demonstrable. And second, the trials were much too small to demonstrate a benefit of coronary care when the base rate of unexpected cardiac arrest was only five per cent. The correct resolution of these questions has come from large multi-centred observational studies of chest pain symptoms presented in emergency wards, which clearly demonstrate both the value of coronary care in saving life and the great importance of the electrocardiogram in clinical triage of patients with acute chest pain (Goldman *et al.*, 1988).

The development of coronary care units has resulted in the development of physicians with better skills in the management of seriously ill cardiac patients. Two major concepts have been tested and validated by randomised controlled trial: limitation of infarct size by techniques that reduce the heart muscle's need for blood flow; and early coronary reperfusion chiefly by means of thrombolytic therapy. These newer concepts have resulted in better use of the coronary care unit facility in reducing early mortality in myocardial infarction, but their overall significance pales in comparison with the overall benefits of immediate detection and effective treatment of cardiac arrest.

Some of the most decisive randomised controlled trials have resulted in proven advances in the management of subacute and chronic coronary heart disease: beta blocker (B Blocker Heart Attack Trial Research Group, 1982) and aspirin (ISIS-2, 1988) are proven advances in the management of patients after discharge from hospital following myocardial infarction, as is the use of non-medical allied health personnel in the vigorous control of risk factors after myocardial infarction (Oldridge *et al.*, 1988). Large trials of coronary by-pass surgery have shown that surgery is the most effective treatment in relieving angina and in improving exercise tolerance. The effect of surgery in prolonging life is still hotly debated: by study design, one trial showed that a policy of early surgery was superior to a policy of medical treatment switching to surgery if medical treatment failed, but two other studies did not confirm this. An overview of those studies suggests that a policy of surgery for patients with angina and advanced coronary artery disease is superior to a policy of watch-and-wait in these cases (Bonow and Epstein, 1985).

Observational studies suggest that the effect of by-pass surgery in prolonging life is greater than that demonstrated in the trials, as many of the obviously sick were excluded from the trials and managed by surgery of choice – that is, pre-randomisation bias (Rahimtoola, 1985). The above laudatory view of randomised controlled trials in the management of patients with subacute and chronic coronary heart disease has overlooked the fact that as yet, community studies have not confirmed that the life expectancy of such patients has been prolonged. Maybe it is too soon to tell? Are these again misleading trials of therapy?

## STRENGTHS AND LIMITATIONS OF RANDOMISED TRIALS

If doubts exist on the relative merits of two forms of treatment, the best way to resolve the doubt is to randomly assign patients to either form of treatment. In doing so one hopes to create groups which are identical in all respects except in the treatment received. Thus any difference in outcome should be attributable to differences in treatment only.

When randomised controlled trials are analysed, most care is given to studying whether the randomisation process resulted in groups similar in all respects in factors known to influence outcome; to counting the numbers of treatment dropouts and analysing their causes and outcomes; and to assessing whether an appropriate statistical test is used to analyse group differences in outcome created by the randomisation process (see Figure 3).

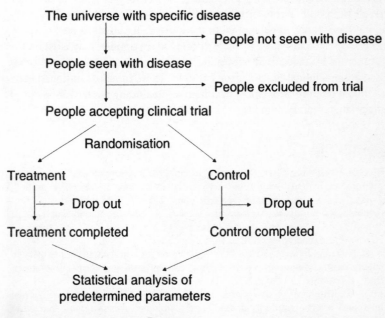

*Figure 3* The randomised controlled trial

Examples exist where randomisation provided prognostically different groups (Lee *et al.*, 1980), and where ignorance of causes and outcomes of dropouts produced a spurious benefit for a particular treatment (Coronary Drug Project Research Group, 1980). Arbitrary decisions at the level of statistical analysis may result in apparent but spurious benefit favouring treatment (Temple and Pledger, 1980).

The major reason for not accepting the results of trials as the basis for clinical practice is the lack of knowledge of patients excluded from trials. These exclusions might be of patients unsuited for trials but who are seen and accounted for – such patients have a higher mortality rate than those included for trial (Hill *et al.*, 1978). More subtle are exclusions because typical patients are not sent for trial by clinicians – 'pre-randomisation bias' (Rahimtoola, 1985). The most excellently conducted trial may have no relevance if its subjects were atypical of the usual patient and, in particular, not like the patient seen by a particular clinician.

## A CLINICAL APPROACH TO CLINICAL TRIALS

The randomised controlled trial provides some of the best evidence on the role of treatment. However, it is fraught with many potential biases described above. It has to be balanced with other evidence of a biomedical, psychological and sociological nature; and with previous experience derived from both a core of relevant literature and of a personal or institutional base. It has to be applied to the individual patient as perceived by both patient and doctor. Legitimate differences in opinion may exist on the relevance of a randomised controlled trial after considering all the other information. Clinical practice is not simple. There remains continued need for clinical input in all areas of health policy including the development of appropriate research methods.

## REFERENCES

B-Blocker Heart Attack Trial Research Group, 1982, 'A randomized trial of propranolol in patients with acute myocardial infarction. 1. Mortality results', *Journal of the American Medical Association*, 247: 1707–14.

Beaglehole, R., Bonita, R., Jackson, R., Stewart, A., Sharpe, N. and Fraser, G.E., 1984, 'Trends in coronary heart disease event rates in New Zealand', *American Journal of Epidemiology*, 120: 225–35.

Bonow, R.O. and Epstein, S.E., 1985, 'Indications for coronary bypass surgery in patients with chronic angina pectoris: implications of the multicenter randomised trial', *Circulation*, 72 (supp V): V-23–V-30.

Cobb, L.A., Thomas, G.I. and Merendino, K.A., 1959, 'An evaluation of internal mammary artery ligature by double blind technique', *New England Journal of Medicine*, 260: 1115–18.

Coronary Drug Project Research Group, 1980, 'Influence of adherence to treatment and response of cholesterol on mortality in the Coronary Drug Project', *New England Journal of Medicine*, 303: 1038–41.

Daly L.E., Mulcahy, R., Graham, I.M. and Hickey, N., 1983, 'Long term effect on mortality of stopping smoking after unstable angina and myocardial infarction', *British Medical Journal*, 287: 324–6.

Dobson, A.J., Gibberd, R.W., Leeder, S.R., Alexander, H.M., Young, A.F. and Lloyd, D.M., 1988, 'Ischemic heart disease in the Hunter region of New South Wales, Australia, 1979–1985', *American Journal of Epidemiology*, 128: 106–15.

Elveback, L.R., 1985, 'Coronary heart disease in residents of Rochester, Minnesota. V. Prognosis of patients with heart disease based on initial manifestation', *Mayo Clinic Proceedings*, 60: 305–11.

Elveback, L.R., Connolly, D.C. and Kurland, L.T., 1981, 'Coronary heart disease in residents of Rochester, Minnesota. II. Mortality, incidence and survivorship, 1970–1975', *Mayo Clinic Proceedings*, 56: 665–72.

Gillum, R.F., 1987, 'Acute myocardial infarction in the United States, 1970–1983', *American Heart Journal*, 113: 804–11.

—— 1989, 'Sudden coronary deaths in the United States, 1980–1985', *Circulation*, 79: 756–65.

Gillum, R.F., Folsom, A., Luepker, R.V., Jacobs, D.R. Jr., Kottke, T.E., Gomez-Marin, D., Prineas, R.J., Taylor, H.L. and Blackburn, H., 1983, 'Sudden death and acute myocardial infarction in a metropolitan area, 1970–1980. The Minnesota Heart Survey', *New England Journal of Medicine*, 309: 1353–8.

Goldberg, R.J., Gore, J.M., Alpert, J.S. and Dalen, J.E., 1988, 'Incidence and case fatality rates of acute myocardial infarction (1975–1984): The Worcester Heart Attack Study', *American Heart Journal*, 115: 761–7.

Goldman, L. and Cook, E.F., 1984, 'The decline in ischemic heart disease mortality rates. An analysis of the comparative effects of medical interventions and changes in lifestyle', *Annals of Internal Medicine*, 101: 825–36.

Goldman, L., Cook, F., Hashimoto, B., Stone, P., Muller, J. and Loscalo, A., 1982, 'Evidence that hospital care for acute myocardial infarction has not contributed to the decline in coronary mortality between 1973–1974 and 1978–1979', *Circulation*, 65: 936–42.

Goldman, L., Cook, E.F., Brand, D.A., Lee, T.H., Rouan, G.W., Weisberg, M.C., Acampora, D., Stasiulewicz, C., Walshon, J., Terranova, G., Gottlieb, L., Kobernick, M., Goldstein-Wayne, B., Copen, D., Daley, K., Brandt, A.A., Jones, D., Mellors, J. and Jannbowski, R., 1988, 'A computer protocol to predict myocardial infarction in emergency department patients with chest pain', *New England Journal of Medicine*, 318: 797–808.

Gomez-Marin, D., Folsom, A.R., Kottke, T.E., Shu-Chen, H.Wu, Jacobs, D.R., Gillum, R.F., Edlavitch, S.A. and Blackburn, H., 1987, 'Improvement in long term survival among patients hospitalised with acute myocardial infarction 1970–1980. The Minnesota Heart Survey', *New England Journal of Medicine*, 316: 1353–9.

Hammond, E.C., 1964, 'Smoking in relation to mortality and morbidity. Findings in first thirty-four months of follow-up in a prospective study started in 1959', *Journal of the Nat Cancer Institute*, 32: 1161–88.

Hill, J.D., Hampton, J.R. and Mitchell, J.R.A., 1978, 'A randomised trial of home versus hospital management for patients with suspected myocardial infarction', *Lancet*, 1: 837–41.

Hobbs, M.S.T., Hockey, R.A., Martin, C.A. and Armstrong, B.K., 1984, 'Trends in ischemic heart disease mortality and morbidity in Perth Statistical Division', *Australia and New Zealand Journal of Medicine*, 14: 381–7.

Hofvendahl, S., 1971, 'Influence of treatment in a coronary care unit on prognosis in acute myocardial infarction', *Acta Medica Scandinavica*, 519 (supp.): 1–78.

ISIS-2 (Second International Study of Infarct Survival) Collaborative Group, 1988, 'Randomised trial of intravenous streptokinase, oral aspirin, both or neither among 17,187 cases of suspected acute myocardial infarction: ISIS-2', *Lancet*, 2: 329–60.

Kannel, W.B., Cupples, L.A. and D'Agostino, R.B., 1987, 'Sudden death risk in overt coronary disease: The Framingham study', *American Heart Journal*, 113: 799–805.

Kuller, L.H., Perper, J.A., Dai, W.S., Rutan, G. and Traven, N., 1986, 'Sudden death and the decline in coronary heart disease mortality', *Journal of Chronic Diseases*, 39, 100: 1–10.

Lee, K.L., McNeer, J.F., Starmer, C.F., Harris, P.J. and Rosati, R.A., 1980, 'Clinical judgement and statistics. Lessons from a simulated randomized trial in coronary artery disease', *Circulation*, 61: 508–15.

Lipid Research Clinics Program, 1984, 'The Lipid Research Clinic's Coronary Primary Prevention Trial Results. 1. Reduction in incidence of coronary heart disease', *Journal of the American Medical Association*, 251: 351–64.

Martin, M.J., Hulley, S.B., Browner, W.S., Kuller, L.H. and Wentworth, D., 1986, 'Serum cholesterol, blood pressure, and mortality: implications from a cohort of 361,662 men', *Lancet*, 2: 933–6.

Medical Research Council Working Party, 1985, 'MRC Trial of treatment of mild hypertension: principal results', *British Medical Journal*, 291: 97–104.

Multiple Risk Factor Intervention Trial Research Group, 1982, 'Multiple risk factor intervention trial. Risk factor changes and mortality results', *Journal of the American Medical Association*, 248: 1465–77.

National Heart Foundation of Australia, 1986, *Heart Facts*, Melbourne: National Heart Foundation.

Oldridge, N.B., Guyatt, G.H., Fischer, M.E. and Rimm, A.A., 1988, 'Cardiac rehabilitation after myocardial infarction. Combined experience of randomized clinical trials', *Journal of the American Medical Association*, 260: 945–50.

Peduzzi, P., Hultgren, H., Thomsen, J. and Detre, K., 1987, 'Ten year effect of medical and surgical therapy on quality of life: Veterans Administration Co-operation study of coronary artery surgery', *American Journal of Cardiology*, 59: 1017–23.

Pell, S. and Fayerweather, W.E., 1985, 'Trends in the incidence of myocardial infarction and in associated mortality and morbidity in a large employed population, 1957–1983', *New England Journal of Medicine*, 312: 1005–11.

Rahimtoola, S.H., 1985, 'A perspective on the three large multicenter randomized clinical trials of coronary bypass surgery for chronic stable angina', *Circulation*, 72 (Supp. V): V-123–V-135.

Rose, G., Hamilton, P.J.S., Colwell, L. and Shirley, M.J., 1982, 'A randomised controlled trial of anti-smoking advice: 10 year results', *Journal of Epidemiology and Community Health*, 36: 102–8.

Stewart, A.W., Fraser, J., Norris, R.M. and Beaglehole, R., 1988, 'Changes in severity of myocardial infarction and three year survival rates after myocardial infarction in Auckland, 1966–7 and 1981–2', *British Medical Journal*, 297: 517–19.

Temple, R. and Pledger, G.W., 1980, 'Special Report. The FDA's Critique of the Anturane Re-infarction Trial', *New England Journal of Medicine*, 303: 1488–92.
Thompson, P.L., Hobbs, M.S.T. and Martin, C.A., 1988, 'The rise and fall of ischaemic heart disease in Australia', *Australia and New Zealand Journal of Medicine*, 18: 327–37.
Weinblatt, E., Goldberg, J.D., Ruberman, W., Frank, C.W., Monk, M.A. and Chaudhary, B.S., 1982, 'Mortality after first myocardial infarction. Search for a secular trend', *Journal of the American Medical Association*, 247: 1576–81.
World Health Organization European Collaborative Group, 1986, 'European collaborative trial of multi-factorial prevention of coronary heart disease: final report on the 6 year results', *Lancet*, 1: 869–73.

# Part III

# Non-experimental quantitative study designs

# 6    Broadening the scope of evaluation
## Why and how

*Christel A. Woodward*

The randomised controlled trial (RCT) is considered to be a design of choice in health care research that assesses the effects of treatment. Well-executed double blind RCT studies can assess the efficacy or the effectiveness of a therapy or diagnostic procedure in a rigorous fashion that will ensure high internal validity. As mentioned previously, generalisability (external validity) may be problematic if those entered into the trial are a highly selected group of patients. Thus, investigators are now sometimes encouraged to study the choices and outcomes of those eligible for but not entered into an RCT. With such a strategy, both a 'quasi-experiment' and an experiment would be included in the final study.

Campbell and Stanley (1966) coined the term 'quasi-experiment' in their 1966 monograph. In a quasi experiment, whether or not a person receives the intervention is often not under the investigator's control. Random allocation of patients to treatments has not occurred and thus various types of selection bias may be present. Yet quasi-experiments aim to approximate, as best as possible, the conditions of an experiment and to apply the logic of an experiment to study execution. In this chapter, several quasi-experimental and observational designs that may be useful in health care research will be described. The use of such designs in evaluation in health care will be illustrated. As well, some of the methodological issues must be considered in the design of such studies and their execution will be explored. Such designs often require considerable creativity on the part of the investigator who must attempt to rule out other plausible, rival hypotheses for the results observed.

## UNDER WHAT CIRCUMSTANCES DO NON-RCT TYPES OF RESEARCH DESIGN BECOME THE DESIGN OF CHOICE?

Quasi-experiments and non-experimental designs are often used in the early stages of our understanding of the possible benefits of a therapeutic intervention or diagnostic test. For example, Chalmers (1981) coined the terms 'Phase I' and 'Phase II' studies to describe the early studies used to develop information about drugs. Such studies have long used historical comparison groups and/or before–after designs to estimate the possible effect and toxicity of a new treatment. They are seen as the precursor to trials since they allow the investigator to estimate the possible potential benefit of a new treatment regimen. Information obtained from Phase II studies is used to estimate the sample size requirements for full-scale RCTs. Such designs may also be used when technology is rapidly changing, and there is a concern that the length of time between the design, execution and reporting of outcomes of RCTs will be too long (i.e. that the treatment investigated will no longer be seen as the treatment of choice by the time the trial results are known). They are also used to study diseases that are thought to be the results of toxic or carcinogenic agents. Here, long latency is often suspected or random allocation of subjects to treatment is seen as unethical. Non-RCT designs may also be used when a treatment has become accepted practice despite the fact that no high-quality information regarding its efficacy or effectiveness exists at the human level, or adverse effects are now suspected. For example, several investigators have used a case control design to evaluate the effectiveness of screening by Pap smears to help prevent cervical cancer (Macgregor *et al.*, 1985) and to examine the relationship between oestrogen replacement and endometrial cancer (Horwitz *et al.*, 1978).

The current AIDS crisis may present another situation where trials become problematic. Since they are dealing with a deadly disease, few people may be willing to enter a trial of vaccine effectiveness, and fewer still are willing to wait until lengthy trials, examining the efficacy and effectiveness of new treatment interventions, are completed before beginning to take the treatment (Booth, 1989). Finally, other types of study designs are needed when the question posed is not a causal one.

## METHODOLOGICAL CHALLENGES INVOLVED IN THE DESIGN OF QUASI-EXPERIMENTS AND NON-EXPERIMENTAL STUDIES

Although different types of quasi- and non-experiment designs share different design features, the investigators nevertheless wish to examine the effect of a particular intervention or exposure. In developing the study, the seasoned investigator will ask, 'What are all the possible outcomes of this study, and how would I explain each?' Usually, this strategy allows the investigator to consider how to rule out the possibility that the patient groups compared are fundamentally different (with the result that the observed difference or lack thereof could be attributable to this). The investigator must also ensure that the effect observed was caused by the intervention or exposure and not something else (e.g. natural history of the disease, another intervention, regression toward the mean). Similarly, possible reasons for lack of effect must be explored. Differences in the groups assembled, lack of compliance with treatment or the presence of contamination (where both groups inadvertently receive the intervention) may lead to a no-difference conclusion. Finally, the investigator must examine whether the method of measurement could produce the result observed. For example, effects observed may be the result of bias introduced by unblinded outcome assessment or rumination bias in the exposed group. On the other hand, insensitive measurement or unreliable measures may result in a no-difference result (Michael *et al.*, 1984). By considering the range of possible outcomes of a study and how they might arise, the investigator can identify methodological weaknesses in study design. This usually leads to gathering considerable collateral information which is used to rule out plausible rival hypotheses, and to improvements in study design (e.g. development of procedures to ensure outcome is assessed without knowledge of treatment group membership).

## QUASI-EXPERIMENTS

### Concurrent comparison group studies

In circumstances where random allocation of subjects to treatments is precluded, the investigator may still assemble a concurrent comparison group. Three general types of concurrent comparison groups may be chosen:

1 based on quasi-random allocation;
2 based on comparing the treated group with a group in another setting where the treatment is unavailable; or
3 by matching those treated with those from another group who have not received the treatment.

Each of these choices has limitations and may lead to selection biases. These will be discussed below.

Quasi-random allocation occurs when subjects are assigned to treatments in a systematic way (e.g. every other patient, patients appearing on odd or even days, etc.). It is often appealing as it is less difficult to implement than random allocation. However, it is also easy to sabotage this effort to obtain comparable groups. Patients and clinicians can readily conspire to get the patient into the group of their preference. The two groups will be distorted to the extent that clinicians are able to distinguish important prognostic factors (confounders) for their patients, and these are unequally distributed between the two groups.

The investigator may also search for an untreated group in another setting that appears similar to the treated group. Here the major question is why the other group has not sought or been referred for treatment. They may be healthier (or sicker) than the treated group or at least different from those treated in some fundamental way. For example, in the early 1970s we were asked to help evaluate a special education program for emotionally disturbed (ED) children run by the local school board. Despite our best efforts, random allocation of children to these classes was not possible. The number of candidates presented each year matched the number of slots available (18). Yet, we felt that many more children with significant emotional problems that interfered with their learning were present in this large school board. We thus sent a child psychiatrist to 'case find' by screening children in another set of special education classes – 'opportunity' classes for slow learners. This group was to be used as a silent control group. As we anticipated, she identified a number of these 'slow learners' as ED children whom she would admit to the ED program if they were presented to the admissions board. The key question here was *why* they had not been identified previously and presented. This became clear when their baseline measures were examined. These were 'quietly crazy' children. Although equally disturbed, they did not act out their problems in the flagrant dramatic ways of the children referred to the program.

Finally, investigators may choose to match experimental subjects to controls. Here the hope is to gain equivalence in groups although, in general, the comparison groups available are different from the controls in prognostic factors. For example, one might wish to compare a treatment patient with a patient who did not receive treatment but who was within 5 years of age, of the same sex and who had similar severity of disease. Matching, unfortunately, becomes quite difficult when it is attempted for more than two or three characteristics. A large pool of control subjects may be needed to find exact matches. Yet patients often have more than two or three characteristics which we would like to match. Further, this method also may have problems. The matched groups may represent extremes within two different populations with different underlying means. An effect may be observed, unrelated to treatment, because members of both groups gradually regress towards the mean for their group (Davis, 1976). The use of repeated baseline measures before the intervention may help ensure that regression towards the mean is not operating.

Another challenge that researchers using quasi-experimental designs face is ensuring the fidelity of the intervention. Often control over the interventions compared is less complete than in an RCT, especially in the standard treatment group. Thus, evidence of how well the treatments were applied, compliance with treatment and lack of contamination and co-intervention (where another unmeasured treatment occurs in one or both groups) must be gathered.

Ascertainment of outcomes must be done in an unbiased fashion. Often the patient and treatment provider are not blind to the treatment received. The use of assessors blinded to the treatment group of the patients and the use of reproducible criteria for this assessment are helpful safeguards. Similarly, the measures used must be sensitive to the types of change expected. Some investigators would add measures *not expected to change in both groups* to ensure the effect observed is related to the intervention and not some other events occurring during the time period (Cook and Campbell, 1979).

Despite these problems, a carefully designed quasi-experiment can sometimes provide useful information. For example, some physicians in a multi-specialty internal medical polyclinic were concerned about their level of use of preventive measures. (The clinic served mainly patients with chronic illnesses, many of whom were age 50 and over). They posed the question: to what extent can influenza vaccination rates in eligible patients who attend our clinic be improved if we delegate the tasks of screening and approaching eligible patients to the nurses (Hoey *et al.*, 1982)? These nurses already administered the vaccine when it was ordered by physicians. Rather than develop a randomisation schedule, the physicians chose to have nurses approach all eligible patients during the morning session of the polyclinic. They compared the vaccination rate achieved with that obtained by physicians who had clinics in the afternoon. They state that these latter physicians were unaware of the change in pattern of delivery of influenza vaccine that occurred during the morning clinics but had been informed that influenza vaccine had been received and was available for use with their patients. In the morning, 56 physicians worked in the clinic while 39 physicians worked in the afternoon. The same eligibility criteria were used to decide who was eligible to receive the vaccine at both sessions of the polyclinic. During the six-week period monitored, 52 per cent of 435 eligible patients seen in the morning were offered vaccine and 35 per cent were vaccinated. Physicians requested vaccination for 2 per cent of 348 eligible patients seen in the afternoon. Although the already busy work schedule of nurses limited their ability to approach all eligible patients, the vaccination rate was markedly higher among patients who attended the clinic in the morning.

In this study, the reproducible criteria for eligible patients, the same rate of eligible patients at both morning and afternoon sessions (44 per cent), the clarity of the intervention and the large difference observed make the study 'believable'. (We must take on faith that the afternoon group had been informed that the vaccine was available for use.) However, what if no difference had been observed? Plausible explanations for such a finding might include awareness of the afternoon group of the change (contamination) which caused them to increase their rate (the 'John Henry' effect) or the unwillingness of nurses to take on the newly assigned task on top of their heavy workload.

## Historical comparison group studies

Historical comparison groups are the least preferred method for examining the effect of a new medical technology (Diehl and Perry, 1986). Although they allow all newly recruited individuals to receive the new treatment, and are thus much faster and less expensive than RCTs, one must be able to rule out that changes in diagnosis or management of the condition have not led to substantial changes in outcome over time. The way patients are selected for treatment must also be equivalent. More stringent criteria (or at least different criteria) may be used to recruit patients now than previously (Green, 1987). The experience of the population now may be different than in the past. An Australian study clearly illustrates these problems (Christie, 1979). The effect of computed tomography (CT) scanning on mortality in stroke patients was examined by comparing the outcomes of patients seen in 1978 (who were investigated with CT) and those of patients seen in 1974, before the CT scanner was available. Patients were matched on all prognostic variables thought to be relevant. Outcomes for 1978 patients were superior to those for 1974 patients. However, to rule out general improvement in the treatment of stroke the investigator examined mortality in another matched group: stroke patients seen in 1978 when the CT scanner was not working. The latter group had the lowest mortality rate of all (although similar to the CT-scanned 1978 group)! This study is a good example of ingenuity in research that can be used to rule out plausible, rival hypotheses.

## Before–after studies

Unfortunately, before–after studies with the same individual are also fraught with problems. Other potential explanations of the difference observed (natural history of the disease, regression towards the mean, placebo effects due to expectation of benefits, etc.) must be ruled out. This cannot usually be done without a comparison group. Such studies can only provide definitive answers about the benefits of a new technology when the natural course of a disease is well known and the effect of the intervention is dramatic. Unfortunately, few new therapies fit these criteria.

## Summary

Quasi-experimental designs should never be substituted for an RCT in a situation where an RCT is possible. The literature contains many examples of reduction in benefit as the type of study design used to explore the effectiveness of a procedure becomes more powerful (avoids bias in subject selection and measurement of outcomes, standardises the treatment; controls for co-intervention, contamination, changes over time in health outcomes and natural history of the disease) (Diehl and Perry, 1986; Christie, 1979; Chalmers *et al.*, 1978). For example, Chalmers *et al.* (1977) compared the results of different types of studies on the use of anticoagulants after a myocardial infarction. In several case series with historical controls, anticoagulated patients had longer survival times. The reported benefit was substantially smaller but still favoured anticoagulation in studies where patients were alternatively assigned to treatment, while with RCTs the benefit is almost non-existent. This suggests that the more enthusiastic we are about a treatment/procedure, the less carefully we evaluated it! However, good quasi-experiments exist that have added to our knowledge. They have done so to the extent that the investigator was able to rule out plausible rival hypotheses by building in design features that protect the study from the influence of various biases.

## NON-EXPERIMENTAL STUDIES

A series of non-experimental designs may also be useful to answer questions of interest to medical researchers. They differ from quasi-experiments in that the investigator lacks control both over who receives the intervention and the nature/extent of the treatment/exposure received. Further, such studies may be done retrospectively or have a retrospective component. Thus, they often rely on the examination of existing data (from clinical or administrative records).

Using existing data sources for research has several potential advantages. Since no new data collection is required, obtaining the needed information is often quicker and less expensive (especially if the database is already computerised). Data may be available on very large groups of people or even entire populations (e.g. medical or hospital insurance claims data). However, use of existing data also has potential pitfalls. The information gathered may not have been gathered in a uniform fashion across time. Definitions may be subtly changed or applied in a different fashion across time. The database may have missing data for some subjects. The accuracy of some data may be suspect (especially such items as diagnosis or cause of death) and it may be difficult to check on its validity. Finally, important variables that affect health (e.g. smoking behaviour, social class) may be lacking or poorly documented.

## Case-control studies

One of the best known non-experimental designs used in medical research is the case-control study (Schlesselman, 1982). Case control studies are particularly useful in health care research which evaluates the effectiveness or impact of a new technology after it has been widely introduced or examines the effects of occupation or environmental exposure. They differ from other types of studies in that having or not having the outcome of interest is the basis on which the study groups are selected. Central to case-control studies is the careful definition of cases, controls and exposure. In defining cases and controls, an essential requirement is that the cases and controls of a matched set can be considered as arising from a population, all of whose members had an equal chance of appearing in the study as cases. Defining this base population is an exercise fraught with difficulty and investigators may not agree on the most appropriate reference group (Sasco *et al.*, 1986). Horwitz and Feinstein (1981) have suggested that the investigator include those who, if there had been a trial, would have been entered as eligible.

Despite careful selection of cases and controls, the investigator must rule out other plausible hypotheses for the association between exposure and outcome. For example, in the study by Clarke and Anderson (1979) on the effectiveness of screening for cervical cancer, only one-third (32 per cent) of cases had one or more screening Pap smears during the five years preceding the year of diagnosis, as compared to 56 per cent of controls. Despite the fact that cases and controls were neighbours, both educational attainment and total family income were significantly lower in one case. These two variables are potential confounders as they are also strongly associated with a history of having a screening Pap smear. To check whether the relative risk of cervical cancer in those who failed to have a Pap smear remained consistently high, the relative risk within each level of education and income was examined. Significant differences between cases and controls on other known risk factors for carcinoma of the cervix were also observed. Thus, they standardised the relative risk for cervical cancer associated with failing to have a Pap smear for marital status, age at marriage, age at first intercourse, regular employment, access to medical care, and smoking history.

Constraints on the selection of cases and controls may also lead to bias. For example, in the Clarke and Anderson (1979) study, nearly one-third of eligible cases were not available for interview, and thus were excluded from the study. To examine potential sources of bias in the selection of cases, investigators examined the first 100 eligible cases. No difference was observed in the proportion who had had a Pap smear before their first symptoms among those interviewed and not interviewed. Similarly, they encountered a success rate of only approximately one-in-twelve in approaching households to obtain neighbourhood controls (five controls per case were enrolled). They examined this problem by separating out those controls who were enrolled immediately after the case (or another control) had been interviewed (i.e. controls obtained without an intervening failure), and estimated the relative risk using only this control group.

Definition and ascertainment of both outcomes and exposure must be done with care to avoid bias in ascertainment of exposure. For example, recall and interviewer bias may occur. Cases may be more likely than the controls to recall details of their past health; or unblinded interviewers may unconsciously be more thorough in their questioning of cases than controls. In the cervical cancer screening study cited, the investigators compared information from physicians' medical records regarding screening for cervical cancer with interview data to assess possible recall and interviewer bias. Again, the methods employed allowed assessment of whether or not these plausible rival hypotheses could explain the results observed.

The interested reader is referred to two articles that outline methodological standards for the evaluation of the adequacy of a case-control study (Horwitz and Feinstein, 1979; Lichtenstein *et al.*, 1987).

## Cohort studies

Another type of non-experimental design often used in health care research is the cohort study (Wolf *et al.*, 1973). Here, a group of individuals, existent in the population at one point in time, are followed forward in time (often after a baseline measurement is taken). Subjects are eventually divided into those who have and have not been exposed or by the extent (duration and intensity) of their exposure to a particular event. The proportion in each group that develops the outcome of interest is ascertained. Although such designs are used mainly to ascertain risk factors for disease development, they can also be used to evaluate the impact of a new technology or to examine the potential harm of an existing technology.

One of the most famous cohort studies which defined the cohort on the basis of geographical boundaries is the Framingham study of the risk factors for cardiovascular disease (Wolf *et al.*, 1973). A cohort of individuals aged 30-59 was defined from the population of this community in Massachusetts and followed prospectively for more than thirty years. Here the cohort is defined without any knowledge of the status of individuals with respect to presumed causal variables, and an internal comparison group was constructed from the members of the cohort with the risk factor.

Cohorts may also be selected because of the special exposure of all members to be studied. Usually attempts are made to classify such individuals on the basis of their level of exposure, at least in broad classes. Data are gathered about both exposure and sociodemographic variables that may affect the disease under investigation. The follow-up period chosen must be long enough to allow the development of the disease studied. For example, Court Brown and Doll (1957) studied the occurrence of leukaemia in patients given X-rays for ankylosing spondylitis (13,352 patients treated between 1934 and 1954). They classified their cohort by dose of radiation received. The outcome evaluated was death from leukaemia or aplastic anaemia, between 1935 and 1954. This cohort study, begun in 1955 when both the exposures and death to be studied had already occurred, was undertaken retrospectively. Such retrospective cohort studies may also have a prospective component. For example, Court Brown and Doll (1957) continued to follow the cohort forward in time to identify deaths occurring after 1955.

When all cohort members have been exposed to the putative causal agent, three types of comparison groups may be employed. First, groups differing in the amount of exposure may be established among members of the cohort. Second, the experience of the general population at the time the cohort is being followed may be used (if the information is available). Age/sex-specific rates of the disease under study in the general population (expected rate) are compared with rates observed in the cohort. Third, comparison cohorts, similar in demographic characteristics to the exposed group, may be constructed.

Unless high-quality information is available in medical, insurance or other record systems, cohort studies must often rely on the information about exposure and/or outcome obtained from study members across time, either by direct examination, mailed questionnaire or interview. Thus, the effects of non-response (study attrition) may present problems. Theoretically, the true relationship between exposure and outcome is distorted only when the loss is biased with respect to both exposure and outcome. In practice, it may be difficult to know whether the loss was selective with respect to exposure, outcome or both. To indirectly assess this problem, a number of procedures are used: a) more intensive efforts may be made to obtain exposure information on a small sample of non-respondents, to see if they are different from respondents with regard to exposure; b) ancillary information (e.g. age, sex, socio-economic status) that can be obtained on both respondents and non-respondents is compared; and c) non-respondents are followed up to obtain information on outcome, even though exposure information is lacking.

A recent study of the mortality experience of Ontario glass fibre workers clearly illustrates some of the problems which may be encountered in historical prospective cohort studies in the occupational health field (Shannon *et al.*, 1987). This study cohort consisted of 2,557 men who were employed at an insulating glass wool plant for at least ninety days between 1955 and 1977. Since no historical data were available on fibre levels within the plant, length of exposure was used as a proxy for quantitative measures such as cumulative dose. Although detailed work histories were compiled for study subjects, such information was not available for some workers. Thus, the workers were divided into three groups: those who worked in the plant only, the office area only, and a mixed exposure group whose job entailed a combination of plant and office work. The follow-up strategy involved searching for the men through various methods including Canada's Vital Statistics and Disease Registry, driver's licence bureau, the US Department of Immigration and Naturalization, former fellow workers, friends, relatives, telephone books in the local area, etc. to ascertain mortality (both date and cause of death). At second follow-up in 1984, 157 deaths were found in the 97 per cent of men traced. The high number traced speaks to the large effort expended to obtain outcome information. Minor corrections were also made in the cohort size (reduced by nineteen) in 1984 when during tracing it was discovered that initially some women had been included and some men had been counted twice. Again, such errors are often found in data taken from historical records.

In this study, mortality was compared by the person-years method to that of the Ontario population. Although overall mortality was below that expected (Standard Mortality Ratio – SMR = 84), cancer deaths were slightly raised owing entirely to an excess of lung cancer (SMR = 176). All but two of these cases occurred among plant-only employees. However, SMRs by length of exposure (number of years employed at the plant) and time since first exposure were not consistent with an occupational cause (did not increase with length of time). Thus, the interpretation of the data is difficult. No information on smoking histories of these workers was available. Such information and better measures of work history, including actual cumulative exposure to fibre dust, would have greatly improved this otherwise carefully executed study. The authors are appropriately cautious about the likelihood of a causal relationship.

**Time series designs**

Another type of observational study, the time series design, is built on the simple idea that an event is embedded in time (Kahn *et al.*, 1988). The analytical procedures used are much more complicated and depend in part on the type of change hypothesised (e.g. change in level of intercept; change in direction or slope, delayed change, etc.). Time series designs can be used when periodic measurement of variable(s) of interest is available over a fairly long period of time, an intervention has occurred during the period of observation and the investigator has hypotheses about the effect of such an intervention.

Soumerai *et al.* (1987) conducted time series analyses of propoxyphene use to examine the effect of combined nationwide government/commercial educational activities and accompanying press reports on the prescribing patterns of physicians and the number of overdose deaths involving propoxyphene. The prescription data used (1974–83) were obtained from an ongoing national prescription audit of a large representative sample of 1,200 retail pharmacies in the United States. Overdose deaths data (1977–83) were obtained from the National Institute of Drug Abuse as reported in the Drug Abuse Warning Network (DAWN). The investigators found that nationwide propoxyphene use during the warnings continued a *pre-existing* decline of about eight per cent per year, but this decline halted after the warnings. The risk of overdose death per propoxyphene prescription had remained constant since 1979. They concluded that sharper declines in misuse of such drugs would require stronger, more sustained regulatory or educational measures. This study is interesting because it used several data sets to explore the issue of impact. Further, monitoring a fairly long period of time before and after the intervention demonstrated that, although a decline was observed in prescriptions during the intervention period, this decline had started *long before* the intervention occurred and began to level off after the intervention.

**Summary**

Three types of non-experimental studies that are used to address causal questions have been described. In case-control studies, the extent to which one can be assured that cases and controls emerged from the same underlying population is often a troublesome issue. The usefulness of information from longitudinal cohort studies depends on the representativeness of the group studied and the lack of selective attrition over time from the cohort. Time series designs can be quite powerful as they incorporate repeated measurement across time. Careful framing of the questions posed, ensuring representativeness of the sample studied, the availability of high-quality data and careful attention to measurement of exposures, outcomes and possible confounding factors can make these designs quite powerful.

## OBSERVATIONAL STUDIES THAT BROADEN THE SCOPE OF EVALUATION

Evaluation of health care is not limited to questions regarding the efficacy or effectiveness of a procedure or the extent to which an exposure/intervention is associated with a later outcome. With the increasing availability of computerised health-care databases, large-scale observational studies that describe health care delivery are now possible. Such studies may examine whether variations are seen in the use of technology across geographical areas and describe the extent of diffusion of new technology. Study designs may be either cross-sectional (and provide a snapshot of one period of time) or may describe changes across time.

### Cross-sectional observational studies

Cross-sectional observational studies may provide information about health care such as a variation in rates of use of technology across geographical areas. For example, large variations in the rates of use of 123 medical and surgical procedures by United States Medicare patients have been reported across geographical areas (Chassin *et al.*, 1986). In this retrospective study, physician claims data were used to establish population-based rates for these procedures. Among the 123 procedures studied, a three-fold difference or more was seen for 67 of the procedures across the 13 geographical regions. A 26-fold difference in the use of injections for haemorrhoids was seen across sites!

Variability in utilisation of medical technology may be seen because diffusion has proceeded more slowly in some areas or because more inappropriate use is occurring in some areas. A subsequent study was done to examine how appropriately one procedure, upper gastrointestinal endoscopy, was being used (Kahn *et al.*, 1988). The authors developed a comprehensive, detailed list of 1,069 indications or specific clinical scenarios for which upper gastrointestinal endoscopy might be used. This list was rated by panels of physicians for appropriateness. Medicare patients who had received upper gastrointestinal endoscopy in 1981 were then randomly selected from three areas. Complete clinical information was obtained for 95 per cent of eligible cases and rated for appropriateness.

When more than one indication was assigned per case, the one with the highest appropriateness rating was used in the analysis. Patient co-morbidity was also assessed by collection of collateral chart information.

Here, study integrity depended on the representativeness of cases studied (random selection and good co-operation in obtaining information for selected cases) and uniformity in data collection across sites. An essential feature of the study was the careful specification of criteria for rating appropriateness. Use of an expert consensus panel ensured that the criteria used would be seen as medically credible. Work was done to show that the criteria could be rated in a reliable fashion. The investigators also examined the extent to which any disagreement among members of the expert group in their definitions of inappropriate, equivocal and appropriate use of the procedure influenced the results. Depending on the extent of agreement among the expert panel used to define inappropriateness, from eleven to seventeen per cent of upper gastrointestinal procedures were found to be done for inappropriate reasons.

## Longitudinal observational studies

Longitudinal observational studies can also supply information about the impact of new technology on health care delivery. Anderson and Lomas (1988) examined the diffusion of a technology into practice in a Canadian province by using existing administrative records from the Hospital Medical Records Institute (HMRI) which receives an abstract for each hospital discharge in the province. Cases were included in the study if a coronary artery by-pass surgery (CABS) procedure had been performed in 1979, 1981, 1983 or 1985 on an individual aged 20 or older who resided in Ontario, the most populous Canadian province. Estimates from the Ontario health insurance plan indicate that more than 98 per cent of CABS received by Ontario residents were performed inside the province. Thus, most procedures done on the population were included. Age-specific rates of CABS were computed for each time period and centre, using census data to estimate the appropriate denominator. Investigators found that the percentage of procedures performed on the elderly (aged 65-plus) more than doubled (from 12.8 per cent to 27.4 per cent) between 1979 and 1985. However, significant regional variation (across centres performing CABS) was seen both in rate of increase and percentage of CABS done for aged 65-plus individuals. The lack of detailed diagnostic information in existing records limited the investigators' ability to assess indications for CABS in their cases and to adjust raw rates of mortality and morbidity associated with CABS. Thus, they could only point to the paucity of evidence for effectiveness of CABS in the 65-plus age group and the large observed differences in CABS rated across regions to raise questions about whether diffusion has been optimal. The study points out both the types of information that can be obtained and carefully examined using an administrative database, and the limitations inherent in such databases.

## MEASUREMENT IN HEALTH RESEARCH

Across study designs, measurement problems continue to slow our progress in evaluation of medical care. Too often investigators have chosen to measure impact in terms of readily measured 'hard' outcomes (e.g. mortality or morbidity) rather than to measure more difficult constructs such as quality of life, differences in functional status, or extent to which treatment is applied appropriately. However, even the measurement of mortality and morbidity often provide methodological challenges in the definition of such events and their careful ascertainment (Haynes, 1988). Measurement challenges face investigators whether they use randomised controlled trials, quasi-experiments or observational studies. These challenges may be more acute in observational studies that rely on existing sources of data. Here the data available are often limited, and measures must be constructed from available information (Horwitz and Yu, 1984). Clear specification of assessment criteria, independent of knowledge of outcome, that can be reliably reproduced is essential. An assessment of the validity of the information contained in the written record should also be made whenever possible (Kosecoff *et al.*, 1987).

In prospective studies which attempt to assess impact of a treatment or exposure on health status, the recent proliferation of measures of quality of life, functional status and health utility leaves the investigator with the difficult task of searching for the measure or group of measures that will best capture the types of social, physical and/or emotional function or changes therein that he/she wishes to assess. Useful guides include several recent reviews of general health status measures in adults (McDowell and Newell, 1987) and proceedings of conferences on health status measurement (Lohr and Ware, 1987; Lohr, 1989; Katz, 1987). The National Center for Health Statistics in the United States also publishes an annotated bibliography on health indices which is periodically updated. Such references speed the work of identifying potentially useful measures for a study that wishes to assess impact of an intervention on the patient's health status. However, investigators are still left to make difficult choices among measures that appear to measure what they wish to measure. What criteria should be used in making a final selection? Again, criteria for selection are available in the published literature but will be summarised below (Haynes, 1988; Horwitz and Yu, 1984; Kosecoff *et al.*, 1987; Mosteller, forthcoming; McDowell and Newell, 1987; Brook *et al.*, 1979; Lohr and Ware, 1987; Lohr, 1989; Katz, 1987; Ware *et al.*, 1981; Ware, 1987; Kirshner and Guyatt, 1985).

## General versus disease-specific measures

Briefly described, one of the first decisions the investigator must make is whether to choose a generic health status measure (which purports to be broadly applicable across types and severity of disease, different medical treatments and different populations) or a disease-specific measure which focuses on measuring areas that are likely to be directly affected by the intervention planned (e.g. dexterity and pain in arthritis treatment). Although the latter may be seen to have greater content validity or relevance in a trial of arthritis medications, the use of disease-specific measures makes comparisons of gains through treatment across different disease types difficult. Disease-specific measures may be more useful as diagnostic tools and are more sensitive to the specific clinical intervention that they were targeted to assess.

Despite careful selection, almost all measures will contain some items where change cannot be expected. Some would argue that only items amenable to change (where improvement is possible) should be used to measure change, irrespective of whether a disease-specific or generic measure is chosen (Guyatt *et al.*, 1986). Such decisions must be made *before* the study begins and not during data analysis.

## Psychometric properties of measures

A minimum criteria for selection of a measure is that it is reproducible. Scores obtained within a short time interval when no change has occurred should correlate highly with each other (test-retest reliability). Scoring criteria applied by different raters should yield highly similar results (inter-rater reliability). Another important psychometric property is content validity. The measures' content should reflect the full domain of situations or activities relevant to the particular assessment. Evidence for construct validity should also exist (i.e. the measure should correlate well with similar measures of function and not correlate with measures that purport to assess unrelated areas of functioning). Further, differences at a point in time should be predictive of future functioning (predictive validity). Responsiveness to change is one of the most important criteria for measures that will be used to assess the effects of interventions. Meaningful clinical change should be reflected in change in the measure. (Measures may be highly reliable because they are insensitive to change.) Internal consistency is important for measures that are seen as unitary scales. Here, it is important that all items included in the measure assess the same dimension (e.g. mobility).

### Respondent burden

Respondent burden must also be carefully considered. If possible, measures should be brief enough to ensure that fatigue does not become a factor. Completing the measures should be palatable to respondents. Measures that take several hours to complete or seem unrelated to their concerns will test the patience and co-operation of even the most compliant patients. Ease of administration and scoring must also be considered. Self-administered measures are often preferable to measures that require elaborate equipment and/or extensive training to ensure standard administration and reliable scoring by the examiner.

Whether proxy respondents will be allowed (for logistical reasons or because of the patient's poor health) must also be considered. Proxy responses usually correlate well with patient responses. However, systematic differences in proxy responses have been reported and these merit attention. Proxies who spent more time per week helping the patient rated the patient's functional status and social activities as more impaired than did the patient (Epstein *et al.*, 1989). These authors caution against intermingling proxy and patient responses as this may lead to biased results.

## ECONOMIC ANALYSIS

The health care research field must also include research designs from health economics in its armamentarium. Much of health care research focuses on potential benefits on new treatments and technologies without spending time examining the cost of these effects or the relative costs of differences in effect. Given the current climate of economic constraints, policy makers are paying more attention to such issues. Two papers in the *How to Read Clinical Journals* series of the McMaster University Department of Clinical Epidemiology and Biostatistics (1984, parts A and B) outline the methodological standards for economic evaluations of health care interventions.

As Himmelstein and Woolhandler (1985) point out, the cost-effectiveness of interventions may appear radically different depending on the alternatives that are compared. This problem is illustrated by their comparison of the net benefit of two interventions: a) cholestyramine therapy to prevent coronary heart disease among those with elevated serum cholesterol levels – the Lipid Research Clinics Coronary Prevention Trial

(Lipid Research Clinics Program, 1984); and b) the effects on health of a variety of health insurances plans varying from complete coverage with no co-payments to fairly high co-payment levels – the Rand Health Insurance Experiment (Brook *et al.*, 1983). Both of these studies used an RCT design and are considered to be methodologically quite sound. The former reported significant benefit from cholestyramine therapy while the latter reported that free health care led to a substantial increase in the use and cost of services and a slightly diminished risk of early death among high-risk individuals. When a cost-effectiveness analysis was done to compare these two interventions, free care was seen to be 3 to 100 times as cost-effective as cholestyramine therapy in preventing death!

Comparisons of *net* cost-effectiveness must be considered when evaluating the impact of a new technology on health status. The cost- effectiveness of entirely different types of intervention must be compared if we are to develop health policy that allocates health care dollars in a rational way.

## CONCLUSION

In this chapter, a pot-pourri of quasi-experimental and observational research designs relevant to assessment of health care and its delivery has been discussed. Study designs that attempt to address causal questions have been highlighted. Such designs are useful to the extent that the design builds in features that will allow the investigator to rule out plausible, rival hypotheses for the effects/lack of effect observed and realises the limitations inherent in the study methods in drawing conclusions from the investigation. A poorly executed study, no matter what its basic design, will yield poor-quality information. Similarly, a well-designed study that is executed with intelligence and care, where the investigators have thought through how they might explain all of the possible findings, need not be an RCT to yield highly credible, useful information. Yet the risk of bias and/or poor data quality is usually greater in non-RCT studies. The emergence of large computerised health care databases provides an opportunity to develop population-based descriptions of the use of health care technologies. Such databases may also be used to obtain random samples of patients who have received a particular treatment and to examine the extent to which the treatment was medically indicated or examine its health outcomes.

Measurement issues loom large in the development of useful data about health care and its delivery. Lack of good measurement often hampers our understanding as much as any other research design issue. An area of measurement often not included in health care research is the cost of the medical technology relative to its effect. There is a need to more frequently incorporate such economic analyses into health care research.

# REFERENCES

Anderson, G.M. and Lomas, J., 1988, 'Monitoring the diffusion of a technology: Coronary artery by-pass surgery in Ontario', *American Journal of Public Health*, 78: 251–4.

Booth, W., 1989, 'NIH Offers AZT to exposed workers', *Science*, 243: 1137.

Brook, R.H., Ware, J.E., Jr., Rogers, W.H., Keller, E.B., Davies, A.R., Donald, C.A., Goldberg, G.A., Lohr, K.N., Masthay, P.C. and Newhouse, J.P., 1983, 'Does free care improve adults' health?: Results from a randomized controlled trial', *New England Journal of Medicine*, 309: 1426–34.

Brook, R.H., Ware, J.E., Davies-Avery, A., Stewart, A.L., Donald, C.A., Rogers, W.H., Williams, K.N. and Johnston, S.A., 1979, 'Overview of adult health status measures fielded in RAND's Health Insurance Study', *Medical Care*, 17 (7 supp.): III–X, 1–31.

Campbell, D.T. and Stanley, J.C., 1966, *Experimental and Quasi-experimental Designs for Research*, Chicago: Rand-McNally.

Chalmers, T.C., 1981, 'The Clinical Trial', *Milbank Memorial Fund Quarterly*, 59, 3: 324–39.

Chalmers, T.C., Matta, R.J., Smith, H., and Kunzler, A., 1977, 'Evidence favouring the use of anticoagulants in the hospital of acute myocardial infarction', *New England Journal of Medicine*, 297: 1091–5.

Chalmers, T.C., Smith, H., Ambroz, A., Reitman, D. and Schroeder, B.J., 1978, 'In defense of the VA randomized control trial of coronary artery surgery', *Clinical Research*, 26: 229–35.

Chassin, M.R., Brook, R.H., Park, R.E., Keesey, J., Fink, A., Kosecoff, J., Kahn, K., Merrick, N. and Solomon, D.H., 1986, 'Variations in the use of medical and surgical services by the Medicare population', *New England Journal of Medicine*, 314: 285–9.

Christie, D., 1979, 'Before–after comparisons: a cautionary tale', *British Medical Journal*, 2: 1629–30.

Clarke, E.A. and Anderson, T.W., 1979, 'Does screening by Pap smears help prevent cervical cancer? A case-control study', *Lancet*, 7 July: 1–4.

Cook, T.D. and Campbell, D.T., 1979, *Quasi-experimentation: Design and Analysis Issues for Field Settings*, Chicago: Rand-McNally.

Court Brown, W.M. and Doll, R., 1957, 'Leukaemia and aplastic anaemia in patients irradiated for ankylosing spondylitis', *Medical Research Council Special Report Series*, No. 295, London: Her Majesty's Stationery Office.

—— 1965, 'Mortality from cancer and other causes after radiotherapy for ankylosing spondylitis', *British Medical Journal*, 2: 1327–32.

Davis, C.E., 1976, 'The effect of regression in epidemiologic and clinical studies', *American Journal of Epidemiology*, 104: 493–8.

Diehl, L.F. and Perry, D.J., 1986, 'A comparison of randomized concurrent control groups with matched historical control groups: Are historical controls valid?', *Journal of Clinical Oncology*, 4: 1114–20.

Epstein, A.M., Hall, J.A., Tognetti, J., Son, L.H. and Conant, L., 1989, 'Using proxies to evaluate quality of life: Can they provide valid information about patients' health status and satisfaction with medical care?', *Medical Care*, 27 (supp.): S91–S98.

Green, S.B., 1987, 'Patient heterogeneity and the need for randomized clinical trials', *Controlled Clinical Trials*, 3: 199–208.

## 112   Non-experimental quantitative study designs

Guyatt, G.H., Bombardier, C. and Tugwell, P., 1986, 'Measuring disease-specific quality of life in clinical trials', *Canadian Medical Association Journal*, 134: 889–95.

Haynes, R.B., 1988, 'Selected principles of the measurement and setting of priorities of death, disability and suffering in clinical trials', *American Journal of Medical Sciences*, 296: 364–9.

Himmelstein, D.U. and Woolhandler, S., 1985, 'Free care, cholestyramine and health policy', *New England Journal of Medicine*, 311: 1511–14.

Hoey, J.R., McCallum, H.P. and LePage, E.M.M., 1982, 'Expanding the nurse's role to improve preventive service in an outpatient clinic', *Canadian Medical Association Journal*, 127: 27–8.

Horwitz, R.I. and Feinstein, A.R., 1978, 'Alternative analytic methods for case-control studies of estrogens and endometrial cancer', *New England Journal of Medicine*, 299: 1089–94.

—— 1979, 'Methodologic standards and conflicting results in case-control research', *American Journal of Medicine*, 66: 556–64.

—— 1981, 'The application of therapeutic-trial principles to improve the design of epidemiologic research', *Journal of Chronic Diseases*, 34: 575–83.

Horwitz, R.I. and Yu, E.C., 1984, 'Assessing the reliability of epidemiologic data obtained from medical records', *Journal of Chronic Diseases*, 37: 825–31.

Kahn, K.L., Kosecoff, J., Chassin, M.R., Solomon, D.H. and Brook, R.H., 1988, 'The use and misuse of upper gastrointestinal endoscopy', *Annals of Internal Medicine*, 109: 664–70.

Katz, S. (ed.), 1987, 'The Portugal conference: Measuring quality of life and functional status in clinical and epidemiological research', *Journal of Chronic Diseases*, 40, 6: 459–63.

Kirshner, B. and Guyatt, G., 1985, 'A methodologic framework for assessing health indices', *Journal of Chronic Diseases*, 38: 27–36.

Kosecoff, J., Fink, A., Brook, R.H. and Chassin, M.R., 1987, 'The appropriateness of using a medical procedure: Is information in the medical record valid?', *Medical Care*, 25: 196–201.

Lichtenstein, M.J., Murlow, C.D. and Elwood, P.C., 1987, 'Guidelines for reading case-control studies', *Journal of Chronic Diseases*, 40: 893–903.

Lipid Research Clinics Program, 1984, 'The lipid research clinic coronary primary prevention trial results: 1. Reduction in the incidence of coronary heart disease', *Journal of the American Medical Association*, 251: 351–64.

Lohr, K.N. (ed.), 1989, 'Advances in health status assessment: conference proceedings', *Medical Care*, 27 (supp.) S1–S294.

Lohr, K.N., Ware, J.E., Jr. (eds), 1987, 'Proceedings of the advances of health assessment conference', *Journal of Chronic Diseases*, 40 (supp.): 15–191S.

McDowell, I. and Newell, C., 1987, *Measuring health: A guide to rating scales and questionnaires*, New York: Oxford University Press.

Macgregor, J.E., Mossi, S.M., Parking, D.M. and Day, N.E., 1985, 'A case-control study of cervical cancer screening in north-east Scotland', *British Medical Journal*, 290: 1543–46.

McMaster University, Department of Clinical Epidemiology and Biostatistics, 1984, 'How to read clinical journals: VII. To understand an economic evaluation (part A)', *Canadian Medical Association Journal*, 130: 1428–33.

—— 1984, 'How to read clinical journals: VII. To understand an economic evaluation (part B), *Canadian Medical Association Journal*, 130: 1542–9.

Michael, M., Boyce, W.T. and Wilcox, A.J., 1984, *Biomedical bestiary: An epidemiologic guide to flaws and fallacies in the medical literature*, Boston: Little, Brown & Co.

Mosteller, F., (ed.), forthcoming, *Quality of life and health status measurement: A report from the Council on Health Care Technology*, Washington, DC: National Academy Press.

NCHS bibliography on health indexes, irregular, Clearinghouse on health indexes, Hyattsville, Maryland: National Center for Health Statistics.

Sasco, A.J., Day, N.E. and Walter, S.O., 1986, 'Case-control studies for the evaluation of screening', *Journal of Chronic Diseases*, 39: 399–405.

Schlesselman, J.J., 1982, *Case-Control Studies: Design, Conduct, Analysis*, Oxford: Oxford University Press.

Shannon, H.S., Jamieson, E., Julian, J.A., Muir, D.C.F. and Walsh, C., 1987, 'Mortality experience of Ontario glass fibre workers – extended follow-up', *Annals of Occupational Hygiene*, 31: 657–62.

Soumerai, S.B., Avorn, J., Gortmaker, S. and Hawley, S., 1987, 'Effect of government and commercial warnings on reducing prescription misuse: The case of propoxyphene', *American Journal of Public Health*, 7: 1518–23.

Ware, J.E., 1987, 'Standards for validating health measures: Definition and content', *Journal of Chronic Diseases*, 40: 473–80.

Ware, J.E., Jr., Brook, R.H., Davies, A.R., and Lohr, K.N., 1981, 'Choosing measures of health status for individuals in general populations: A shopping guide', *American Journal of Public Health*, 71: 620–5.

Wolf, P.A., Kannel, W.B., McNamara, P.M. and Gordon, T., 1973, 'The role of impaired cardiac function in atherosclerotic brain infarction: The Framingham Study', *American Journal of Public Health*, 63: 52–8.

# 7 Advantages and limitations of the survey approach
## Understanding older people

*John B. McKinlay*

## INTRODUCTION

I have been asked to discuss the advantages and limitations of the survey in practice and to focus not so much on substantive as on methodological detail. In making a case for the socio-medical survey I will illustrate my points with specific reference to surveys of older people – say those over the age of 70 years. This will set some limits on the range of topics considered. It also focuses attention on the fastest growing demographic category, where a great deal of information is needed concerning health and social functioning. If it is to be useful for policy and planning, this information must be valid, reliable and inferentially sound. Focusing on older people will also let us see how inappropriate many of our survey techniques are, because they generally derive from studies of younger populations. There is some doubt as to how applicable or even adaptable current survey methods are to the study of older people, particularly those free-living in the community: they present their own unique problems and challenges to socio-medical researchers.

There is obviously no right or wrong way to do field-work and while all field approaches are useful, some are more useful than others. As Dillman (1978: 39), in his assessment of the relative merits of surveys (mailed questionnaires, telephone interviews, and face-to-face interviews) states, '. . . it all depends. Until the attributes of each method are considered in relation to the study topic, the population to be surveyed, and the precise survey objectives, the question of which is best cannot be answered.'

The chapter that follows is deliberately practical. It is based on recent experience with social and epidemiological surveys and experiments with older populations conducted by New England Research Institute (NERI) staff in the north-eastern United States.

## SPECIAL CONSIDERATIONS IN STUDYING THE SOCIO-MEDICAL BEHAVIOUR OF OLDER PEOPLE

Surveying the socio-medical behaviour of older people requires special approaches and some appreciation of the psychological, psychosocial and pathological impacts of aging.

### Similarities with other populations

Researchers must be aware of the ways in which older people are, in various respects, like all other, some other, and no other demographic category.

Studies of predominantly sick populations or the users of particular health services are likely to emphasise the distinctiveness of those populations. Not surprisingly, research based on representative community-based samples uncovers their similarity and continuity with other population groups. Generally speaking, normally aging people use health care services like their younger, similarly circumstanced counterparts. There are dangers in accepting the view that the behaviour of older people is essentially different from the remainder of the population. If we do so, we risk propagating obtrusive, over-medicalised policy and inattention to the reasons why older people cope with problems and changes in the ways that they do.

### Multiple conditions

The proportion of people with multiple and often unrecognised conditions rises with age.

Studies of people over age 75 in different national settings report an average of approximately 3.5 clinical conditions per person, a considerable proportion of which are unrecognised by the regular medical care provider (Williamson, 1981; South East London Screening Study Group, 1977). As Brotherston puts it, 'Old people disobey the rule which doctors have invented that a person is entitled to only one disease at a time' (Brotherston, 1981: 125).

### Lack of homogeneity

Older people are not a homogeneous, undifferentiated group. Age divisions among older people are, in important respects, more significant than differences between older people as a whole and younger age groups (Maddox, 1962). With respect to service utilisation, one Canadian study of

5,000 older individuals over a two-year period uncovered considerable differentiation: 20 per cent never visited a doctor during the study period, while 8 per cent accounted for 35 per cent of the visits (Roos and Shapiro, 1981). Hospital utilisation was even more differentiated: 80 per cent reported no hospital treatment, and 3 per cent used 67 per cent of all of the hospital days, meaning that 10 per cent of those surveyed accounted for 78 per cent of all hospitalisation.

## Under-utilisation of health care

Contrary to popular view, older people may under-utilise health care, and many serious and treatable conditions often go unreported. Population studies over the last thirty years have documented the extent to which illness is 'private business' (Rowe, 1983; Anderson, 1966; Besdine, 1982). Typically only about a quarter of reported illness episodes lead to the use of formal services, a fact that appears unrelated to the severity of symptoms (Pearse and Crocker, 1944; Dunnell and Cartwright, 1972; Hannay, 1979). One Oxford survey identified an average of 2.6 conditions per older patient – one of which was, on average, unknown to the patient's physician and a high proportion of which were amenable to medical amelioration.

## Variations in symptoms

The signs and symptoms of the same disease may vary in different age groups. Such variations can take two forms. First, the characteristic symptoms of a disease in middle age may be replaced by other symptoms in old age. For example, older people are less likely than younger adults to present symptoms of chest pain as a result of myocardial infarction (Pathy, 1967). Second, older people are more likely to present non-specific signs and symptoms, such as confusion, weakness, weight loss, or the hoary catch-all 'failure to thrive', rather than specific symptoms indicating specific organ or systemic dysfunction (Rowe, 1985; Kart, 1981; Besdine, 1982). We must disentangle age-related physiological changes from specific disease processes.

An untoward laboratory finding may be incorrectly attributed to 'old age' when the actual cause is some specific pathological process. Conversely, physiological changes may be attributed to diseases and treated as an illness when some age-related process is actually responsible. Older people who have low haematocrit levels may erroneously be categorised as having 'anaemia of old age', despite the fact that epidemiological studies of healthy older people in the community uncover no age-related reduction in the haematocrit. There are many other common clinical tests (e.g. that of blood glucose level, serum electrolyte concentration, certain hormones, and blood gas values) that are not or only minimally influenced by age (Rowe, 1985; McKinlay *et al.*, 1989).

Some physiological changes associated with normal aging are, of course, separable from the effects of disease. Progressive age-related reduction in the function of many organs – arteriosclerosis; losses in renal, pulmonary and immune functions; modification of central lens proteins resulting in increased opacity and lens inflexibility – is one set of examples. Age-related sensory losses have been reported (Hickey, 1980) as well as apparent increases in introspection. Not all of these age-related physiological changes have adverse clinical sequelae, however. For example, we have shown that menopause, although often accompanied by vasomotor symptoms (hot flushes and sweats), generally does not result in poorer health status, increased use of health services, or increased levels of depression (McKinlay and McKinlay, 1985; McKinlay *et al.*, 1987; Avis *et al.*, 1991).

## Revisions in methodologies

Research on the utilisation behaviour of older people often requires revision of established methodologies derived from studies of other, usually younger, populations.

NERI's studies concerning the social networks of frail older people have required some modification of Dillman's (1978) well-established and highly successful total design method (TDM) in order to accommodate the fear of outsiders, the reluctance to identify informal caregivers, speech pathology, hearing deficit, and limitation of vision, among other problems. We all know that there is some disjunction between the way field-work ought to be done, as discussed in methodology texts and college courses, and the way that it sometimes has to be done in order to generate meaningful data from particular populations.

## The social circumstances and health characteristics of older people

Available socio-demographic data on persons classified as old or elderly point to one conclusion: the group is highly heterogeneous (Rosenwaike, 1985). This variability in characteristics among people, which increases with age, has important implications for the selection of appropriate field methods in order to ensure adequate response rates and high-quality data collection. The data that follow are taken from the US National Health Interview Survey (National Center for Health Statistics, 1985) and the Supplement on Aging to the National Health Interview Survey, completed in 1984 (Kovar, 1986; Fulton *et al*., 1989), and highlight the need for accommodation in traditional field approaches.

In general, older people today are healthier and more active than is often realised. Almost 11 per cent of those aged 65 and over report that 'working' is their usual activity; another 43 per cent cite 'keeping house'. Just over one-half (54.7 per cent) are married, with almost as many (46 per cent) living with a spouse. Yet a sizeable proportion (31 per cent) live alone. While the level of education is relatively low (probably reflecting a cohort effect), about one-fifth are college graduates. Although 60 per cent of the older people living in the community report partial limitations, the majority are in good health; however, when data for various age groups are analysed, important differences emerge, differences that have implications for how research should be conducted. The biggest differences generally occur at age 85 years and over.

Although the majority of older people living in the community are in the 65–74 age group, approximately two million are aged 85 and over. In the US this group of 'oldest-old' is of interest to researchers because of their rapidly increasing numbers as well as their potential need for human services. They also present a challenge to researchers because their social and physical characteristics influence their willingness and/or ability to participate in research studies. Most people in this age group are women (71 per cent), have been widowed (72 per cent), are living alone (45 per cent), and have relatively little formal education (48 per cent have eight years or fewer).

Perhaps the factor having greater potential impact on the participation of older people in research, however, is their health and functional status. A shift in this community-based population towards poorer health with in-creasing age is evidenced in such indicators as health status, bed-days, and limitation of activity. Limitation of activity shows the largest difference in relation to advanced age. Among people aged 65–74 years, 37 per cent reported some limitation in activity, with 11 per cent completely unable to perform their usual activity. By contrast, 60 per cent of people aged 85 and over reported limitations in activity, with 20 per cent completely unable to perform their usual activity. These data are consistent with other findings (Feller 1983) that indicate that the need for help with daily living activities from another person increases with age (35 per cent for those aged 85 and over compared to 5 per cent for those aged 65–74).

Table 7 summarises some pertinent health statistics for older people in the US. Researchers give insufficient attention to these physical impair-ments among older people, even though they obviously affect the success of different field research approaches. Non-response may result from an inability to respond to an inappropriate field approach, rather than simply

*Table 7* National estimates of physical limitations and social conditions by age and sex (%)

| Physical limitations and social conditions | Age | | | | Total |
| | 75–84 | | 85+ | | |
| | M | F | M | F | |
|---|---|---|---|---|---|
| Hearing | 39.9 | 28.2 | 58.3 | 44.3 | 27.8 |
| difficulty even with hearing aid* | 52.3 | 40.6 | 66.1 | 60.9 | 38.9 |
| Vision | 16.7 | 15.6 | 25.0 | 27.5 | 12.8 |
| difficulty even with glasses** | 38.0 | 40.0 | 45.0 | 55.9 | 31.1 |
| Difficulty getting out of bed or chair | 5.9 | 11.2 | 12.7 | 22.2 | 8.0 |
| Difficulty grasping small objects | 9.6 | 14.1 | 10.3 | 16.4 | 10.7 |
| Lives alone | 19.0 | 52.9 | 28.3 | 52.9 | 31.8 |
| Lacks telephone | 4.4 | 2.5 | 5.4 | 3.7 | 3.1 |
| Less than 5 years at current address | 13.9 | 15.9 | 14.1 | 20.1 | 17.2 |

* among individuals who use hearing aids
** among individuals who wear glasses
*Source*: The National Health Interview Survey: United States, January–June 1984

reflecting an unwillingness to respond. Culpability for failure must rest not with a 'recalcitrant' respondent, but with the survey researcher who repeatedly employs the same inappropriate field approaches (e.g. repeat mailings of a questionnaire to a visually or cognitively impaired respondent). Social survey research presupposes that respondents accurately respond to items in a questionnaire or interview schedule. Herzog and Dielman (1985), however, examined age-specific accuracy across a variety of responses from several surveys and found no evidence for less accurate reporting by elderly respondents. Rodgers and Herzog (1987), using different external sources for validating information, detected few age differences in reporting accuracy. In fact, where age differences were observed, the older respondents were sometimes more accurate than younger respondents. While recognising the serious consequences of measurement error, Rodgers and Herzog (1987) concluded that this problem is no more common among older respondents than among any other age group.

In addition to functional status, some other social characteristics of older people influence the success of different field approaches. For example, the proportion of older people living alone, which is the situation for one out of every two women aged 85 and over, may affect the success of in-person interviewing in the community. From data presented by Lebowitz (1975), 71 per cent of people who are aged 60 and over and who live in large cities are fearful for their personal safety and, therefore, are likely to exhibit reluctance to permit strangers (i.e. field workers) to enter their homes to ask personal questions. Recognising such risks, many community organisations serving the needs of older people specifically advise them not to answer personal questions on the telephone or to let strangers into their homes.

## MOVING BEYOND THE IN-PERSON INTERVIEW

For a long time, the in-person interview has been thought to be the only way to obtain valid and reliable information; it has become the 'gold standard' for field methods in social and epidemiological research. However, that situation seems to be changing quite rapidly for a number of reasons:

1   the temporal decline in response rates in in-person surveys;
2   the prohibitive expense of in-person interviewing of large numbers in the community, primarily because of labour costs for field workers;
3   the public concern about strangers and issues of security, making it more difficult for field workers to obtain access to respondents' homes; and
4   a perceived danger to field workers, although I have yet to uncover evidence of any actual harm coming to workers in the field.

Alternative field approaches (e.g. telephone interviewing and mailed questionnaires) have become more attractive because of developments relating to those approaches. When in-person interviewing became well established in the 1940s and 1950s, only 40–50 per cent of the American public had telephones. Today, however, an estimated 93 per cent of the population have telephones. As reported by Thornberry and Massey (1988), some population subgroups exhibit high levels of telephone non-coverage – not the elderly. For people aged 65 and over, telephone coverage is relatively complete (97 per cent), regardless of race or income. While there is some regional variation in non-coverage in the US (i.e. 2.2–2.5 per cent in the Northeast, Midwest and West and 4.9 per cent in the South), the difference is small compared to other age groups. Even though 20–30 per cent of potential respondents have unlisted telephone numbers, random-digit dialling techniques permit easy contact with otherwise unreachable respondents (Thornberry and Massey, 1988; Lepkowski, 1988).

As a result of the improved and well-tested techniques developed by such researchers as Dillman (1978, 1982), mail questionnaires have also become more feasible and attractive. Acceptable response rates are now ensured by a sequence of tested steps: accurate formatting of questions, size of print, length of instrument, weight and colour of paper, accessible folds in inserts, careful selection of days on which mailings should occur. In addition, technological advances in word processing and database management facilitate initial and follow-up mailings to respondents and make use of mailed questionnaires in large-scale surveys more feasible.

Table 8 summarises some of the advantages and limitations of the three major field approaches: in-person interviewing, telephone interviewing, and mail questionnaires (Fowler and Mangione, 1984; Kish, 1965; Hochstim, 1967; Siemiatycki, 1979; Siemiatycki and Campbell, 1984; Siemiatycki *et al;*., 1984; Groves and Kahn, 1979). In my experience, there is no self-report information that cannot be reliably obtained over the telephone with a well-designed instrument and appropriately trained interviewers. Even information on sexual activity and income (subjects about which it is notoriously difficult to obtain information in the United States) is being successfully gathered by NERI researchers from older people using this mode (the Massachusetts Male Aging Study). In summary, alternatives

*Table 8* Advantages and limitations of three major field approaches

|  | In-person face-to-face | Telephone interview | Mail questionnaire |
|---|---|---|---|
| Cost | I | A | H |
| Sample size | I | A | H |
| Geographic dispersion | I | A | H |
| Response rates | H | A | I |
| Duration of study | I | H | A |
| Length of interview | H | A | I |
| Type of information | H | A | I |
| Data quality: | | | |
|   correct respondent | H | H | I |
|   comprehension | H | H | I |
|   item non-response | H | H | I |

A = appropriate
H = highly appropriate
I = inappropriate

122    *Non-experimental quantitative study designs*

to the in-person interview, in particular telephone interviews, are feasible and may be preferred, especially during economically stringent times, for social and epidemiological research.

## SOME RECENT METHODOLOGICAL DEVELOPMENTS

The last decade has witnessed advances in the understanding of fundamental cognitive processes and the refinement of research methods and analytic techniques particularly suited to studies of older people. By way of illustration, a few of the more important ones are discussed here.

### Development of instruments for identifying psychosocial and physiological processes

Valid and reliable instruments are now available for the measurement of frailty and the multi-dimensional assessment of functional limitation (Fillenbaum and Smyer, 1981; Morris *et al.*, 1984); of depression (Radloff, 1977); of chronic pain episodes (Fienberg *et al.*, 1985b; Kent, 1985); of life history of occupation/residence/education and smoking (Baumgarten *et al.*, 1983; Coggon *et al.*, 1985; Gerlin *et al.*, 1985; Pechacek *et al.*, 1984); of dietary behaviour (Mullen *et al.*, 1984; Posner *et al.*, 1982; Todd *et al.*, 1983; Van Staveren *et al.*, 1985; Willett *et al.*, 1987); of physical activity (Washburn and Montoie, 1986), and of functional capacity limitations (Branch and Meyers, 1987; Gresham and Labi, 1984; Kane and Kane, 1981; Katz, 1983), to list just a few.

In recent years, considerable progress has also been made in the understanding of the fundamental cognitive processes that respondents employ during the survey response process (Brown *et al.*, 1985; Fienberg *et al.*, 1985a, 1985b; Jabine *et al.*, 1984; Lessler *et al.*, 1985; Lessler and Sirken, 1985; Loftus and Fathi, 1985; Loftus *et al.*, 1985; Loftus and Marburger, 1983; Sirken, 1986). Recognising that little use is made of controlled laboratory experiments to investigate the manner in which respondents and interviewers process the information presented by the survey instruments, the US Federal Government has recently established a Questionnaire Design Research Laboratory (QDRL) as a resource for developing and testing questionnaires for health surveys (Royston *et al.*, 1986).

### Emergence of strategies for in-home collection of information

In the past, even older people have been requested to attend some central clinic or hospital location for physiological measurements (urine samples, blood pressure, height and weight, physical activity, blood samples, and pulmonary function). For poor health and other reasons unrelated to health, older people are unlikely/unable to meet such requests. As the famous Framingham Heart Study cohort has aged, home visits have been instituted to compensate for the problem of increasing non-response. This non-response has been due primarily to ill health among the men – but not among the women – in the study. The ongoing Pawtucket Heart Health Program reveals that most physiological data can be obtained in the home as reliably as, more cost-efficiently than, and with significantly higher response rates than in a clinic or a hospital (McKinlay and Kipp, 1984). This development is especially important when examining the socio-medical behaviour of older, less mobile populations. Some data (e.g. medication usage) can be obtained more reliably in the home. Our research team, in collaboration with the Harvard School of Dental Medicine, has developed and implemented an in-home protocol for conducting oral health examinations with older people. NERI staff have also pioneered the reliable use of a 12-lead electrocardiogram during in-home protocols in the most disadvantaged of inner-city areas to estimate the prevalence of 'silent' myocardial infarctions. NCHS is also using in-home protocols for obtaining measurements on respondents aged 65 and over, as well as on non-respondents to the Mobile Examination Center appointment in the third US National Health Examination Survey.

### Proxy or surrogate interviewing

Informed consent by proxy, sometimes necessary in studies of older patients, presents unique challenges. Although interviews with older people sometimes have to be conducted by proxy, heretofore the quality of the data gathered has been suspect. Proxy interviews now appear to hold considerable promise, especially when the alternative is no data at all.

There are obvious criticisms of proxy data gathering, in particular the suggestion that proxy respondents (usually female) tend to under-report illnesses of absent persons (usually male), which suggests that any purported gender differences in morbidity may be a function of this methodological artefact (Nathanson, 1975; Clarke, 1983; Verbrugge, 1976; Koons, 1973). Mechanic (1978) observes, on the basis of his studies, that gender differences in morbidity rates cannot be attributed simply to proxy respondents. Proxy interviews, while perhaps not ideal or desirable, are necessary with some types of studies, particularly with older or other particular population groups.

To summarise, my preference is for self-reports wherever possible. I recognise the potential limitations of proxy interviews despite recent studies reporting their successful use in diverse areas of inquiry. In some situations, with particular groups or unique areas, proxy respondents may be required; in these cases, some information may be preferred to none at all.

### Self-reports as 'objective' data

For some reason, what people say about their behaviour has never been considered to be as valid, or as reliable, as that which clinicians measure during the occasional observation. Supposedly, the social sciences deal with 'soft data', while the natural sciences deal with 'hard data'. The devaluation of self-reports has complex and sociologically interesting causes. More than a decade has passed since the milestone paper by Maddox and Douglass (1973) showed: a) a persistent and positive congruence of self and physician's ratings of health; b) wherever incongruity did occur, individuals tended to overestimate rather than underestimate their health; c) substantial stability of both self- and physician-health ratings was observed through time, with the self-health rating showing slightly more stability; and d) the self-health rating was a better predictor of future physicians' ratings than the reverse (Maddox and Douglass, 1973; Maddox, 1962). (See also Tissue, 1972; Stoller, 1984; Ferraro, 1980; Massey and Shapiro, 1982; Linn and Linn, 1980).

### MIXED-MODE FIELD APPROACHES WITH OLDER POPULATIONS

### Advantages

Following Dillman (1978) I have suggested that the choice of an optimal field approach depends upon the topic of the research, the study objectives, and the population being surveyed. Given the common impairments of older people, however, choosing an appropriate field approach requires even further discrimination. According to Table 9, what may be appropriate and acceptable to some respondents, even within a single study, may be quite inappropriate and disagreeable to others. For example, it is appropriate to distribute mailed questionnaires to people who are hard-of-hearing, but unrealistic to undertake telephone interviews. However, it may be possible, depending on the skill of the interviewer, to conduct an in-person interview in this situation.

The necessity to employ different field approaches in studies of older people is illustrated by the recent experience in the US of the Established Populations for Epidemiologic Studies of the Elderly, supported by the National Institute on Aging. This project, conducted in four different locations – Iowa; New Haven, CT; Durham, NC; and East Boston, MA – involved a baseline in-home interview survey, followed by annual interviews conducted mainly by telephone (Brock, personal communication). Data from two sites are reported to illustrate the need for flexibility in field approach.

In Iowa, 3,673 subjects aged 65 and over responded at baseline to an in-house interview (response rate: 80 per cent). A total of 3,497 were re-interviewed, primarily by telephone, at the first follow-up. Among the remaining 176, 128 had died, 47 refused to be re-interviewed, and one was not interviewed because he was incorrectly coded as dead. At the first follow-up, 5.3 per cent of the subjects required an in-home interview, rather than a telephone interview, because of hearing problems. Another 8.2 per cent of the interviews were conducted with proxy respondents (telephone or in-home) because the subject was too ill, was mentally incompetent, or was out working on his farm.

In New Haven, 2,811 subjects aged 65 and over responded in person at baseline (response rate: 82 per cent). A total of 2,562 were re-interviewed at the first follow-up. Among the remaining 249, 145 had died, 91 refused to be re-interviewed, and 13 are unaccounted for at present. At the first follow-up, 11.6 per cent of the interviews were done face-to-face in the subject's home because of hearing or language problems (Italian or Russian as a first language). Another 6.1 per cent were done by proxy (telephone or in-home) because the respondent was too ill or was mentally incompetent. A noteworthy feature of these results is the substantial variation, between

*Table 9* Advantages and limitations of three major field approaches, given the impairment and attitudes of the oldest old

|  | In-person face-to-face | Telephone interview | Mail questionnaire |
| --- | --- | --- | --- |
| Hard of hearing (deaf) | ? | I | A |
| Sight impaired (blind) | A | A | I |
| Speech language pathology | ? | I | A |
| Arthritis/tremors/paraplegia | A | A | I |
| Fear of strangers | I | A | A |

A = appropriate
H = highly appropriate
I = inappropriate
? = possible

survey locations, in the reasons for doing something other than interview the chosen subject on the telephone.

These mixed-mode surveys are often viewed as a means of achieving higher response rates by getting responses from people who otherwise will not respond (Brambilla and McKinlay, 1987a; Dillman and Tarnai, 1988). They may, however, be particularly useful in studies of older people who experience the types of impairments and limitations described above because they may be a means of getting responses from people who simply cannot respond. Mixed-mode approaches, then, are not only a desirable method for improving response rates, but in community-based studies of older people, in particular, they may also be essential if reliable data are to be obtained (Herzog *et al.*, 1983).

Most mixed-mode surveys start with either mailed questionnaires or telephone interviews (Hochstim, 1967; Hochstim and Athanasopoulos, 1970; Goudy, 1978; Siemiatycki, 1979; Brambilla and McKinlay, 1987a). Follow-up of non-respondents typically involves the other of these two, face-to-face interviews, or a combination of approaches. The sequence usually ranges from the least expensive (mailed questionnaires) to the most expensive (in-person interviewing), thereby devoting resources to the hardest to reach. Obviously, it is not cost efficient to use in-person interviewing if the same data and quality can be obtained by using a cheaper mode. There are quantum leaps in costs from mailed questionnaires to telephone interviewing to in-person interviewing. While cost is usually the major determinant of mode sequence, other considerations – such as time constraint and study content – can also be important factors.

When compared with in-person interview surveys, mixed-mode designs cost less and yet have produced the same high response rates (Hochstim, 1967; Siemiatycki, 1979; Woltman *et al.*, 1980; Whitmore *et al.*, 1985). If subjects are geographically dispersed (Brambilla and McKinlay, 1987a), a reduction in survey costs from a fixed budget can mean a greater sample size. Compared with surveys by either mail or telephone alone, the mixed-mode approach has not only produced higher response rates but, more importantly, also less socio-economically biased responses (Hochstim and Athanasopoulos, 1970; Siemiatycki and Campbell, 1984; Brambilla and McKinlay, 1987a). In-person follow-up after non-response to telephone calls has also improved coverage and reduced non-coverage bias.

### Disadvantages

Although mixed-mode surveys offer considerable promise, particularly in studies of older populations, they have their disadvantages and limitations. This discussion will focus on three concerns: costs, missing data and response validity. Follow-up constitutes work in excess of the effort normally expended in single-mode mail or telephone surveys. Therefore, mixed-mode surveys are always more expensive than surveys by the initial mode alone but less expensive than using the follow-up mode alone (Hochstim, 1967; Siemiatycki, 1979).

Aside from a few well-known items (e.g. household income), item non-response is most frequent on mailed questionnaires (Hochstim, 1967; O'Toole *et al.*, 1986; Brambilla and McKinlay, 1987a). Thus, mixed-mode surveys that include this mode may produce somewhat higher levels of missing data. Much of the problem is apparently caused by inadvertent respondent error, a problem that can be reduced through careful instrument design (Brambilla and McKinlay, 1987b).

Data missing for other reasons are of greater concern. The propensity for item non-response can vary with respondent characteristics, especially on mailed questionnaires (Brock *et al.*, 1986). These data are clearly not missing at random and can bias survey results (Rubin, 1976). We have found in health-related surveys that item non-response is related to health status (Brambilla and McKinlay, 1987a; 1987b). Unfortunately, estimates of bias are not yet available and more work is needed in this area.

## FURTHER MEASURES TO ENHANCE SUCCESS

Field-work success can be related to any number of factors. In studies of frail older people, however, our experience shows that measures can be taken to enhance the likelihood of success. These measures relate principally to accessing a study population, improving response rates, and ensuring collection of high quality data. Although the importance of the measures discussed below probably increases with the age of the study population, these measures are obviously useful in any social research.

### Gaining access to a study population

In our experience with surveys of older people, they are often understandably cautious about providing personal data, especially about their health and functionality, because they think that such data might influence their eligibility for benefits or services. Endorsement by local, widely recognised agencies or community leaders establishes the legitimacy of the study and often addresses respondents' concerns about participation.

This endorsement may take several forms, such as a letter to potential respondents, a notice of the study in organisational newsletters, or an article in the local newspaper. For statewide surveys, endorsement by the state unit on aging or other appropriate state agency is suggested. Not only can this endorsement be used with potential respondents, but it may also be helpful in gaining the co-operation and endorsement of local organisations.

Two other ways to reassure respondents of the legitimacy of a study exist: using the letterhead of a sponsoring organisation to indicate affiliation with a legitimate and recognisable organisation and using identification cards complete with the name of the project and sponsoring organisation as well as a picture of the field worker. These methods establish the legitimacy of the workers and their connection with both the project and the sponsoring organisation. In all contacts with the respondent (mail, telephone, or in-person), the name and telephone number of the project director should be provided in case the respondents have residual concerns about the study and/or their participation in the study.

In addition to obtaining local endorsements for the study, it is essential to have in-depth knowledge of the study community: its resources, its services for older people, and both its formal and informal leaders. Qualitative methods and ethnographic techniques can often provide this important contextual information. As part of the public relations activities carried out prior to the start of field-work, all relevant people should be contacted and informed of the study. Networking techniques facilitate the identification of key people who may not be known to the project staff (e.g. an influential church leader) and who, if not contacted, might block access to a study population or discourage participation. These contacts can avoid turf struggles or a community's tendency to 'protect' older clients, especially if the sponsoring organisation or project staff are seen as 'outsiders' or as a threat. These local contacts may also facilitate access to a study population by explaining the purpose of the study, by translating it for respondents, by encouraging participation, or by serving as proxy interviewers where appropriate. Such support permits more complete data gathering.

**Using local trackers**

Employing part-time local people who are very familiar with a particular study community to locate hard-to-find respondents can also enhance data collection and response rates. Because they do not collect data, these local trackers need not be experienced interviewers. We have found that the ideal tracker is a long-term resident of the community who knows its formal and informal resources well and can utilise these resources to find potential respondents who might otherwise be lost. Respondents can be tracked through letter carriers, town clerks, churches, senior centres, social clubs, home care agencies, public housing authorities, rental/management companies in private apartment complexes, and even funeral directors. A good local tracker can often uncover new resources. Care must be taken in training these trackers regarding the limited information they may give in attempting to locate respondents so that confidentiality of study participation is maintained.

## Staffing issues

Respondent burden is often of concern in studies of older people. Little is said, however, about the potential for interviewer burden. Field interviewers frequently face such problems as locating hard-to-find respondents, dealing with sensory and other functional or cognitive impairments that interfere with study participation, and establishing trust to gain entry. Several practical issues that improve field staff performance, thereby producing a satisfactory response rate and reducing interviewer burden (or 'burn-out'), are discussed below.

## The interviewer

Fowler and Mangione (1984) observe that, although crucial to any study's success, interviewers and the quality of interviewing in a survey are typically ignored. Groves and Kahn (1979) have shown that a fourth to a third of survey items are subject to significant interviewer effects (Kish, 1962; Hyman *et al.*, 1954). Interviewers can affect quality in two principal ways. First, if interviewers are inconsistently standardised, survey-based estimates are less precise, thereby increasing the amount of random error around the survey estimates and decreasing the extent to which the differences among respondents are detectable in the answers. Second, interviewers can systematically bias data and render them invalid. In one recent study, thirty per cent of the variation in some key outcome variables (social support networks and symptom reporting) was explained by interviewer differences!

The pace at which an interview is conducted, the kind of respondent behaviours interviewers elicit and reinforce, and the goals that interviewers communicate to respondents have been shown to relate to data accuracy (Cannel *et al.*, 1977a; 1977b). Similarly, interviewer vocal characteristics have been related to non-response in telephone surveys (Oksenberg and Cannel, 1988). A field experiment recently examined the potential that various training and supervision programs had to affect the performance of health survey interviewers as well as the quality of the data that they collect (Fowler and Mangione, 1984). Fowler and Mangione found that interviewers receiving less than one day of basic training generally displayed inadequate interviewing skills. Training and supervision were found to be related to data quality. Attention to aspects of interviewer management – training and supervision, design of questions to reduce the need for probing, procedures to be used and the size of assignments – are cost-effective ways to improve the quality of survey-based estimates. We concur with Fowler and Mangione (1984) who suggest that, despite a history of research showing that interviewers matter, standards for the way interviewers are trained and managed are long overdue.

When interviewing older people, particular attention must be paid to the type of interviewer one hires. A sensitive, compassionate, mature individual who is accustomed to dealing with this particular population group and who, preferably, is trained or experienced in the human services is most desirable. Although students are readily available and using them is relatively inexpensive, on the basis of experience we advise against recruiting them to do field studies of older people. This is supported by the work of Oksenberg and Cannel (1988) who found that faster rate of speaking, louder pitch of voice, and confidence in the voice were significantly related to lower refusal rates in telephone surveys.

## Specialised interviewer training

Field research with older populations requires special training for interviewers. First, many older respondents have difficulty processing and giving clear responses to an apparently straightforward question. For example, it may take up to five minutes to establish whether or not a respondent has arthritis. With older populations, such a question will often elicit prolonged descriptions of disabilities, the medications, and the utilisation behaviour associated with the condition, which has important implications for the cost of field-work. Interviewers must be trained to sensitively keep the respondent focused and to elicit clear responses in an economical fashion.

Second, in studies of older populations, particular attention must be devoted to concluding an interview. In our experience, respondents frequently enjoy discussing their problems and lives with the interviewer. The telephone call from the interviewer may be the only call that they have recently received. Older respondents often perceive the interviewer as someone who is interested in their situation and circumstances; therefore, the interviewer must know how to sensitively and not abruptly terminate interviews with obviously interested, talkative respondents. Extending the interview beyond the time necessary to obtain the required data has obvious cost implications. And, as in all types of research, one wants to close the interview as gently as possible, so that the next researcher who calls will encounter an interested respondent and one who will be inclined to participate again.

## Work atmosphere

Following recruitment and training, efforts should be made to create a work climate that will encourage capable and experienced field interviewers to stay with the project. Our experience shows that the development of a spirit of teamwork and co-operation and the sense of belonging to a cohesive, viable and important research project cannot be under-estimated, and that maintaining a pleasant and humane work atmosphere, in which individuals at every level feel part of the study, is critical.

To create an open, communicative work environment, concerns about the project must be openly discussed and problems dealt with regularly. Weekly staff meetings provide an excellent opportunity to air concerns, foster a sense of teamwork, and communicate expectations. A daily field log book facilitates communication among field staff who are on different schedules and usually on the road, which limits opportunities for regular face-to-face meetings.

A comfortable and secure working environment is also important for telephone field staff. Adequate space and a place to call their own can have a tremendous impact on the interview environment. A quiet, dedicated telephone-interviewing work space is essential.

### SUMMARY AND CONCLUSION

The widely discussed, rapid increase in the numbers of older people challenges researchers to provide valid and reliable data with which to inform health and social policy about this demographic category. No one can question the importance of gathering accurate information so that policy can be guided and focused by data, and the effectiveness of programs evaluated. Research methods derived from and useful in studies of younger populations or convenience samples may be inappropriate and require modification for use with older people whose health status and social circumstances preclude their use. Some socio-medical researchers are not well prepared to meet this challenge.

I do not argue for one ideal way of conducting survey research with older populations (or any other social category for that matter); rather, my essential message is the *need for flexibility*. While all field approaches are useful, some appear more useful than others. Their usefulness depends on the topic and objective of the study and characteristics of the population under investigation. Although the limitations of mixed-mode surveys are well recognised, I view them as particularly promising with older populations. Certainly, in-person interviews are no longer the 'gold standard' and may indeed be too costly, especially during economically stringent times for socio-medical research. Based on recent experience with surveys and experiments with older people in the Northeast US, some suggestions are offered with the intention of assisting colleagues embarking on socio-medical surveys of older people.

## ACKNOWLEDGEMENTS

This chapter draws on recent experience with several socio-medical field studies of primarily older populations conducted by New England Research Institute staff: specifically 'An Epidemiological Investigation of Menopause' (Grant AG03111), 'Health and Effective Functioning in the Normally Aging' (Grant AG04673), 'Hypertension in the Elderly' (Grant HL18318-11), 'Pathways to Provision of Care for Frail Older Persons' (Grant AG07182), 'Validation and Field Tests for Risk Appraisal Instruments' (HL3214), 'Oral Health of Older Adults' (5RO1 AG07139-02) and 'Follow-up Tracking on the Framingham Heart Study' (HL38038). These studies were supported by the National Institute on Aging and the National Heart, Lung and Blood Institute of the National Institutes of Health, Washington, DC. I am indebted to my colleagues Donald Brambilla, PhD; Cheryl Caswell, MBA; Sonja McKinlay, PhD; and Sharon Tennstedt, PhD, for their valuable contributions to this chapter.

## REFERENCES

Anderson, W.F., 1966, 'The Prevention of Illness in the Elderly: The Rutherglen Experiment in Medicine in Old Age', proceedings of a conference held at the Royal College of Physicians, London: Pitman.

Avis, N., McKinlay, S.M., Brambilla, D. and Vass, K., 1991, 'A Longitudinal Analysis of the Association of Menopause and Depression: Results from the Massachusetts Women's Health Study', unpublished manuscript under review.

Baumgarten, M., Siemiatycki, J. and Gibbs, G.W., 1983, 'Validity of Work Histories Obtained by Interview for Epidemiologic Purposes', *American Journal of Epidemiology*, 118: 583–91.

Besdine, R.W., 1982, 'The Data Base of Geriatric Medicine', in Rowe, J.W. and Besdine, R.W. (eds), *Health and Disease in Old Age*, Boston: Little, Brown & Co.

Brambilla, D.J. and McKinlay, S.M., 1987a, 'A Comparison of Responses to Mailed Questionnaires and Telephone Interviews in a Mixed-Mode Health Survey', *American Journal of Epidemiology*, 126: 962–71.

—— 1987b, 'Item Nonresponse and Response Bias in Mixed-Mode Surveys', in *Proceedings of the Public Health Conference on Records and Statistics*, DHHS Pub. No (PHS) 88-1214, Hyattsville, MD: Public Health Service, US Government Printing Office.

Branch, L.G. and Meyers, A.R., 1987, 'Assessing Physical Function in the Elderly', *Geriatric Assessment*, 3: 29–51.

Brock, D.B., Lemke, J.H. and Woolson, R.F., 1986, 'Identification of Nonrandom Item Nonresponse in an Epidemiologic Survey of the Elderly', in *Proceedings of the Section on Survey Research Methods*, Washington, DC: American Statistical Association.

Brotherston, J., 1981, 'Policies for the care of the elderly: An overview' in Kinnaird, J., Brotherston, J. and Williamson, J. (eds), *The Provision of Care for the Elderly*, Edinburgh: Churchill Livingstone.

Brown, N.R., Rips, L.J. and Shevell, S.K., 1985, 'The Subjective Dates of Natural Events in Very-long-term Memory', *Cognitive Psychology*, 17: 139–77.

Cannel, C.F., Marquis, K.H. and Laurent, A., 1977a, 'A Summary of Studies', in *Advance Data from Vital and Health Statistics*, Series 2, No. 69, Hyattsville, MD: Public Health Service, US Government Printing Office.

Cannel, C.F., Oksenberg, L. and Converse, J.M., 1977b, *Experiments in Interviewing Techniques: Field Experiments in Health Reportings, 1971–1977*, Hyattsville, MD: National Center for Health Services Research.

Clarke, J.N., 1983, 'Sexism, Feminism and Medicalism: A Decade of Literature on Gender and Illness', *Sociology of Health and Illness*, 5, 1: 62–82.

Coggon, D., Pippard, E.C. and Acheson, E.D., 1985, 'Accuracy of Occupational Histories Obtained from Wives', *British Journal of Industrial Medicine*, 42: 563–4.

Dillman, D.A., 1978, *Mail and Telephone Surveys: The Total Design Method*, New York: John Wiley & Sons.

—— 1982, 'Mail and Other Self-administered Questionnaires', in Rossi, P., Wright, J.D. and Andersen, A.B. (eds), *Handbook for Survey Research*, New York: Academic Press.

Dillman, D.A. and Tarnai, J., 1988, 'Administrative Issues in Mixed-Mode Surveys', in Groves, R., Biermer, P., Lyberg, L., Massey, J., Nicholls, W. and Waksberg, J. (eds), *Telephone Survey Methodology*, New York: John Wiley & Sons.

Dunnell, S. and Cartwright, A., 1972, *Medicine Takers, Prescribers and Hoarders*, London: Routledge & Kegan Paul.

Feller, B.A., 1983, 'Americans Needing Help to Function at Home', *Advance Data from Vital and Health Statistics*, No. 92, DHHS Pub. No. (PHS) 83-1250, Hyattsville, MD: Public Health Service, US Government Printing Office.

Ferraro, K.F., 1980, 'Self-ratings of Health Among the Old and the Old-Old', *Journal of Health and Social Behavior*, 21: 377–83.

Fienberg, S.E., Loftus, E.F. and Tanur, J.M., 1985a, 'Cognitive Aspects of Health Survey Methodology: An Overview', *Milbank Memorial Fund Quarterly*, 63: 547–64.

—— 1985b, 'Recalling Pain and Other Symptoms', *Milbank Memorial Fund Quarterly*, 63: 582–97.

Fillenbaum, G.G. and Smyer, M.A., 1981, 'The Development, Validity, and Reliability of the OARS Multidimensional Functional Assessment Questionnaire', *Journal of Gerontology*, 36: 428–34.

Fowler, F.J. and Mangione, T.W., 1984, *Reducing Interviewer Effects on Health Survey Data*, unpublished NCHS Grant No. 3-R18-HS04189.

Fulton, J. and Hendershot, G., 1986, 'Functional Limitation of Older Americans: Provisional Data from the National Health Interview Survey, United States, January–June 1984', in *Advance Data from Vital and Health Statistics*, DHHS

## 134 Non-experimental quantitative study designs

Pub. No. (PHS) 86-1250, Hyattsville, MD: Public Health Service, US Government Printing Office.

Fulton, J., Katz, S., Jack, S. and Hendershot, G.E., 1989, 'Physical Functioning of the Aged: United States, 1984', in *Advance Data from Vital and Health Statistics*, Hyattsville, MD: Public Health Service, US Government Printing Office.

Gerlin, M., Siemiatycki, J., Begin, H. and Begin, D., 1985, 'Obtaining Occupational Exposure Histories in Epidemiologic Case-control Studies', *Journal of Occupational Medicine*, 27: 420–6.

Goudy, W.J., 1978, 'Interim Nonresponse to a Mail Questionnaire: Impacts of Variable Relationships', journal paper no. I-8456, Ames, IA: Iowa Agriculture and Home Economics Experiment Station.

Gresham, G.E. and Labi, M.L.C., 1984, 'Functional Assessment Instruments Currently Available for Documenting Outcomes in Rehabilitation Medicine', in Granger, C.V. and Greer, G.E. (eds), *Functional Assessment in Rehabilitation Medicine*, Baltimore, MD: Williams and Wilkins.

Groves, R.M. and Kahn, R.L., 1979, *Surveys by Telephone: A National Comparison with Personal Interviews*, New York: Academic Press.

Hannay, D.R., 1979, *The Symptom Iceberg: A Study of Community Health*, London: Routledge & Kegan Paul.

Haug, M.R., 1986, 'Aging in the Eighties: Impaired Senses for Sound and Light in Persons Age 65 Years and Over: Preliminary Data from the Supplement on Aging to the National Health Interview Survey: United States, January–June 1984', in *Advance Data from Vital and Health Statistics*, Hyattsville, MD: Public Health Service, US Government Printing Office.

Herzog, A. and Dielman, L., 1985, 'Age Differences in Response Accuracy for Factual Survey Questions', *Journal of Gerontology*, 40: 350–7.

Herzog, R., Rodger, W.L. and Kulka, R.A., 1983, 'Interviewing Older Adults: A Comparison of Telephone and Face-to-face Modalities', *Public Opinion Quarterly*, 47: 405–18.

Hickey, T., 1980, *Health and Aging*, Monterey: Brooks/Cole Publishing Co.

Hochstim, J.R., 1967, 'A Critical Comparison of Three Strategies of Collecting Data from Households', *Journal of the American Statistical Association*, 62: 976–89.

Hochstim, J.R. and Athanasopoulos, D.A., 1970, 'Personal Follow-up in a Mail Survey: Its Contribution and Its Cost', *Public Opinion Quarterly*, 43: 69–81.

Hyman, H.H., Cobb, J., Feldman, J. and Stember, C, 1954, *Interviewing in Social Research*, Chicago: University of Chicago Press.

Jabine, T.B., Straf, M.L., Tanur, J.M. and Tourangeau, R., 1984, *Cognitive Aspects of Survey Methodology: Building a Bridge Between Disciplines*, Washington, DC: National Academy Press.

Kane, R.A. and Kane, R.L., 1981, *Assessing the Elderly: A Practical Guide to Measurement*, Lexington, MA: DC Heath.

Kart, C., 1981, 'Experiencing Symptoms: Attribution and Misattribution of Illness Among the Aged', in Haug, M.R. (ed.), *Elderly Patients and Their Doctors*, New York: Springer Publishing Co.

Katz, S., 1983, 'Assessing Self-maintenance: Activities of Daily Living, Mobility, and Instrumental Activities of Daily Living', *Journal of the American Geriatrics Society*, 31: 721–7.

Kent, G., 1985, 'Memory of Dental Pain', *Pain*, 21: 187–94.

Kish, L., 1962, 'Studies of Interviewer Variance for Attitudinal Variables', *Journal of the American Statistical Association*, 44: 380–7.
—— 1965, *Survey Sampling*, New York: John Wiley & Sons.
Koons, D.A., 1973, 'Quality Control and Measurement of Non-Sampling Error in the Health Interview Survey', in *Advance Data from Vital and Health Statistics*, Series 2, No. 54, Hyattsville, MD: Public Health Service, US Government Printing Office.
Kovar, M.G., 1986, 'Aging in the Eighties: Preliminary Data from the Supplement on Aging to the National Health Interview Survey, United States, January–June 1984', *Advance Data from Vital and Health Statistics*, No. 115, DHHS Pub. No. (PHS) 86-1250, Hyattsville, MD: Public Health Service, US Government Printing Office.
Lebowitz, B., 1975, 'Age and Fearfulness: Personal and Situational Factors', *Journal of Gerontology*, 30: 696–700.
Lepkowski, J., 1988, 'Telephone Sampling Methods in the United States', in Groves, R., Biemer, P., Lyberg, L., Massey, J., Nicholls, W. and Waksberg, K. (eds), *Telephone Survey Methodology*, New York: John Wiley & Sons.
Lessler, J.T. and Sirken, M.G., 1985, 'Laboratory-based Research on the Cognitive Aspects of Survey Methodology: The Goals and Methods of the National Center for Health Statistics Study', *Milbank Memorial Fund Quarterly*, 63: 565–581.
Lessler, J.T., Bercini, D., Tourangeau, R. and Salter, W., 1985, 'Results of the Cognitive/Laboratory Studies of the 1986 NHIS Dental Care Supplement', in *Proceedings of the Survey Methods Section*, Washington, DC: American Statistical Association.
Linn, B. and Linn, M., 1980, 'Objective and Self-assessed Health in the Old and Very Old', *Social Science and Medicine*, 14A: 311–15.
Loftus, E.F. and Fathi, D.C., 1985, 'Retrieving Multiple Autobiographical Memories', *Social Cognition*, 3: 280–95.
Loftus, E.F. and Marburger, W., 1983, 'Since the Eruption of Mt St Helens, Has Anyone Beaten You Up? Improving the Accuracy of Retrospective Reports with Landmark Events', *Memory and Cognition*, 11: 14–120.
Loftus, E.F., Fienberg, S.E. and Tanur, J.M., 1985, 'Cognitive Psychology Meets the National Survey', *American Psychologist*, 40: 175–80.
McKinlay, J.B. and McKinlay, S.M., 1985, 'Health, Status, and Health Care Utilization by Menopausal Women', in Mastroianni, L. and Paulsen, C.A. (eds), *Aging, Reproduction and the Climacteric*, New York: Plenum Publishing Press.
McKinlay, J.B., McKinlay, S.M. and Brambilla, D., 1987, 'The Relative Contribution of Endocrine Changes and Social Circumstances to Depression in Mid-age Women', *Journal of Health and Social Behaviour*, 28: 354–63.
McKinlay, J.B., Longcope, C. and Gray, A., 1989, 'The Questionable Physiologic and Epidemiologic Basis for a Male Climacteric Syndrome: Preliminary Results from the Massachusetts Male Aging Study', *Maturitas*, 11: 103–15.
McKinlay, S.M. and Kipp, D., 1984, 'A Field Approach for Obtaining Physiologic Measures in Surveys of General Populations: Response Rates, Reliability and Costs', in Cannel, C. (ed.), *Health Survey Research Methods, Fourth Conference, Research Proceedings Series*, DHHS Pub. No. (PHS) 84-3346, Hyattsville, MD: National Center for Health Services Research.
Maddox, G.L., 1962, 'Some Correlates of Differences of Self-Assessments of Health Among the Elderly', *Journal of Gerontology*, 17: 180–5.
Maddox, G.L. and Douglass, E.B., 1973, 'Self-assessment of Health', *Journal of Health and Social Behavior*, 14: 87–93.

136 *Non-experimental quantitative study designs*

Massey, J.T. and Shapiro, E., 1982, 'Self-rated Health: Predictor of Mortality Among the Elderly', *American Journal of Public Health*, 72: 800–08.

Mechanic, D., 1978, 'Sex, Illness, Behavior and the Use of Health Services', *Social Science and Medicine*, 12 3B: 207–14.

Morris, J., Sherwood, S. and Mor, V., 1984, 'An Assessment Tool for Use in Identifying Functionally Vulnerable Persons in the Community', *The Gerontologist*, 24: 373–79.

Mullen, B.J., Krantzler, N.J., Grivetti, L.E., Schutz, H.G. and Meiselmen, H.L., 1984, 'Validity of a Food Frenquency Questionnaire for the Determination of Individual Food Intake', *American Journal of Clinical Nutrition*, 39: 136–43.

Nathanson, C., 1975, 'Illness and the Feminine Role: A Theoretical Review', *Social Science and Medicine*, 9: 57–62.

National Center for Health Statistics, 1985, 'Current Estimates from the National Health Interview Survey, United States, 1982', in *Advance Data from Vital and Health Statistics*, Series 10, No. 134, DHHS Pub. No. (PHS) 81-1562, Hyattsville, MD: Public Health Service, US Government Printing Office.

Oksenberg, L. and Cannel, C., 1988, 'Effects of Interviewer Vocal Characteristics on Nonresponse', in Groves, R., Biemer, P., Lyberg, L., Massey, J., Nicholls, W. and Waksberg, J. (eds), *Telephone Survey Methodology*, New York: John Wiley & Sons.

O'Toole, B.I., Battistutta, D., Long, A. and Crouch, K., 1986, 'A Comparison of Costs and Data Quality of Three Health Survey Methods: Mail, Telephone and Personal Home Interview', *American Journal of Epidemiology*, 124: 317–28.

Pathy, M.S., 1967, 'Clinical Presentation of Myocardial Infarction', *British Heart Journal*, 29: 190–9.

Pearse, I. and Crocker, L., 1944, *The Peckham Experiment*, London: Allen & Unwin.

Pechacek, T.F., Fox, B.H., Luepker, D.M. and Luepker, R.V., 1984, 'Review of Techniques for Measurement of Smoking Behavior', in Mattarazzo, J.D., Weiss, S.M., Herd, J.A. and Miller, N.E. (eds), *Behavioral Health: A Handbook of Health Enhancement and Disease Prevention*, New York: John Wiley & Sons.

Posner, B.M., Borman, C.L., Morgan, J.L., Borden, W.S. and Ohls, J.C., 1982, 'The Validity of a Telephone-administered 24-hour Dietary Recall Methodology', *American Journal of Clinical Nutrition*, 36: 546–53.

Radloff, L.S., 1977, 'The CES-D Scale: A Self-report Depression Scale for Research in the General Population', *Applied Psychological Measurement*, 3: 385–401.

Rodgers, W.L. and Herzog, A.R., 1987, 'Interviewing Older Adults: The Accuracy of Factual Information', *Journal of Gerontology*, 42: 387–94.

Roos, N.P. and Shapiro, E., 1981, 'The Manitoba Longitudinal Study on Aging: Preliminary Findings on Health Care Utilisation by the Elderly', *Medical Care*, XIX: 6.

Rosenwaike, I., 1985, 'A Demographic Portrait of the Oldest Old', *Milbank Memorial Fund Quarterly*, 63: 187–205.

Royston, P., Bercini, D., Sirken, M. and Mingay, D., 1986, 'Questionnaire Design Research Laboratory', presented at the Survey Methods Section, Meetings of the American Statistical Association.

Rowe, J.W., 1983, 'Systolic Hypertension in the Elderly', *New England Journal of Medicine*, 309: 1246–7.

—— 1985, 'Health Care of the Elderly', *New England Journal of Medicine*, March 28: 827–35.
Rubin, D.B., 1976, 'Inference and Missing Data', *Biometrika*, 63, 581-92.
Siemiatycki, J., 1979, 'A Comparison of Mail, Telephone, and Home Interview Strategies for Household Health Surveys', *American Journal of Public Health*, 69: 238–45.
Siemiatycki, J. and Campbell, S., 1984, 'Nonresponse Bias and Early Versus All Responders in Mail and Telephone Surveys', *American Journal of Epidemiology*, 120: 291–301.
Siemiatycki, J., Campbell, S. and Richardson, L., 1984, 'Quality of Response in Different Populations Groups in Mail and Telephone Surveys', *American Journal of Epidemiology*, 12: 302–14.
Sirken, M.G., 1986, 'Error Effects of Survey Questionnaires on the Public Assessments of Health Risks', *American Journal of Public Health*, 76: 367–8.
South East London Screening Study Group, 1977, 'A Controlled Trial of Multiphasic Screening in Middle Age: Results of the South East London Screening Study', *International Journal of Epidemiology*, 6: 4.
Stoller, E.P., 1984, 'Self-assessments of Health by the Elderly: The Impact of Informal Assistance', *Journal of Health and Social Behavior*, 25: 260–70.
Thornberry, T. and Massey, J., 1988, 'Trends in United States Telephone Coverage Across Time and Subgroups', in Groves, R., Biemer, P., Lyberg, L., Massey, L., Nicholls, W. and Waksberg, J. (eds), *Telephone Survey Methodology*, New York: John Wiley & Sons.
Tissue, T., 1972, 'Another Look at Self-Rated Health Among the Elderly', *Journal of Gerontology*, 27: 91–4.
Todd, K.S., Hudes, M. and Calloway, D.H., 1983, 'Food Intake Measurement: Problems and Approaches', *American Journal of Clinical Nutrition*, 37: 139–46.
Van Staveren, W.A., de Boer, J.O. and Burema, J., 1985, 'Validity and Reproducibility of a Dietary History Method Estimating the Usual Food Intake During One Month', *American Journal of Clinical Nutrition*, 42: 554–9.
Verbrugge, L.M., 1976, 'Females and Illness. Recent Trends in Sex Differences in the United States', *Journal of Health and Social Behavior*, 17: 387–403.
Washburn, R.A. and Montoie, H.J., 1986, 'The Assessment of Physical Activity by Questionnaire', *American Journal of Epidemiology*, 123: 563–76.
Whitmore, R.W., Mason, R.E. and Hartwell, T.D., 1985, 'Use of Geographically Classified Telephone Directory Lists in Multi-Mode Surveys', *Journal of the American Statistical Association*, 80: 842–4.
Willett, W.C., Reynolds, R.D., Cottrell-Hoehner, S., Sampson, L. and Brown, M.L., 1987, 'Validation of a Semi-quantitative Food Frequency: Comparison with a 1-year Diet Record', *Journal of the American Dietetic Association*, 87: 43–7.
Williamson, J., 1981, 'Screening, Surveillance, and Case Finding', in Arie, T. (ed.), *Health Care of the Elderly*, London: Croom Helm.
Woltman, H.F., Turner, A.G. and Bushery, J.M., 1980, 'A Comparison of Three Mixed-Mode Interviewing Procedures in the National Crime Survey', *Journal of the American Statistical Association*, 75: 534–43.

# 8 Comparing alternative methodologies of social research
## An overview

*Jake M. Najman with John Morrison, Gail M. Williams and Margaret J. Andersen*

Any assessment of the relative merits or disadvantages of different research methods in sociology must begin by acknowledging that research is not conducted in a social, intellectual or political vacuum. To the extent that overt or covert objectives underlie social research, judgements about the appropriateness and adequacy of a chosen methodology are dependent upon whether these objectives have been met. Thus methodologies which are suspect or weak from a quantitative perspective, e.g. case studies, may nevertheless prove persuasive and important.

This overview then does not seek to advance one methodology as intrinsically better than another, nor to suggest that there is a single methodological approach which has advantages over all others. Indeed it argues that a final judgement of the value of a methodology depends upon the aims and objectives of those undertaking the research and the extent to which there emerges a consensus that these have been achieved. Yet we will advance three qualifications to the above proposition. First, whatever the methodology used, it is important to carefully distinguish between the data or findings and their interpretation. Much of the time the data are not in dispute, except where errors of observation or measurement are suspected, but it is their potential alternative interpretations which are of concern. Irrespective of the methods used, if the researcher fails to consider alternative interpretations of the findings and to discuss the merits of these alternatives, then there remain questions which serve to limit the confidence one might have in the conclusions the author derives.

Second, there are some commonly accepted methodological criteria which may be applied to any study or method. These criteria can be thought of as a guide or checklist against which much (but presumably not all) research can be judged. A short list of such criteria would include the following:

1 estimates of the reliability of the measurements;
2 estimates of the validity of the measurements;

3 sampling and the consequent generalisability of the results;
4 whether observed differences are statistically significant or possibly represent chance variations;
5 whether observed associations reflect strong or weak effects;
6 whether the observed associations are possibly attributable to confounding or to other intervening or like variables;
7 whether the data have been collected in a manner consistent with their interpretation. This is particularly important where a method of cross-sectional data collection is used to infer a causal sequence more appropriately addressed using longitudinal methods; and
8 whether the results are consistent with previous research, i.e. whether the findings have been replicated.

Third, we will suggest that much research seeks to argue for a particular causal sequence. We will advance this argument despite occasional denials to the contrary, noting that the most interesting questions in social research concern whether some events or situations precede others (e.g. whether poverty precedes disease, whether professional socialisation is a consequence of medical education or whether male/female differences in health-related behaviour are the result of socialisation or differential access to medical care). If the implicit aim of research is to suggest a causal sequence which might be the subject of policy proposals (e.g. to reduce inequality, improve medical education, decrease gender-related health inequalities) then additional methodological considerations confirming or denying the proposed causal sequence should be considered.

This chapter provides an overview of the methodologies used by sociologists and other social researchers whose primary research concerns are health related. It begins by considering the range of methodologies used by sociologists and the extent to which they involve various mixtures of observation and interpretation. It then discusses the criteria which might be applied to judge the contribution of a particular study, and there follows a consideration of the issue of causality and its determination in sociological research. At various points in the argument data from a number of sources are used to illustrate the main thrust of this chapter, namely that the determination of cause and effect are a high priority in sociological research and that such a determination requires, at least, a disciplined adherence to specific principles of research – known more colloquially as 'the scientific method'.

## METHODS OF SOCIAL RESEARCH: INDUCTION VS. DEDUCTION

Sociological research is characterised by its acceptance of a wide variety of research methods and research orientations (Table 10). While some might wish to include survey research under a separate methodological heading, it could be argued that the social survey is a particular approach to data collection and therefore is only part of a broader methodological orientation. Methodological orientations can be categorised in six broad headings in terms of the extent to which their approach is inductive or deductive. Qualitative methods essentially proceed from an inductive approach generating analyses based upon the continuing refinement of observations.

Of course elements of hypothesis testing (deduction) are sometimes to be found in qualitative research, but the overriding thrust of qualitative research is hypothesis generating rather than hypothesis testing. By contrast, experimental and quasi-experimental methods generally begin with a specific hypothesis (or hypotheses) which are accepted or rejected (perhaps with qualifications). The experiment is deliberately ranked below the panel/longitudinal study on the criterion of hypothesis testing. This is justified because experiments are necessarily limited in scope: they tend to be restricted to small samples and often take place in an artificial or contrived context. By contrast, the panel study allows the researcher access to a more 'real world' situation, to consider the role of a number of independent variables and to predict in a natural context (see Biddle, *et al.*, 1983, for a discussion on this point).

Three issues are worth emphasising in relation to the above analysis. First, in an important sense, it is not possible to prove a hypothesis, since there are likely to be many ways in which a single hypothesis might be tested. One might fail to refute the hypothesis a number of times yet still recognise that a further test might still deny its validity. According to this

*Table 10* The focus of various methods of social research

---

*Qualitative*

| (hypothesis-generating) | * | observation and related qualitative data collection (e.g. participant observation, case studies) |
| | * | unstructured interviews, focused groups |
| | * | analysis of documentary and historical sources |
| | * | analysis of official statistics |
| | * | experimental and quasi-experimental studies |
| (hypothesis-testing) | * | panel/cohort/longitudinal studies. |

*Quantitative*

---

(Popperian) view it is the repeated (not single) failure to reject the hypothesis that increases one's confidence in its probable validity. Second, social surveys may be used in conjunction with a number of different methodologies which may be qualitative, quantitative or experimental in orientation. To report that one has done a social survey is to provide little detail of one's methodology. Finally, the methodologies listed in Table 10 do not 'belong' to any single discipline, with the possible exception of the qualitative methodologies. Thus, for example, psychologists, demographers, historians, epidemiologists, economists, and geographers have used these methods at various times. It is arguably only the qualitative methods that have been developed largely by sociologists (and anthropologists) and that are largely restricted to these disciplines (although market researchers are developing focused group interviews as a qualitative methodology).

## THE SCIENTIFIC METHOD AND ITS APPLICATION TO SOCIAL RESEARCH

Some would argue that a true (read correct) understanding of society will not result from the application of 'the scientific method' to social phenomena. It is suggested that the desire to emphasise scientific methods reflects an outdated positivist orientation which is doomed to failure not only because the subject matter is extremely complex but also because all research begins with presuppositions and assumptions (read bias) which then direct both the preferred research method and the interpretation of the results. My colleague Claire Williams (1988), who writes of 'feminist methodologies', reflects this type of argument. At its most extreme form, this criticism of positivist methods takes its arguments from a sociology-of-knowledge perspective, raising questions about whether it is possible to know reality outside one's own socialisation.

Positivists have tended to respond to these claims by acknowledging their fundamental accuracy (all research reflects qualities of the researcher as well as the subject matter of the research) but denying that such an acknowledgement is a threat to the preference for a scientific methodology. Indeed if, as those who criticise the positivist school of research argue, social reality is both complex and selectively perceived and interpreted by positivist researchers, then the same criticisms must apply equally to those who prefer inductive/qualitative methods. If errors of observation and measurement are a problem in social research, as undoubtedly they are, then methods which more tightly control the process of data collection appear a better response than methods which allow such a process to continue. On this point the positivists would appear to have the argument in their favour since they rely on replication and repeated hypothesis testing, thus providing opportunities for the individual bias of researchers to be factored out.

An extension of this view argues that the methods of the physical sciences have been inappropriately applied to human and social phenomena. This use of physical science methods, it is suggested, is an impossible task doomed to failure because of the interdependent and holistic nature of the (sociological) subject matter. Efforts to disaggregate the whole into its components and thus permit some gains in understanding are further criticised because it is the whole which is believed to be of primary interest. The whole is believed to be of a different character than suggested by its parts. An additional argument questions the need for scientific rigour, suggesting that all research is political and therefore should be undertaken to serve the needs of those disadvantaged by the existing political process, rather than to exhibit a misplaced concern with methodological sophistication. Whatever the merits of the above propositions, and some have merit, it is absurd to suspend efforts to improve the quality of social research because doubts have been raised about some aspects of this effort.

It is unclear whether our understanding of society will be most advanced by:

1  better holistic interpretations (grand theory);
2  better qualitative research; or
3  a greater emphasis on scientific method and carefully collected, high-quality data.

Probably all of the above will contribute to advancing the cause of social research, but not unless researchers attend to improving the quality of existing research methods. A case could be made that the major deficiencies of social research have been a reluctance to question findings and too great a willingness to accept results and theories at face value, irrespective of their methodological strengths and weaknesses. If, as we have suggested, the findings (read data) may be less important than their interpretation, then the criteria used to make such judgements must be clearly understood. It is to these criteria that we now turn.


## RELIABILITY

The concepts of reliability and validity are, at the simplest level, a concern about the consistency and accuracy of measurement. There is reason for social researchers to be greatly concerned with the validity of their measurements. Thus in-depth interviews following administration of questionnaires have shown that even very simply framed questions are misunderstood by a majority of respondents (e.g. 'How many hours of television do you watch in an average week?').

Other studies have shown that characteristics of the interviewer or respondent or their rapport may influence the answers they give. Data from the Danish National Morbidity Survey (Nathanson, 1978: 259) show that males appear to report higher levels of morbidity when they are interviewed by females and lower when interviewed by males (Table 11). This result might be attributed to the perception male respondents are believed to hold that female interviewers are more accepting of illness than are male interviewers.

*Table 11* Reported illness among male respondents, Denmark, 1952–4

| | *Illness per 1,000 respondents by age* | | |
|---|---|---|---|
| *Interviewer and respondent's sex* | *15–39* | *40–59* | *60+* |
| Males interviewed by males | 301 | 359 | 497 |
| Males interviewed by females | 412 | 534 | 832 |

*Source*: Nathanson, 1978

It is difficult to ignore the possibility that a lack of reliability may permeate the whole research process from data collection to data coding. A lack of reliability creates imprecision or 'noise' for the analysis and can provide misleading trends and information. Regardless of the method of research adopted, it would appear of fundamental importance that social researchers report details of how they have gone about determining the reliability and validity of their methods.

Quantitative researchers have begun to use in-depth and group interviews to review the meanings respondents give to their questions; and the use of test–retest correlations, balanced scales and scale reliability coefficients are other approaches commonly used to ascertain the reliability of the measuring instruments. Generally, experimental methods attend to reliability issues as an integral part of the methodology. Qualitative researchers have generally not addressed the issue of reliability in a systematic and consistent fashion, presumably because their resources are limited. There is, for example, no obvious reason why a number of observers could not independently witness the same situation or event and describe it, though such checks are rarely reported. Similarly the coding of qualitative data could be undertaken by a number of researchers, and reliability coefficients produced.

## BIAS

A significant problem faced by many social researchers is that their measurements are consistently inaccurate and misleading. Such problems arise not only in relation to attitudes which may be subject to conformity, desirability or acquiescence bias but to a whole range of health, substance use and demographic data. While McKinlay (1989) may be correct in noting that questions concerning cigarette use turn out to be reasonably valid, only about half the amount of alcohol consumed is admitted to by respondents on questionnaires. Others have noted that heavy drinkers may selectively under-report, with young employed males being particularly prone to selectively understating their level of alcohol consumption (Cooke and Allan, 1983). The interview situation has been found to influence reports of alcohol use, with contact with an interviewer being associated with reduced estimates of alcohol consumption (Crawford, 1987: 170). Interestingly, preferences for different modes of data collection (face-to-face interview, questionnaire, telephone survey) do not appear to greatly influence the answers provided, although there may be exceptions to this. It is arguable that anonymous forms of data collection (telephone, self-completed questionnaires) may produce more valid results.

Bias is of serious concern not only because respondents may have a particular reason for misleading the interviewer but also because many of the concepts being measured can be reflected in a number of ways – some of which give answers that are inconsistent with one another (e.g. 'Is social class best indicated by assessing occupational skill, education, income prestige or status, quality of housing, area of residence, etc.?'). It is not surprising that ten different measures of class may produce conflicting results, nor that a researcher will select and report that result which is 'most interesting'.

Quantitative researchers have tended to use a variety of means to determine the bias in their measures, including comparisons with objective indicators, clinical judgements, criterion groups, predictive accuracy and so on. While some of these approaches may serve to institutionalise existing and erroneous criteria, the broad acceptance of a need to validate measures serves to enhance the quality of the data.

Unfortunately, qualitative researchers have tended to take less interest in the validation of their measurements, though this could be defended by their general willingness to treat their findings as hypotheses which remain to be evaluated.

## SAMPLING

The method used to select a sample for a study determines the extent to which it can be seen to have external validity (i.e. generalisability). Some key aspects of sampling are worthy of elaboration.

It is relatively rare to find researchers who limit their discussion of findings to the sample they have selected. This is because results which cannot be generalised are of relatively little interest, remembering here that a sample chosen at a point in time may be generalised not only to other like groups but to members of the study group existing prior or subsequent to the time the study was undertaken. This desire to generalise, either implicitly or explicitly, seems to underpin most social research.

The major requirements for a representative sample are that the sample be chosen in a random manner from a known population. Only rarely does this prove practicable, and most studies vary from these requirements, whether they acknowledge such variation or not. Thus skid row derelicts, persons of no fixed residence or those in prison are rarely included in even the best sampling frames. This is not a trivial set of exclusions since it is precisely the group excluded which may manifest the greatest coincidence of social and health disadvantages. Further, while a random sample is likely to produce representativeness, there is no guarantee that it will. Alternately, it is possible that a sample chosen via a number of non-random means may produce results which are broadly consistent with those which might have appeared had a random sample been used. Thus, a study of smoking by British doctors (Doll and Hill, 1956) and a study of self-selected members of a voluntary organisation (Hammond and Dorn, 1958) both produced results, subsequently confirmed by numerous other studies, that smoking was causally related to lung cancer.

The key issues, then, in judging a sample are the extent to which it is necessary or practicable to select a sample in a restricted manner (e.g. persons who work at one place, who live in one or more areas, who can read and write) and the impact this has on the findings of interest. This is not a totally unknown quantity as some of the characteristics of the sample can be compared to the population from which it is drawn and as the relationship between some observed biases of sampling can be statistically controlled in the process of data analysis.

The real problem in selecting a sample is to do so in a way which allows one to make judgements about the extent to which it is unrepresentative and the likely impact of this unrepresentativeness. It is also worth emphasising that a sample may be unrepresentative in some respects, but that this may not influence the generalisability of results (unrelated to the hypothesis of interest).

In judging the representativeness of a sample it is necessary to consider the manner in which the sample was obtained, the characteristics of those finally selected compared to the population they are believed to represent, and any grounds for asserting external validity if this is not clear. Perhaps most important in this process is a detailed description of response rates and the documentation of how refusals differed from the participants in the study. Without these details it is difficult to distinguish results which reflect nothing other than the peculiar features of some unusual individuals fortuitously included in a study, from those which reflect more prevalent social processes.

## STATISTICAL SIGNIFICANCE

If one is seeking to generalise beyond the chosen sample to a population then two questions arise. First, could the observed differences reflect random variations in the distribution of the data? Are the differences such that they could arise by chance? Second, are the observed differences in the groups being compared such that they are likely to reflect differences in the population from which these groups are drawn?

If, as we have argued, the external validity (generalisability) of results is a key issue, then the testing of results to determine whether they could arise by chance would seem fundamental. Two arguments are sometimes advanced to divert a reader from a concern with the significance of differences (or their possible lack of significance). The first of these is that the researcher admits to choosing an unrepresentative sample and reports that there is no intent to generalise and that therefore a test of significance is inappropriate. The second is that the researcher has sampled the whole population (presumably a small population) and therefore a test of significance is inappropriate. Both these claims can be disputed and should be tested more frequently than they are. Such a test could involve asking whether the results would be worth considering if:

1   they reflect idiosyncrasies of a peculiar sample;
2   they are limited to that sample at that point in time, i.e. the association is no longer believed to exist.

Even if one has a whole population at a point in time, it is arguably a sample of those who are in this population over different time periods. On this ground the use of inferential statistics is appropriate. In any event, the failure to test for significance of differences leaves open the possibility that the differences are due to chance and should therefore be ignored.

In recent literature a further debate has arisen that is concerned with the use of point estimates of the significance of differences. Point estimates provide a 'greater or less than' indication of the likelihood that differences between the groups being compared could arise by chance. Such estimates, it is suggested, are crude and relatively uninformative (e.g. If $p<05$, then how far below .05 is it? Similarly, if .05, how far above $p>.05$ is it?). Reporting the actual $p$ value allows the readers to judge for themselves whether a difference ought to be taken seriously. Even more informative, it is suggested, are confidence limits because they provide the reader with additional information about the distribution of *p* values for an observed difference or association. Some journals now require their contributors to include confidence limits in their papers and they routinely reject papers which do not provide these details (see Walker, 1986, and Fleiss, 1986, for examples of this debate).

Irrespective of where one stands in relation to these debates, they emphasise the need to consider the possibility that any observed difference is potentially a chance observation. Unless a researcher performs the appropriate tests of significance it is potentially misleading to even note that a difference has been observed.

## STRENGTH OF ASSOCIATION

If a difference has been found, or an association between two or more variables is believed to exist, then the next question of concern is usually whether the association or difference is of sufficient magnitude to matter. Here one should judge whether the association is weak, moderate or strong. This is particularly pertinent where, say, one group is believed to differ from another in their attitudes, values, beliefs or behaviours. A weak association suggests that perhaps a majority of persons in the groups being compared manifest similar characteristics, and that there is only a tendency for one group to have somewhat more persons of one characteristic than the other group(s). In this latter instance a claim that the groups differ should be accompanied by the qualification that the differences are weak (despite being significant). Whether or not the researcher details the strength of the association, readers should consider this issue and base their interpretation on this judgement.

Estimates of the strength of association are broadly of three types, each with somewhat different utility. Correlation coefficients (strictly Pearson product moment) can provide an estimate of the amount of variation in one variable possibly attributable to its association with another variable. Such statements as 'class differences could account for twenty per cent of the variation in birthweight' are informative and provide a basis for comparing the importance of different independent variables. A second approach derives from analysis of variance and, for an interval-dependent variable, can indicate how much of a difference exists between groups (e.g. 'lower-class women have babies, on average, 150 grams lighter than those of upper-class women'). Whether such a difference is worthy of attention becomes a matter of informed judgement. Finally, one may directly compare groups using either crude percentage differences or odds ratios (or relative risks). This can produce such claims as 'lower-class women were twice as likely to be heavy smokers'. A further refinement of presentation can involve the production of confidence limits either for correlations or odds ratios, further facilitating the interpretation of results.

If no claims regarding the strength of an association are made then readers must seek to make the appropriate judgement themselves or, failing that possibility, must take the conservative view that the differences may not be great. It could reasonably be suggested that it is for the researcher to present sufficient information to enable the reader to judge whether an association is weak or strong, and that a failure to do so can be interpreted as a deficiency of the research.

## CONFOUNDING

The determination of confounding is a special aspect of efforts to determine whether an association is causal. A conservative view is that confounding can be said to occur when an association between, say, two variables is interpreted as real when it is an artefact. A broader approach would include under the heading of confounding those variables which elaborate the relationship between the dependent and independent variables. Rosenberg (1968) many years ago elegantly described the range of types of confounding variables and saw the task of the data analyst as one which involves the elaboration of a causal sequence. When faced with numerous computer-generated tables which suggest that a number of variables may be related to the dependent variable, Rosenberg advocates a stepwise process to determine which are antecedent, independent, intervening, extraneous, component and masking variables.

One example serves to illustrate the underlying methodological principle and how it can be addressed. Assume that we are testing a hypothesis that mental illness rates in the community have increased partly as a result of historical changes in the nature of society. More specifically it is suggested that the decline in religious observance, the change from an extended family to a nuclear family, increased acceptance of *de facto* unions, high mobility levels and high divorce and child abuse rates in contemporary society all contribute to increased levels of mental illness. We could test this hypothesis by examining a number of contemporary societies, say between 1900 and 1970, and determining whether the number of persons in mental institutions during that period of time has increased. Such a study would confirm that indeed there has been an increase consistent with the hypothesis. Are we then to argue that the hypothesis is correct? Before a convincing argument to this effect can be mounted, the existence of other factors and other variables explaining the observed association must be considered. One such factor would be whether the clinical composition of patients in psychiatric institutions has changed dramatically since the beginning of this century. For example, with the aging of the population we would expect more people, some of whom are institutionalised in psychiatric units, to manifest symptoms of senility. If the association between rapid social change and increasing rates of psychiatric hospital admission over time are an artefact, attributable to an aging population, then this will be evident once we compare rates of psychiatric admission by specific ages. Indeed, the data are consistent with this interpretation, and the changes that occurred between 1900 and 1970 were largely attributable to the aging of the population.

Of course even if testing had not demonstrated that the changing age structure of the population accounts for variations in psychiatric admissions over time, it remains possible that other factors might account for these observed differences – for example, changing definitions of what constitutes mental illness, changing forms of treatment, etc. Any observed association could be attributed to a range of other factors. It is for the researcher or critic to identify these potential confounders and seek to determine whether the alternative explanations they raise are plausible.

A number of well-established statistical procedures are available to facilitate this type of analysis. The presentation of three- or n-way tables provides the most simple mode of analysis, but partial correlation, multiple correlation and regression and the analysis of variance and co-variance all provide examples of ways of elaborating an association. Such methods presuppose sample sizes that are substantial and measurement procedures that are largely quantitative. For the qualitative researcher the determination of confounding is more difficult and may require alternative approaches, but it is difficult to see how any research can ignore the possibility that an observed effect may be an artefact.

## DATA COLLECTION: SIMULTANEOUS OR SEQUENTIAL?

Many of the most important and interesting questions in social research are concerned with the relationship between events, as for example between attitudes and behaviour, knowledge and performance and social structural location and its consequences. While passing acknowledgement has been given to the now cliché that 'correlation is not causation', in practice researchers have simply proceeded as if it is possible to disentangle cause and effect from data collected simultaneously (i.e. cross-sectionally).

The need for methods which directly address issues of cause and effect is reflected in the growth of the 'modelling' school, that is of those researchers who reconstruct a causal model from data collected simultaneously. On theoretical grounds these researchers generally purport to 'test' the validity of a (usually) non-recursive model or sequence of events. In more recent times path analysis has given way to logistic regression and the use of a goodness-of-fit statistic to 'confirm' the model. Biddle *et al.* (1983: 17) note the deficiencies of this approach and label its proponents' claims that they are testing a causal sequence as 'silly'. They note that confirming a regression model is not equivalent to confirming the existence of a causal relationship and add that the majority of those researchers who use these methods violate the statistical assumption underpinning the methods they use (thus LISREL and related programs assume a variable is normally distributed for values of other variables in the equation, a condition which is rarely met).

Of course there are many circumstances where asserting cause and effect from, say, a single social survey does not do great injustice to the data. Thus, one might correlate age and alcohol consumption and argue for the causality of the association on logical grounds. In the majority of instances, however, it is not possible to confidently arrange the data collected cross-sectionally into a causal sequence. In other circumstances one might contrive a set of questions which involve the recall of past events, and thus argue a causal sequence. The credibility of this latter approach is dependent upon the accuracy of the events recalled and the extent to which subsequent situations influence this level of accuracy. Events in the past take their meaning from the present and with the benefit of hindsight; consequently such recall is generally suspect (Janson, 1981: 36).

In 1938 Paul Lazarsfeld and Marjorie Fiske introduced the panel study as a method of social research which was perhaps more efficient for collecting data than the usual cross-sectional social survey. Almost as an aside they noted the suitability of this approach to data collection for identifying factors producing change (see Lazarsfeld, 1940, for a more extended discussion of this point). Others have since argued this proposition more aggressively, suggesting that '[s]tatic research makes it impossible to carry out any definitive causal analysis' (Caplovitz, 1983: 327).

Simply put, surveys represent a static method of collecting data, whereas our major concerns tend to be with the process of change. The case for longitudinal methods of data collection has led to some seventy such studies being undertaken in Europe (until 1981) and a number of others in the United States, New Zealand and Australia. Unfortunately, longitudinal research designs still represent only a small proportion of all studies. The need for more such studies is evident from a few illustrations which follow.

## COMPARING RESULTS DERIVED FROM SIMULTANEOUS AND SEQUENTIAL APPROACHES TO DATA COLLECTION

The Mater University of Queensland Study of Pregnancy (MUSP) began in 1978 as a collaborative study which has focused upon both substantive and methodological issues in social research. The main component of the longitudinal study began in 1981 when all women attending a large obstetrical hospital in Brisbane were invited to participate in a study of their own health and that of their soon-to-be-born children (n = 8556). Details of reliability, validity, sampling, significance testing, and major findings have been documented in a number of published papers (see Keeping, *et al.*, 1989, and others listed below). To date the results have addressed four main issues:

1  In qualitative and quantitative studies, we have found that women fail to obtain the information that they would like from their obstetricians (Shapiro, *et al.*, 1983). In particular, lower-class women want more information but obtain less than their higher-class counterparts (Shapiro and Najman, 1987).

2  There is little reason to be concerned about the pregnancy health of employed women, though unemployed women appear to constitute a group at high risk of some negative outcomes (Najman, *et al.*, 1983; Najman, *et al.*, 1989b).

3  There are significant social class differences in the outcomes of pregnancy but these differences are largely attributable to the lifestyle and other demographic differences which distinguish the social classes (Najman, *et al.*, 1983; Morrison, *et al.*, 1989).

4  There are important differences in the pregnancies and pregnancy outcomes of women who belong to different religious groups. Women members of minority Christian sects manifest both a very healthy lifestyle and superior pregnancy outcomes (Najman, *et al.*, 1988a; Najman, *et al.*, 1988b).

Further work is now proceeding in a number of areas, including assessment of the long-term consequences of having an unwanted baby, characteristics of women who give up their children for adoption, social factors influencing babies' birth weight and so on. While such broad-ranging studies permit researchers to 'build up' a research area, it is the longitudinal nature of the study which is of particular importance.

Taking data from the MUSP, a three-wave longitudinal study, it is possible to emphasise the problems associated with causal assertions derived from simultaneously collected data. The data which follow were collected at six-month intervals: the first wave at the mother's first clinic visit, the second some four days after the birth and the third wave when the baby was six months old. Stress is measured using the Reeder *et al.* (1973) scale from the international collaborative study of heart disease. Anxiety is measured using seven items from the Delusions-Symptoms-States-Inventory of Bedford and Foulds (Bedford and Foulds, 1977; 1978). Both measures have been categorised into four groups with the extreme groups representing persons who are stressed or anxious. Table 12 presents data comparing the correlation between stress and anxiety at each phase of the study, as well as across phases of the study. The diagonal that is highlighted represents the estimates of association based upon simultaneously collected data. All other figures represent causal sequences with stress preceding anxiety or vice versa. If we square the correlations to get an approximation of the amount of variation in one variable, possibly a consequence of its association with other variables, then the estimates derived from simultaneously collected data are about 16 per cent while the sequentially collected data provide estimates of 8–9 per cent, i.e. half the magnitude of the simultaneously collected data. Thus, based on cross-sectional surveys, we might argue that 16 per cent of the variance in anxiety is attributable to stress, while longitudinally collected data indicates that about 8 per cent of the anxiety variance is attributable to stress.

*Table 12* The association between stress and anxiety estimated using both simultaneous and sequential data collection methods (Kendall TAU B correlation coefficient)

|  | *Stress Phase A* | *Stress Phase B* | *Stress Phase E* |
|---|---|---|---|
| Anxiety *Phase A* | **.41** | .26 | .25 |
| Anxiety *Phase B* | .29 | **.41** | .27 |
| Anxiety *Phase E* | .31 | .31 | **.49** |

Thus, it appears that a cross-sectional survey may produce estimates of association considerably greater than those which would have resulted had the data been obtained using panel or longitudinal means. Of course, one could argue that the better estimate of association is the one derived from the simultaneously collected data, as the time period (lag) between surveys using the panel data may be too long. Possibly had the phases of data collection been more proximate, the two estimates might have been more similar. The essential concern, however, is that obtaining the data simultaneously can do nothing to resolve which comes first, anxiety or stress.

Tables 13 and 14 address the latter point. In Table 13 we have excluded all women who were classified as anxious at phase A. Thus, cases of anxiety identified at phases B and E represent new cases, following the experience of stress. It is clear that while the correlations are attenuated when compared to those in Table 12, they are both significant (all correlations in all tables are significant) and of modest size.

*Table 13* The association between stress and anxiety (I) (Kendall TAU B) (excludes all women anxious at Phase A)

|                    | Stress Phase A | Stress Phase B |
|--------------------|:--------------:|:--------------:|
| Anxiety Phase B    | .22            | —              |
| Anxiety Phase E    | .25            | .27            |

Similarly, Table 14 excludes all women who reported they were stressed at phase A, and the resulting correlations suggest that women who are anxious are more likely, subsequently, to report they experience stress. Again, the size of the correlations is modest and similar to those derived from Table 12.

Thus, it appears that stress levels can increase anxiety levels about as often as anxiety leads to subsequent stress. This suggests a better conceptualisation of the phenomenon, namely that changes in mood and emotional state reinforce each other and that it is probably inaccurate to think in terms of discrete causes and effects, at least insofar as the relationship between mental health and stress are concerned.

Would other associations be similarly brought into doubt if we were to compare data derived simultaneously and sequentially? What is the

*Table 14* The association between stress and anxiety (2) (Kendall TAU B) (excludes all women stressed at Phase A)

|                    | Stress Phase B | Stress Phase E |
|--------------------|:--------------:|:--------------:|
| Anxiety Phase A    | .22            | .21            |
| Anxiety Phase B    | —              | .24            |

'correct' time lag between measurements and how do estimates of association change as we vary this lag? How should time-lagged data be analysed? The results of panel studies present us with another way of looking at many of the causal associations we have taken for granted, and they raise fundamental questions of methodology which need to be considered.

## SEQUENTIAL METHODOLOGIES AND THE SOCIAL SURVEY

Although it is the case that surveys have been the most commonly used approach to collecting longitudinal data, there are some conspicuous instances where this is not the case, and indeed there is no intrinsic reason why the social survey need be used to do longitudinal research. The rationale for longitudinal methods is that they provide better information about a process than can be obtained from simultaneous data collection.

Of course, the most commonly used research methods for dealing with the delineation of processes are qualitative in orientation. Such qualitative methods are ideal for studying processes because they allow the investigator to follow events as they unfold – to report the process rather than present, as a survey does, a snapshot or, as sequential surveys do, a series of snapshots. Whereas sequential surveys require attention to time lags and a prior decision about the variables of interest, qualitative methods allow the subjects a greater role in defining what is important and why.

There are other alternatives to obtaining sequential data, and many of these are under-used. Thus medical records, death certificate data, employment records and the approach of 'record linkage' are promising alternatives. Further, there is no reason why a number of alternative methods of data collection could not be incorporated in a particular study. Potentially, qualitative and quantitative methods of data collection (at different points in the investigation) could deal with the methodological problems each method is seen to have.

It is also worth noting that the advantages of sequential methods of data collection are likely to be limited and need to be weighed against the additional cost of multiple phases of data acquisition. Where the purpose of the research is exploratory (hypothesis generating), or where issues of cause and effect are self-evident or irrelevant, then the longitudinal approach is unlikely to be appropriate. Alternatively, where a field has been developed over a number of years and issues of cause and effect are of interest, then longitudinal methods are likely to represent the best option.

## CONCLUSION

C. Wright Mills' call for a 'sociological imagination' (1959) to inspire and direct the sociological research effort was heeded by many – and the result (though perhaps not directly attributable to his call) is an emergence of varied and diverse sociological methodologies. Much creative and exciting work has consequently appeared. Now there is arguably a need to place a greater emphasis on discipline and rigour in all these research methodologies. The problem today is simply that little of the work being done survives because it is poor in quality and easily dismissed by critics and because the divisions within the discipline of sociology have denied any group of researchers universal legitimacy.

Mechanic (1989), in a recent paper reviewing research methods in medical sociology, points to the need for a reconciliation between those who advocate the qualitative and those the quantitative methods. His argument is simply that each of these methodological orientations has strengths which its opponents would be wise to incorporate. Perhaps such a call is as optimistic as Solomon's initial attempts to decide which of two mothers should receive the one child. Is this demarcation dispute beyond resolution?

Although only time may provide an indication of this, it is patently clear that medical sociologists operate in an environment which places them under pressure to improve the quality of their research. This poor quality is the subject of discussion by our medical and other professional colleagues, and significantly undermines our potential contribution to knowledge. In medical sociology we are often asked to address issues of considerable political and social significance and to provide advice about the most appropriate policies for government and industry. It is of fundamental importance that we 'get it right', and that our research survive not only the scrutiny of our sociological colleagues but of our other professional colleagues as well. We will only succeed in these efforts if we understand and adapt (but not always adopt) the scientific method of research. Whether the research is qualitative or quantitative, cross-sectional or longitudinal, exploratory or confirmatory, the same criteria are used to judge its contribution – and it is only through the creative and insightful use of methods which address these criteria that we can expect to improve the quality of our contribution to knowledge.

## REFERENCES

Bedford, A. and Foulds, G., 1977, 'Validation of the Delusions-Symptoms-States-Inventory', *British Journal of Medical Psychology*, 50: 163–71.
—— 1978, *Delusions-Symptoms-States-Inventory/State of Anxiety and Depression*, Windsor: NFER-Nelson.

Biddle, B.J., Sclavings, R.L. and Anderson, D.S., 1983, 'Panel studies and casual inference', draft paper submitted to *Sociological Methods and Research*, 1, 23.

Caplovitz, D., 1983, *The Stages of Social Research*, New York: Wiley-Interscience.

Cooke, D.J. and Allan, C.A., 1983, 'Self-reported alcohol consumption and dissimulation in a Scottish urban sample', *Journal of Studies on Alcohol*, 44: 617–29.

Crawford, A., 1987, 'Bias in a survey of drinking habits', *Alcohol and Alcoholism*, 22, 2: 167–79.

Doll, R. and Hill, A.B., 1956, 'Lung cancer and other causes of death in relation to smoking: A second report on the mortality of British doctors', *British Medical Journal*, 2: 1071.

Fleiss, J.L., 1986, 'Significance tests have a role in epidemiologic research: Reaction to A.M. Walker', *American Journal of Public Health*, 76, 5: 559–60.

Hammond, E.C. and Dorn, H.F., 1958, 'Smoking and death rates: Report on forty-four months of follow-up of 187,783 men: 2. Death rates by cause', *Journal of the American Medical Association*, 166: 1294.

Janson, C., 1981, 'Some problems of longitudinal research in the social sciences', in Schulsinger, F., Medrick, S.A. and Krop, J. (eds), *Longitudinal Research: Methods and Class in Behavioural Science*, The Hague: Martinus Nyhoff.

Keeping, J.D., Najman, J.M., Morrison, J., Western, J.S., Andersen, M.J. and Williams, G.M., 1989, 'A prospective longitudinal study of social, psychological and obstetrical factors in pregnancy: response rates and demographic characteristics of the 8,556 respondents', *British Journal of Obstetrics and Gynecology*, 96: 289–97.

Lazarsfeld, P.F., 1940, '"Panel" Studies', *Public Opinion Quarterly*, 4, 1: 122–8.

Lazarsfeld, P. and Fiske, M., 1938, 'The "Panel" as a new tool for measuring opinion', *Public Opinion Quarterly*, 2, 4: 596–612.

Lin, N., Dean, A. and Ensel, W.M., 1986, *Social Support, Life Events, and Depression*, New York: Academic Press.

McKinlay, J.B., 1989, 'Advantages and limitations of the survey approach: understanding older people', paper presented to the Researching Health Care Symposium, Ballarat.

Mechanic, D., 1989, 'Medical sociology: some tensions among theory, method and substance', *Journal of Health and Social Behaviour*, 30 (June): 147–60.

Mills, C.W., 1959, *The Sociological Imagination*, New York: Oxford University Press.

Morrison, J., Najman, J.M., Andersen, M.J., Keeping, J.D. and Williams, G.M., 1989, 'Socio-economic status and pregnancy outcome: an Australian study', *British Journal of Obstetrics and Gynecology*, 96: 298–307.

Najman, J.M., Keeping, J.D., Chang, A., Morrison, J. and Western, J.S., 1983, 'Employment, unemployment and the health of pregnant women', *New Doctor*: 9–12.

Najman, J.M., Morrison, J., Keeping, J.D., Andersen, M.J. and Williams, G.M., 1988a, 'A comparison of the lifestyle and pregnancies of women members of minority Christian sects', in Sheppard, J.L. (ed.), *Advances in Behavioural Medicine*, Sydney: Cumberland College of Health Sciences.

Najman, J.M., Williams, G.M., Keeping, J.D., Morrison, J. and Andersen, M.J., 1988b, 'Religious values, practices and pregnancy outcomes: A comparison of the impact of sect and mainstream Christian affiliation', *Social Science and Medicine*, 26, 4: 401–7.

Najman, J.M., Morrison, J., Williams, G.M., Keeping, J.D. and Andersen, M.J., 1989a, 'The employment of mothers and the outcomes of their pregnancies: An Australian study', *Public Health*, 103: 189–98.

—— 1989b, 'Unemployment and reproductive outcome. An Australian study', *British Journal of Obstetrics and Gynecology*, 96: 308–13.

Nathanson, C.A., 1978, 'Sex roles as variables in the interpretation of morbidity data: A methodological critique', *International Journal of Epidemiology*, 7, 3: 253–62.

Reeder, L.G., Schrama, P.G.M. and Dirken, J.M., 1973, 'Stress and cardiovascular health: An international co-operative study', *Social Science and Medicine*, 7: 573–84.

Rosenberg, M., 1968, *The Logic of Survey Analysis*, New York: Basic Books.

Shapiro, M.C. and Najman, J.M., 1987, 'Socio-economic status differences in patients' desire for and capacity to obtain information in the clinical encounter', *Australian Journal of Social Issues*, 22, 2: 465–71.

Shapiro, M.C., Najman, J.M., Chang, A., Keeping, J.D., Morrison, J. and Western, J.S., 1983, 'Information control and the exercise of power in the obstetrical encounter', *Social Science and Medicine*, 17, 3: 139–46.

Walker, A.M., 1986, 'Reporting the results of epidemiologic studies', *American Journal of Public Health*, 76, 5: 556–7.

Williams, C., 1988, 'Patriarchy and gender: Theory and methods', in Najman, J.M. and Western, J.S. (eds), *A Sociology of Australian Society*, South Melbourne: Macmillan.

# Part IV
# Qualitative research methods

# 9 'Don't mind him – he's from Barcelona'

## Qualitative methods in health studies

*Robert Dingwall*

When I first admitted to thinking about *Fawlty Towers* as a theme for a paper on qualitative methods, an American colleague suggested that I compare the ethnographer with Manuel the waiter, permanently harassed by those in authority and failing to communicate urgent news because he cannot speak their language. It is a nice idea, but my own intentions are rather different, partly because I want to take a broader view of qualitative methods and social science. I shall begin with a brief discussion of what I think health policy research is about and why current practice leaves important gaps in our knowledge. I shall then attempt to share with you something of the thought processes that go into doing qualitative work. When you watch a comedy like *Fawlty Towers*, you are behaving in much the same way as an ethnographer observing a research site. So, by discussing how the programme achieves its effect, I can, I hope, also explore the nature of qualitative methodology in social science.

But I do not want to focus too narrowly on observational studies, although they may be the most controversial element of the methodology. Various forms of interview and documentary analysis also have their part to play and it would be a rare study that depended on a single technique. Thus, much of what I have to say speaks as much to the anthropological or the historical study of health care as it does to sociology. Indeed, I would insist on the fundamental unity of the human sciences and argue that they are distinguished mainly by the simple differences in practice dictated by their subject matter, whether this is the investigation of our own time and place, of societies in the past or of communities made strange by barriers of language and culture.

## WHY DO RESEARCH AT ALL?

Health policy is a matter of concern for all citizens in modern societies. The health care system is one of the few institutions that virtually everybody will use at some point in their lives and, consequently, will be called upon to pay for. The precise mechanisms of payment and service delivery may vary but only the most marginal members of our society will avoid them. Our different relationships to the system may give us different interests: those of providers are not necessarily those of consumers. We may require different amounts of information: no one citizen can be an expert on everything in a complex modern society, so we have to take many things on trust (Simmel, 1950). Nevertheless, part of that trust may well derive from the assurance that those whose words we accept have a properly founded basis for their statements. In other words, that, where appropriate, they rest on some relatively objective study which has been carefully considered in the context of a well-articulated set of values.

There seem to be four basic dimensions on which we are likely to require information in order to evaluate any human service organisation, whether it is a hospital, a school or, for that matter, a seaside hotel (Strong and Dingwall, 1989). Is it *efficient*, in the sense that it consumes the minimum of human and material resources appropriate to the achievement of its goals? Is it *effective*, in that the work of the organisation contributes to the outcomes desired by its clients? Is it *equitable*, in that its services are equally available to all those who need them? Is it *humane*, in that both clients and staff are treated in a civilised fashion? In practice, of course, there are likely to be trade-offs between these various goals and other values that enter into the decision about which are to be given priority in any particular situation.

In compiling this assessment, we are likely to take into account three different aspects of the organisation: structure, process and outcome (Donabedian, 1976). Recent experience in the UK, however, has been dominated by outcome evaluation. What outputs can one get for a given basket of inputs? This reflects the ascendancy of utilitarian approaches to social analysis, especially from neoclassical economics, which do not acknowledge any influences intervening between individuals and the incentives and sanctions of the market or its proxy in the shape of the performance indicators imposed on them. These approaches are reasonably well suited to the provision of information about the relative efficiency of different organisations and can throw some light on the dimensions of effectiveness and quality, particularly if coupled with a structural study. They are, however, comparatively ill suited to any assessment of the humanity of the service and lack any real power to explain the relationships which they find. The link between inputs and outputs is left as a 'black box'. At best, this may be partially filled by a formal description of the organisation's structure.

But an account of *Fawlty Towers* purely in terms of the official roles of a manager, a receptionist, a waiter and a cook, would, I suggest, convey rather little about the factors involved in translating the inward flow of goods, services and guests into bed-nights or meal-units. In the same way, it is well established that official statistics and formal charts can only give a limited portrait of the organisation they purport to describe (Bittner, 1965; Cicourel, 1964, 1968; Cicourel and Kitsuse, 1963; Garfinkel, 1967). Performance indicators are just that: indicators of the performance of the organisation in constructing its activities in their terms. If a hospital is assessed in terms of its mortality rate, its staff are likely to devise ways of ensuring that patients are recorded as dying somewhere else. You may recall Basil Fawlty's attempt to achieve a similar objective. In the same way, if insurers restrict reimbursement for particular diseases, health care workers are likely to find ways of reclassifying patients who seem to need treatment. Cost-containment efforts in health care are a battle of wits between insurers attempting to draft watertight rules and providers attempting to find ways round them (Buckholdt and Gubrium, 1979; Gubrium and Buckholdt, 1982). These behaviours can only be identified by process studies.

Process evaluation demands a methodology which is capable of capturing the dynamic aspects of the organisation rather than simply logging its movements from one point in time to another. This can only be accomplished from the inside, by watching and listening and by studying the documents which its members produce to orchestrate or justify their activities. The problem for qualitative researchers is to achieve this understanding by means that command the confidence of the policy audience. It is exactly the same problem as health planners themselves face in relation to their constituency. Its resolution involves the same considerations, that our procedures for arriving at a conclusion are public and reproducible, that the role of values is clearly identified and that we have abided by what I shall call the 'ethic of fair dealing' in giving due weight to competing hypotheses or interpretations and to deviant cases in our data. One of the great methodological fallacies of the last half century in social research is the belief that science is a particular set of techniques; it is, rather, a state of mind, or attitude, and the organisational conditions which allow that attitude to be expressed.

## THE PLACE OF THEORY

For a health planner or a professional, policy research is always likely to start from a practical problem. Many social scientists, however, will probably respond by turning this into a theoretical problem, a trait which frequently irritates prospective clients (Ashmore, *et al.*, 1989).

Why don't we just set to and answer the policy question? The trouble is that, in research just as much as in clinical practice, it is not always clear that a presenting problem is the real problem for the people who are expressing it. The body of past experiences and observations which is summed up in the theory of any social science provides a way of identifying the presenting problem as a potential member of a class of problems which have certain properties in common and for which particular research strategies have been found to be more or less appropriate. Just as importantly, it also recalls the dimensions of those problems which were unanticipated by the people who originally framed them but which may give some clues to the way the present investigation should be carried out.[1]

Social theories are rarely expressed in law-like forms, and it is doubtful whether they ever should be. History and anthropology abandoned this goal more than a generation ago. Mainstream sociology has largely adjusted to this, although true believers can still be found in areas like exchange theory or rational choice theory. Even those social sciences like psychology or economics which have had stronger aspirations to identify laws of behaviour have increasingly been forced to recognise the large margin of uncertainty which attaches to any predictive statement about human beings (Hayek, 1945; Harree and Secord, 1972).

These doubts partly account for the preoccupation of many social scientists with writers of the past, including philosophers, essayists, novelists and dramatists, which sometimes puzzles people from other scientific fields. This is understandable when you are working in a discipline where the leading edge is discovering previously unknowable phenomena. Warm superconductors might be a current example. Even the journals are out of date by the time they are published. In the human sciences, however, the picture is rather different. People have been thinking and writing about society and interpersonal behaviour for as long as records survive.[2] There is, then, a fair chance that some previous analyst will have discussed a problem which has contemporary relevance.[3] If we are to create a cumulative science of human society, we need to embrace the past rather than dismiss it as a mere canon of errors. Our distinctive contribution may lie in technical skills which allow us to pursue our inquiries more systematically, although there have only been two evolutionary leaps in three thousand years: the invention of the survey in the seventeenth century[4] and the introduction of electronic audio and video recording in the last twenty years. Even then, people have always made statements of a quantitative kind or tried to describe talk or body movement. Observation and the analysis of documents are the original methods of social analysis.

## THEORY AND DATA COLLECTION

If we pose as our equivalent of some policy problem the question 'How do the writers of *Fawlty Towers* get their audience to laugh?', you should, then, expect me to begin by looking at some theoretical ideas about the nature of comedy. In real life, I would undertake a more exhaustive literature review, but for my purposes here I am just going to use one source, an essay by the French philosopher Henri Bergson (1980), first published in 1900 and based on a fair number of nights out observing the Paris theatres of his day. The questions that I am going to ask are those that I would raise in the background to any problem proposed to me for investigation.

The first thing to consider is whether this is indeed a social scientific question. This forces us to distinguish our field of activity from those problems which can be more appropriately addressed by the natural sciences, on the one hand, and those which are not scientific questions at all, on the other. If asked to explain why children giggle when they are tickled, for example, I would probably defer to a neuroscientist. However, as Bergson shows, comedy only exists in relation to human action: there is nothing intrinsically comic about a piece of wood, except to the extent that it may resemble and caricature some human figure or be treated as if it were human.[5] In the same way, there is nothing intrinsically comic about the changing patterns made by electrons hitting a TV screen. They become comic as a result of the way we organise and interpret the shapes and the sounds transmitted with them.

This point is important in understanding the boundaries between social and natural scientific studies in medicine. There are no diseases in nature, merely relationships between organisms (Dingwall, 1977; Sedgwick, 1982). Diseases are produced by the conceptual schemes imposed on the natural world by human beings, which value some states of the body and disvalue others. This is not to say that biological changes may not impose themselves upon us, but rather that the significance of those changes depends upon their location in a human society. The normal physiology of aging is relevant in very different ways to an East African herdsman who sees it as a mark of advancing status, power and sexual attractiveness and to a Californian actress who sees it as the beginning of her decline as a social being.

The study of classificatory systems in medical thought is still a neglected area, despite the efforts of a small number of anthropologists and historians (e.g. Frake, 1971; Fabrega and Silver, 1973; Fabrega, 1974; King, 1954, 1963). When we look at the conceptual schemes used in our own past or in other cultures, our first response is too often to see them as deficient versions of our own and to try to map their correspondence to the 'real' diseases of Western medical science. Instead, we should be trying to reconstruct their own internal logic and, in particular, to apply the same principles to our own medical system, treating Western medicine as a form of folk medicine which happens to have achieved a particular social and legal status.

But it is important to recognise that this is a scientific principle rather than a political programme. If we regard all systems of medical practice as equal for the purpose of analysis, this does not compel us to regard them as equally capable of re-establishing a condition of homeostasis in the human organism. This is a matter for traditional outcome evaluations to distinguish effective treatment from quackery. One of the crueller ironies of sociology's critique of medicine is the way it has led to the celebration of alternative medicine theories, which might liberate patients' psyches at the expense of denying them life-saving interventions. The real purpose of recognising the element of arbitrariness in the relation between any conceptual scheme and the material world of nature is to enhance the work of the medical scientist. It should free an investigator to respond more critically to problems in reconciling theories and evidence and to examine assumptions rather than locating all difficulties in the data (Kuhn, 1962; Gilbert and Mulkay, 1984).

I have already begun to touch on the second aspect of the question. If I had been asked '*Should* we laugh at Basil Fawlty?', I would have to say that it all depends. When he is not talking about the war in front of his German guests, for example, ought we to find this funny or should we be angered by the writers' milking of the Holocaust for laughs.[6] In the same way, if you were to ask me 'Should we provide health care through an NHS, a public insurance system or a private insurance system?', the answer is to a considerable extent a matter of personal values. I can give you some sort of estimate of the likely matrix of costs and benefits from each option, but it is not my place to tell you how to weight them. Even if the question were more limited, such as whether doctors should have longer consultations with patients, I could find out what they would do in that extra time and an economist could find out what it would cost, but you would have to decide how to trade off the extra expenditure against the gains in accuracy of diagnosis or patient satisfaction or the losses in terms of medical intrusions on patient privacy. Policy makers cannot escape the burden of choice: the best they can hope for is to choose with their eyes open.

The second issue that arises in preparing for field-work is that of identifying the theoretical terms that are relevant. As we have seen, this is important both in terms of the cumulation of knowledge and design of the study.

Here, for example, we have Bergson's observation that comedy grows out of failures of human action. The comic figure displays rigidity and lack of self-awareness, 'a certain *mechanical inelasticity* just where one would expect to find the wideawake adaptability and the living pliableness of a human being' (Bergson, 1980: 67) (original emphasis). One dimension of laughter, then, is its role as a means of social control.

This links humour to one of the core problems of the social sciences: the maintenance of order in human existence. Again it is important to distinguish this from the bastardised version which has gained currency in the last twenty years or so. Social control is not about the oppression of individuality: it is a necessary condition for the formation of any kind of group, from a family to a nation–state. It refers to the means by which human behaviour is rendered sufficiently stable for interaction to be possible, while remaining sufficiently flexible to respond to environmental change. This latter is the particular contribution of the comic, whose logic is an inversion of common sense: instead of reacting to the environment, the comic figure tries to force it into his or her own preconceptions. Laughter ridicules this intransigence. It is the motivation behind reciprocity in social interaction, moderation in the pursuit of individual goals and accommodation to circumstance. Without such checks, we would merely be an aggregate of selfish automata, eventually succumbing to environmental change, rusting up in a shower of rain like the Tin Man in *The Wizard of Oz*. The human groups that did not learn to laugh probably died out on the African savannah before any historical record began.

Medicine is a control system which tends to work in the opposite direction. It homogenises the relationship between human beings and their bodies. It defines some states of that relationship as undesirable and provides the means of correction. It plays a role in the resolution of disputes, in adjudicating on the legitimacy of claims to dependency, whether on family members or in the state, and it complements the activities of the legal system in distinguishing between those acts of deviance arising from the exercise of the human will, which may result in punishment, and those acts which are essentially unintended, for which a therapeutic response may be appropriate. Something like these activities seems to occur in all human societies, although in many simpler societies the various control systems are less differentiated than in our own (Spencer, 1896).

This theoretical framework is not, of course, peculiar to qualitative researchers. But then I am not trying to draw sharp distinctions between various types of social investigator. Expressed in these terms, however, I hope that it captures the dynamic nature of human society, and where we are talking about dynamic phenomena there is a place for qualitative work. If we abandon the idea that medical knowledge is a picture of the natural world, then we need to study doctors at work matching events to it. Medical knowledge is its use, not just its textbooks. If we understand that there is no intrinsic rationality to the delivery of health care, then we need to study the services at work as they try to make it appear a rational enterprise. Health care organisations are what they do, not just the statistics they produce or the formal accounts that they deliver to their publics.

## WEIGHING THE EVIDENCE

Many textbooks have been written about the various techniques of qualitative research: however, those of us who are called upon to teach students about it know how difficult it can be to translate their abstract descriptions into practical means of collecting data. In sociology, at least, this is because so many of the authors have got caught up in the philosophical defence of their approach and the sterile debate over positivism. As Professor Silverman has observed elsewhere (1989), it is actually very difficult to say who is and is not a positivist. I would go further and argue that all social scientists are required to be to some extent positivist if the idea of a social science is to have any meaning at all. The four principal tenets of positivism – phenomenalism, nominalism, the separation of facts and values, and the unity of scientific method (Kolakowski, 1972: 9–19)[7] – are fundamental to the possibility of any empirical study of society. What is at issue is the hijacking of those principles and their restrictive interpretation by an influential minority (Giddens, 1974: 3–4). The effort to create a non-positivist base for sociology has simply led us into unnecessary intellectual contortions.

In the remainder of this chapter, then, I shall simply pick out three aspects of practice which I think mark the most successful research and which can be used as a basis for assessing the rigour with which the activity has been performed. They can be thought of as the equivalent of the policy makers' legitimations. They relate to the recording of data, to the constant comparison of data and to the extent to which the interactive character of social life has been captured.

There is, of course, no way in which the literal truth of any observation can be preserved by the recording of a researcher. Our vision of the field is no less selective than the directed lens of the television camera. Think of the sequences in *Fawlty Towers*, for example, when the camera remains in the dining room, pointing at the kitchen doors while various noises go on and a character, usually Manuel, re-emerges. The viewer is forced at that moment to take the role of a guest and to make the inferences from partial data that a participant would have to make. Similarly, in social science, we can only work through the perceptions of the investigator, whether that person is watching some event, questioning an informant or reading a document. Given this, it is essential that the investigator create a record that can stand independently of the observer, in the way that a film does. If I had the tapes with me, I could play you a sequence from *Fawlty Towers* or an audio recording of a doctor–patient encounter, and we could compare our analyses, pointing to specific fragments of the events recorded as our evidence. The challenge to the participant observer or the searcher in archives is no different. Can he or she create a document which is the best available approximation within the terms of the chosen technology of recording for his or her perception of the original event? The choice of technology will depend on the level of analysis which is ultimately required: what is not a matter of choice is the relationship between the researcher and the data.

The first criterion that I would propose for the evaluation of a qualitative report, then, is the extent to which it is possible for readers to separate data and analysis. Clearly, it is no more possible to reproduce all the data than it is for a film-maker to show every inch of film, and I shall need to say more about that problem. What I am taking exception to, though, is the kind of report that is purely a redescription of the researcher's impressions or sensations. Empathy has its place in ethnography but it should enter after recording rather than being confused with it.

The second element of practice that I noted was the importance of comparison and contrast. Social science deals in a vocabulary of types. The typical can only emerge from the collection of numerous instances which can then be compared to induce a classification which reflects their similarities and differences. There are two ways in which such collections of data can be assembled. One, clearly, is the systematic sampling of a universe of events. The fundamental considerations here are similar to those involved in any other form of population sampling. The main difference, in practice, tends to be a greater use of theoretical sampling, which proceeds by specifying critical tests for the general validity of hypotheses and seeking to establish to what extent they hold true under a range of conditions. There is no particular reason why randomised sampling should not be used, except that it is likely to be more time consuming and expensive for no very great increase in validity.

What is often more controversial, however, is the use of the single case study. This tends to be the dominant mode of qualitative work in the UK because of the difficulty of funding the kind of large-scale, multi-site project team that is needed to tackle sampling problems by internal means. What we need to be clear about here is the way in which a case study fits into a body of theory or other findings. It is that background which makes for the intelligibility of the particular case.

As Bergson notes, this has much in common with the method of the comic writer. Comedy can only contribute to social control by making general statements, in contrast to the tragedian's exploration of individuals. We have never met a Basil Fawlty; we have all met people who display some of his characteristics. The writer's art is to assemble those features of real people into a plausible whole, which can define a social type.

This dictates a particular method of working. According to Bergson, no one person could assemble a Lear, an Othello or a Macbeth from observation. These are the product of a writer's self-examination, of mental experiments which imagine the person into extreme situations. The comic writer, however, works by

> bringing together scattered data, by comparing analogous cases and extracting their essence; in short by a process of abstraction and generalisation similar to that which the physicist brings to bear upon facts with the objective of grouping them together under laws. In a word, method and object here are of the same nature as in the inductive sciences, in that observation is always external and the result always general.
>
> (Bergson, 1980: 169–70)

This is equally the method of the qualitative human scientist. In many ways the two crafts mirror each other. The comedian exaggerates types in order to ridicule excess. The social scientist strives for fidelity to life in order to capture the adaptations which make it possible. Comedy corrects the normal by its portrayal of deviance. Much social science normalises the deviant by identifying its adaptive elements.

Comedy is notoriously difficult to translate because so much of its effect derives from the way it plays off the customs of a particular society. The international success of *Fawlty Towers* reflects the widespread experience of formal organisations in modern societies. This is how it can transcend the barriers of culture and language, even if the Spanish version makes Manuel an Italian from Milan! It reproduces the dual life of any organisation: on the one hand, Basil pursuing the official goals of an owner or manager; on the other, the below-stairs characters trying to reconcile these official goals with their personal goals and the resources of time, energy or materials available to them. We can all recognise aspects of the hotel in our own experience, whether of universities, hospitals or public bureaucracies.

*Fawlty Towers* functions as a case study in the pathology of organisations. At the heart of the comedy is the stiff-necked and autocratic Basil, with his desire to run the most genteel hotel in Torbay at the lowest cost to himself in terms of staff or provisions. The result is a conspiracy among his staff to maximise their gains while attempting to keep the hotel functioning to a degree that will safeguard their jobs. The manager's unbending pursuit of his objectives, regardless of circumstances or their human costs, results in the subversion of the whole enterprise. *Fawlty Towers*' contribution to social order is as a dire warning for managers who are too attached to formal rationality.

The comic writer will rarely make explicit reference to the context that makes the humour possible (except perhaps to parody those literary forms like academic writing where this happens constantly). However, as Mitchell (1983) has pointed out in his influential defence of the single case study as a method, its validity in social science depends crucially upon that context. In its absence, the report becomes no more than an exercise in traveller's tales or investigative journalism. The power of Goffman's (1968) work in *Asylums*, for example, has much to do with the way in which he constantly insists on presenting the mental hospital as an instance of a class of institutions and exploring what it implies for prisons, concentration camps, boarding schools and religious orders, all of which share some features in common.

The second test of a field-work report, then, is the way in which it deals with the logic of its own design. In particular, does it spell out clearly its own search for contradictory or negative evidence or the way in which it has set out to test statements proposed on theoretical grounds or established in previous studies? The one-off case study, conceived and executed in magnificent isolation, has no place in modern social science and little more than anecdotal value to a policy maker trying to understand how an organisation works.

The third dimension I would propose for the evaluation of an ethnographic report is the extent to which it recognises the interactive character of social life and deals even-handedly with the people it is studying. Basil Fawlty can only display the inflexibility that makes us laugh through his encounters with the other inhabitants of his hotel. It is their challenges that reveal his limitations as a human being. But many of those challenges reflect the failures of others. Manuel's problem, for example, is his over-eagerness to please. This is adaptability carried to a ridiculous extreme. In their interactions, Manuel becomes as much an automaton as Basil: each is similarly lacking in any indication of a self that might set limits to the inappropriateness of their behaviour. In other situations, of course, the failures are material. Basil's car breaks down and he beats it with the branch of a tree. Without the breakdown, however, the scriptwriter could not introduce the behaviour.

The importance of an interactive understanding of social behaviour was grasped by an early generation of ethnographers. Willard Waller (1936), for example, discussed the need for any analysis of social problems to incorporate both the study of the groups perceived as problematic and the constitution of the definitions of normality that identified them in this way. Since the 1960s, however, ethnography has taken on a more romantic coloration. It is as if we should only be concerned with the Manuels of this world, sympathising with their bewilderment at the forces which oppress them and celebrating the ingenuity of their resistance. As Strong (1988) has recently remarked, a whole generation of British sociologists have been more concerned with being 'right on' than with being right. Ethnography has been defined as an underdog enterprise, speaking for the poor, the lowly and the dispossessed. But, as he and I have argued, this denies us the understanding of the Basils of this world which is just as important in any programme for change (Strong and Dingwall, 1989). Basil is not an evil man. He is as much the creation of his past and present circumstances as is Manuel. Indeed, there are points in his script where he almost becomes an object of pathos much as Malvolio does at the end of *Twelfth Night* or as does Moliere's Harpagon, the miser whose wealth is lost at the conclusion of *L'Avare*. We are allowed to glimpse the humanity behind the obsessions, to get a sense of the person brought low by a lack of self-knowledge and to suspend for a moment the frame between the comic type and the tragic individual. In the same way, our science will never progress if we simply assume that all those white middle-class male heterosexuals leading orderly lives represent some sinister force opposed to our underdog heroes or heroines and never acknowledge that they too are human beings making their way in an uncertain world.

My third criterion then would be the extent to which an ethnographic report displays its adherence to an ethic of fair dealing or what I think you might call 'a fair go'. Does it convey as much understanding of its villains as its heroes? Are the privileged treated as having something serious to say or simply dismissed as evil, corrupt or greedy without further inquiry?

Social inequalities are the outcomes of processes of social relations, which it falls to the social scientist to describe as dispassionately as he or she can. This marks another boundary, between social science and muck-raking journalism. The social scientist's message is 'Look, this is how it is', not 'Isn't this outrageous?'. To the extent that it is outrageous, of course, the force of that argument is likely to be enhanced rather than diminished by its self-control.

## CONCLUSION

Social research is a pre-condition of modern democracy. It is only by the systematic study of our social existence, of how we live, where we have come from and what the possible varieties of human social organisation might be that we can make available to all citizens, directly or indirectly, the knowledge that makes informed choices in social or economic policy possible. This is not an easy banner to carry: even self-styled liberal democracies can be dominated by conviction politicians who believe that their ideology allows them to deduce the answers to all problems of human life. But we must struggle against this. The comedian reminds us of the value of diversity, and that a society which fails to cherish differences is one doomed to stagnation and decay. It is no accident, if not necessarily a conscious plan, that *perestroika* has led to the rebuilding of Soviet sociology. If there is only homogeneity, there is no basis for evolution, for adaptation to a changing environment.

But there are derivative obligations on our own professional communities. The call to let a hundred flowers bloom in British sociology was about as genuine as the Cultural Revolution in China. Why do we have no significant body of liberal sociology or, for that matter, Marxist economics? And why do we remain at war with each other across the disciplines of social science when their boundaries are of no more significance than the demarcations made by any other classificatory scheme? Sociology, economics, history, anthropology and the rest are mere points on a continuum. To the extent that we accept each other's unique skills, we are all strengthened. That continuum is one which must also find a place for the traditional liberal arts, for the incorporation of those observations on the human condition which extend our whole range of experience and our ability to imagine new possibilities for the world.

There will always be a place for the quantitative study of social behaviour. Some questions arise naturally in a quantitative form: How many? How much? How often? But others are intrinsically qualitative: For what reason? In what manner? How justly? The answers to those questions require qualitative investigations as rigorously designed and as dispassionately executed as any sample survey. A government is entitled to demand high standards before investing public money. But a modern society which fails to make full use of all the techniques available to the human sciences deserves to find that it is being run like *Fawlty Towers*.

## ACKNOWLEDGEMENTS

I am grateful for the comments and suggestions of Tom Durkin, Phil Strong, David Silverman and Pam Watson, although the paper would, of course, have been much better if I had incorporated more of them.

## NOTES

1 The classic example, of course, is one of the first pieces of empirical work in sociology, Durkheim's (1952) study on suicide. This seems like the most individual of all acts, but Durkheim's dissection of the official statistics showed

174 Qualitative research methods

its social patterning. Suicide was the act of people who belonged to particular groups under particular circumstances. Any subsequent answer to the question 'Why do people kill themselves?' has had to make some reference to their group affiliations. In the last twenty years we have come to wonder whether this pattern may actually be created by the decisions of those who have to interpret deaths – doctors, police officers, coroners, etc. (Douglas, 1967; Atkinson, 1978). Perhaps the original question is just unanswerable, because we have no access to the mind of the deceased, and what we should concentrate on is understanding how some deaths come to be labelled as suicide and others as accidental and the implications of this distinction.

2 Indeed, there is some reason to think that prehistoric humans would have required much the same sort of skills in social analysis as we use today in evaluating our relationships with each other, in assessing the moral and intellectual competence of others and in determining who should be treated as a friend and who as an enemy.

3 In a recent paper, for example, Philip Strong and I (Strong and Dingwall, 1989) showed that some of the ideas of Stoic philosophers working in Greece two to three hundred years before the birth of Christ could contribute to debates in modern sociology about the relationship between science and policy.

4 Although even this has recognisable antecedents in the censuses of the Roman Empire or the Domesday Book of William the Conqueror.

5 There is a classic Monty Python sketch on this theme, where a human chat show host interviews three blocks of timber.

6 This point was posed even more sharply by the film *A Fish Called Wanda* and its treatment of stammering, which caused a major dispute at one snack lunch of amateur film critics on the staff of the American Bar Foundation.

7 *Phenomenalism* is the denial of any differences between essence and phenomenon. We can only record what is actually manifested in experience. *Nominalism* follows from this and is the belief that the world can only be known through the language we use to describe it. Words are a way of organising experience but have no significance independent of the objects they refer to.

# REFERENCES

Ashmore, M., Mulkay, M. and Pinch, T., 1989, *Health and Efficiency: A sociology of health economics*, Milton Keynes: Open University Press.

Atkinson, J.M., 1978, *Discovering Suicide: studies in the social organization of sudden death*, London: Macmillan.

Bergson, H., 1980, 'Laughter', in Sypher, W. (ed.), *Comedy*, Baltimore: Johns Hopkins Press (first published 1900).

Bittner, E., 1965, 'The Concept of Organization', *Social Research*, 32: 239–55.

Buckholdt, D.R. and Gubrium, J.F., 1979, *Caretakers: Treating emotionally disturbed children*, Beverly Hills: Sage.

Cicourel, A.V., 1964, *Method and Measurement in Sociology*, New York: Free Press.

—— 1968, *The Social Organisation of Juvenile Justice*, New York: John Wiley & Sons.

Cicourel, A.V. and Kitsuse, J.I., 1963, *The Educational Decision-Makers*, Indianapolis: Bobbs-Merrill.

Dingwall, R., 1977, *Aspects of Illness*, London: Martin Robertson.
Donabedian, A., 1976, *Some Issues in Evaluating the Quality of Health Care*, Kansas City: ANA Publications.
Douglas, J.D., 1967, *The Social Meanings of Suicide*, Princeton: Princeton University Press.
Durkheim, E., 1952, *Suicide: A Study in Sociology*, London: Routledge & Kegan Paul (first published 1897).
Fabrega, H., 1974, *Disease and Social Behaviour: An interdisciplinary perspective*, Cambridge: MIT Press.
Fabrega, H. and Silver, D., 1973, *Illness and Shamanistic Curing in Zinancantan: An ethnomedical analysis*, Stanford: Stanford University Press.
Frake, C.O., 1971, 'The Diagnosis of Disease among the Subanun of Mindanao', *American Anthropologist*, 63: 113–32.
Garfinkel, H., 1967, *Studies in Ethnomethodology*, Englewood Cliffs, NJ: Prentice Hall.
Giddens, A., 1974, *Positivism and Sociology*, London: Heinemann.
Gilbert, G.N. and Mulkay, M., 1984, *Opening Pandora's Box: A sociological analysis of scientists' discourse*, Cambridge: Cambridge University Press.
Goffman, E., 1968, *Asylums: Essays on the social situations of mental patients and other inmates*, Harmondsworth: Penguin.
Gubrium, J.F. and Buckholdt, D.R., 1982, *Describing Care: Image and practice in rehabilitation*, Boston: Oelgeschlager, Gunn and Hain.
Harree, R. and Secord, P.F., 1972, *The Explanation of Social Behaviour*, Oxford: Basil Blackwell.
Hayek, F.A., 1945, 'The Use of Knowledge in Society', *American Economic Review*, 35: 519–30.
King, L.S., 1954, 'What is Disease?' *Philosophy of Science*, 21: 193–203.
—— 1963, *The Growth of Medical Thought*, Chicago: University of Chicago Press.
Kolakowski, L., 1972, *Positivist Philosophy: From Hume to the Vienna Circle*, Harmondsworth: Penguin.
Kuhn, T.S., 1962, *The Structure of Scientific Revolutions*, Chicago: University of Chicago Press.
Mitchell, J.C., 1983, 'Case and Situation Analysis', *Sociological Review*, 31: 187–211.
Sedgwick, P., 1982, *Psychopolitics*, London: Pluto.
Silverman, D., 1989, 'Telling convincing stories: a plea for cautions positivism in case studies', in Glaser, B. and Moreno, J. (eds), *The Qualitative–Quantitative Distinction in the Social Sciences*, Dordrecht: Kluwer.
Simmel, G., 1950, 'The secret and the secret society', in Wolff, K.H., *The Sociology of Georg Simmel*, New York: Free Press.
Spencer, H., 1896, *The Principles of Sociology: Volume III*, London: Williams and Norgate.
Strong, P.M., 1988, 'Qualitative Sociology in the UK', *Qualitative Sociology*, 11: 13–28.
Strong, P.M. and Dingwall, R., 1989, 'Romantics and Stoics'. in Silverman, D. and Gubrium, J.F. (eds), *The Politics of Field Research: sociology beyond enlightenment*, London: Sage.
Waller, W., 1936, 'Social Problems and the Mores', *American Sociological Review*, I: 922–33.
Wolff, K.H., 1950, *The Sociology of Georg Simmel*, New York: Free Press.

# 10 Applying the qualitative method to clinical care

*David Silverman*

## DEFINITIONS AND MATERIALS

'Qualitative research' has a problematic meaning in that:

1 it involves the problem of false polarities in social research (qualitative/ quantitative; structure/process, etc.); and
2 it is a negative definition applied to any research that does not follow the favoured (quantitative) model.

It is more sensible to think of models from anthropology, such as ethnography or field research – i.e. those involving understanding in detail, without prior hypotheses, the social organisation/practices of a delimited unit (tribe, organisation, etc.). This does not rule out:

1 the use of comparative method;
2 counting, where appropriate;
3 the *generation* of hypotheses and their testing.

For purposes of simplification, I shall use the term *field research* to refer to the study of naturally occurring social situations using appropriate rigorous methods deriving from a well-developed theoretical and conceptual basis. I would expect good field research to generate (and perhaps) test hypotheses derived from a dialogue between the theoretical apparatus used and the field data. Where appropriate, field research provides a good basis to assess the effectiveness of different forms of social organisation, including health care delivery. Indeed, it is uniquely qualified to examine how well a procedure works in practice because it alone looks at practices *in situ*. This is not to say that field research, like other approaches, does not have problems of its own (see sources cited below and Silverman, 1989b, 1989c).

As requested I will develop my argument using examples from my own research: a study of decision-making about the surgical treatment of

Down's Syndrome children with congenital heart disease (Silverman, 1981, 1987) and current work on counselling for patients who may be HIV-positive (Silverman, 1989a, 1990, Silverman and Perakyla, 1990).

The Down's Syndrome (DS) study was an offshoot of research funded by the British Social Science Research Council into doctor–parent–patient encounters in a paediatric cardiology unit and cleft-palate clinic. The original aim was to examine the degree of variance in these encounters according to their very different trajectories and forms of treatment. Only after intensive work on the 'normal form' of the consultation at the cardiology unit did the significance of the Down's consultation emerge – as a deviant case which made problematic 'reformist' assumptions about the necessarily enlightened character of 'patient-centred medicine' (see Byrne and Long, 1976).

The work on HIV counselling (HC) is funded by the English Health Education Authority (HEA) and Glaxo Holdings plc. The HEA is concerned about the nature and effectiveness of counselling about 'safer sex' that patients receive before and after being tested for antibodies to HIV and once diagnosed as seropositive. This is particularly important at a time when, despite extensive Government-funded health education campaigns, there is little evidence of heterosexuals (and many drug-users) having changed their sexual habits.

Both studies are based on audio-tapes of consultations between patients and professionals which are then carefully transcribed and analysed (there are videotapes available at one of the centres being studied). Although the emphasis is on such 'naturally occurring' data, the DS study also used home interviews with parents of the children seen at the hospitals, while in the HC study we are interviewing professionals to discover how care is organised at each centre, philosophies of care, patient turnover, etc.

## HIV COUNSELLING: THE LOGIC OF FIELD RESEARCH

Given the nature of the problem, why study it this way? A descriptive survey of HIV counselling in the UK had been carried out earlier (Chester, 1987), so why not follow that up with the development of clear hypotheses about the effectiveness of different forms of counselling and their test? A brief examination of the limits of different styles of research should clarify the potential strengths of field research.

### Quantitative, hypothesis-testing research designs

This could proceed by the definition of different methods of counselling, based on the earlier descriptive work, followed by an examination of their effectiveness. Two formats might be used:

I  An experimental design where we offer volunteers different forms of counselling and then interview them subsequently about their uptake of information (followed up some weeks later with a further interview about the effects, if any, on their behaviour).

II A non-experimental design where existing counselling procedures are evaluated by a cohort of patients (with a later follow-up).

The advantage of such research designs is that they permit large-scale studies which generate hard data apparently based on unequivocal measures. However, a number of difficulties present themselves:

1 How relevant is information uptake? Good information can coincide with the continuance of risky practices (e.g. cigarette smoking and health).

2 How seriously are we to take patients' accounts of changes in their behaviour? Will they not tend to tell interviewers what they think they will want to hear? May there not be a 'halo-effect'?

3 Doesn't Study I ignore the *organisational* context in which health care is delivered (relations between physicians and other staff, tacit theories of 'good counselling', resources available, staff turnover, etc.) which shape its nature and effectiveness in actual situations?

4 Don't both studies treat subjects as 'an aggregation of disparate individuals' who have no social interaction with one another (Bryman, 1988: 39)? Yet surely sexual behaviour has a large social component where people respond to their partners and to culturally provided versions of appropriate and inappropriate behaviour?

5 Are we any wiser about how the different forms of counselling work in practice? In Study I, we make a dangerous leap from descriptive work to 'operationalisation'. How do we know that the counselling methods that we have created in the laboratory bear much relation to those found in the field? In Study II, we examine the effects of actual methods *without* knowing what those methods (in detail) are. Hence if counselling in a particular centre seems to be effective, we don't know what about it is effective and so we cannot replicate it more generally. This problem has a general relevance to policy-oriented research, e.g. attempts to reduce inequalities in education by structural changes which are not based on understanding the ways in which teaching works in practice (see Mehan, 1979).

6 If our interest is in the relation of counselling to sexual practices, does either study tell us how people talk about sex (if at all) with each other and with professionals as opposed to via responses to researchers' questions? Hence, the apparently unequivocal measures of information retention, attitude and behaviour that we obtain via laboratory or

questionnaire methods seem to have a tenuous basis in what people may be saying and doing in their everyday lives.

## Qualitative or quantitative studies of sexual vocabularies

To counter problem 6 above, work is being carried out on understanding how people ordinarily describe their own and others' sexual activities. This currently takes two forms:

1 asking respondents what they understand by a series of terms used by professionals to describe sexual activities (e.g. heterosexual, intercourse, etc.). Using this method, Wellings (1989) discovered that many of the terms used in British government health education campaigns on AIDS were misunderstood. Many people simply did not use such terms to describe their own or others' behaviour – indeed they were strikingly reticent about using very many sexual terms (at least to an interviewer).
2 Asking people to keep diaries about their sexual encounters in which they record, in their own terms, the number and nature of their sexual activities over many months. This method is currently being used by Coxon (1986) with a cohort of gay men in Britain. The aim is to discover everyday vocabularies for describing sexual activity without formulating them previously (as in most survey research).

## Problems common to both: the missing phenomenon

Despite the apparent (and real) differences between experimental designs and qualitative research, both share an unwillingness to examine how, for example, 'safe sex' comes to be constituted as a topic in real-life situations (keeping a diary about one's sexual activities is unlikely to be a routine real-life situation!). This is because both kinds of research are fundamentally concerned with the environment around the phenomenon rather than with the phenomenon itself. This arises within the following kind of decision-making strategy:

1 decide whether you are concerned with the 'objective' or 'subjective' aspect of the social world;
2 if you are concerned with the objective world, look at the causes and consequences of social phenomena (e.g. the effects of counselling methods); if you are concerned with the subjective world, look at how people respond to it and define it (e.g. the descriptions they attach to sexuality); and
3 solve the problem of defining your 'variables' in the following way: according to the 'objective' approach, use 'operational definitions'

(based on a nominalist theory of meaning where terms can mean what we say they are and the major requirement is clear 'operational' definition); according to the 'subjective' approach, the phenomenon is simply how people define it.

There are a number of difficulties with both these approaches to variable and concept definition described in paragraph 3 above. Defining variables at the outset has the advantage that it appeals to funding agencies whose models are usually taken from the natural sciences in which clear definition of variables is a basic feature of research design. But if we regard the social world as 'pre-defined' in the everyday activities of its participants (see Schutz, 1964), then the use of 'operational' definitions at an early stage of social research can be an arbitrary process which deflects attention away from the everyday sense-making procedures of people in specific milieux. For example, how do we know what a counselling 'method' is until we have examined in detail how professionals talk to clients in a variety of settings?

Adopting the alternative approach and saying the phenomenon is how people define it seems to overcome this difficulty. However, it generates two intractable problems in its turn:

1  it may overlook the 'situated' character of talk, i.e. that the way in which we speak is related both to the setting in which we are talking and to the way we position our utterances in relation to those that precede them (see Sacks, *et al.*, 1975). So, for instance, how we define our behaviour in a diary to be read by researchers has an unknown relationship to how we talk about that behaviour (if at all) with our sexual partners or with professionals; and

2  it fails to realise that in everyday life we normally function quite successfully without ever having to define our terms. So the laughter that is usually generated by researchers' accounts of the apparently 'inept' way in which laypersons 'misunderstand' sexual terms is misplaced. People's everyday practices are much more sophisticated than they can tell us in response to interview questions. Another way of putting this is that we are all cleverer than we can say in so many words.

In both 'objective' and 'subjective' approaches, we are deflected away from the phenomenon ('counselling' and/or 'talking about sex') towards what precedes and follows it (causes and consequences in the 'objective' approach) or towards how people respond to it (the 'subjective' approach). This can be illustrated in a simple diagram (Figure 4).

Both approaches derive their sense from what I have described as a false polarity in social research. The social world is neither simply objective nor subjective but consists of a set of practices that researchers need to

'*Objectivism*'

Causes > The phenomenon > Consequences

'*Subjectivism*'

Perceptions > The phenomenon > Responses

*Figure 4* Objectivism and subjectivism

describe. One of those practices is distinguishing reality from illusion or thought from fact. This lay distinction is regularly seen at work in the practices of, say, police officers and stockbrokers. It is these practices and routines (and others like them) which constitute the phenomenon that social research should address. Another way of putting this is to say that in social research the objective/subjective distinction should be treated as a topic but not as a resource (see Garfinkel, 1967).

## The HC research: studying the practice(s) of counselling

Having explained why this study of HIV counselling is *not* using commonly employed methods of social research, what are the gains of using audio- and videotapes in the analysis? The major strength of such a database is that it preserves a naturally occurring phenomenon for analysis. Although neither the tapes nor the transcripts can offer a *complete* record of what occurred (camera angles, varying sound quality and the limits of transcription symbols preclude that), they make the phenomenon *in situ* available for analysis in a relatively efficient way. This has already allowed the examination of four crucial areas which are not readily available using other approaches:

1 How sexuality (including 'safer sex') is introduced – usually by counsellors; how the topic is taken up by patients, how counsellors respond to patients' formulations and how the parties exit from the topic. Early work on videotapes from one centre suggests the presence of 'turbulent' talk (i.e. pauses, 'repairs' or self-corrections often coupled with considerable body movement) when patients first use sexual terms (ranging from 'intercourse' to 'condom'). In response, counsellors at this centre regularly *replicate* such turbulences at their next turn at talk. However, after this has been done once by each party, subsequent mentions of the term in question regularly are accomplished with

minimal turbulence (see Silverman and Perakyla, 1990). While this replication of patient utterances by counsellors fits the theory they employ (systems counselling; see Miller and Bor, 1988), staff were only aware that they tried to reproduce patients' own vocabulary – they had not perceived their elegant replication of the *form* of their patients' talk. This apparently trivial practice may have a crucial bearing on the effectiveness of this method of counselling (see below). However, the mere ability of staff to fulfil theoretical precepts *without realising what they are doing* supports my earlier contention that we are cleverer than we can say in so many words. (The same applies to patients whose turbulent utterances can be seen *not* as a communication difficulty but as a communication *skill* – revealing that they are attending to culturally shared assumptions about the dispreferred character of sexuality as a conversational topic. It seems that, having displayed that attendance once, and having had it reproduced by the counsellor, the cultural task is accomplished and further hesitations around the term in question become redundant.)

2  Having established the basic format of 'sex talk' in these professional client encounters, it now becomes possible to identify deviant cases and thus to revise and strengthen the analysis. This follows the method of 'analytic induction' in which hypotheses are generated (and then tested) in the course of research (see Denzin, 1970; and Silverman, 1987). Note that this method, coupled with a close attention to the character of the phenomenon *in situ*, means that we can be more confident that deviant cases derive their status from a comparison with knowledge of participants' routine practices rather than with idealised conceptions of those practices – a frequent concomitant of deploying hypotheses, couched in 'operational definitions' of variables, *prior to* entry into the field.

3  The revised analysis can subsequently be applied to tapes of counsellor patient consultations gathered at other centres, allowing for further revision. This reveals that the comparative method has no less a place in the detailed analysis of naturally occurring situations than in more conventional experimental, interview or life-history methods. So, contrary to the usual perception, *generalisability* need not be a problem in qualitative research.

4  In principle, the practical pay-off of research grounded in understanding of 'real life' practices should be considerably more than work based simply on 'face-sheet' data (e.g. statistical tables showing correlations between pre-defined variables) and experimental studies based on idealised conceptions of the phenomena in question. In the HC study, we are some way off in reaching the policy-recommendation stage.

Two applications may nevertheless turn out to be fruitful. If, as we suspect, the barrier to safer sex is *not* lack of knowledge, then counselling methods which generate a relatively large amount of patient talk about sex *may* serve as a role model. So these patients may be in a better position to discuss sexual practices with their partners and so able, if they choose, to negotiate safer sex. So far, this conclusion is entirely deductive but, given the signal failure of large-scale health education campaigns to change heterosexuals' behaviour, it seems worth exploring.

Second, we need have no reservations about the value of such research in the *training* of counsellors. A common complaint about training for professional skills is that it is over-abstract and thus unrelated to the work task or, conversely, that it is anecdotal, reflecting merely the assumptions of 'old hands'. Neither of these complaints should apply to this kind of research. Careful analysis linked to tapes of actual practice is an invaluable method of teaching professional skills.

## THE DOWN'S SYNDROME STUDY: ANALYSING MEDICAL DECISION-MAKING

The Down's Syndrome (DS) study emerged as an offshoot of a study of doctor–patient–parent encounters in a prestigious paediatric cardiology unit (PCU). It was discovered that consultations with the parents of DS children were longer and more 'open-ended' than others – for instance, even at a first visit, parents were given the right to choose whether their child should have the routine diagnostic test (at that time cardiac catheterisation) which might see them on the path to corrective surgery. This was unlike other consultations where physicians would typically simply tell parents what was proposed at that stage (although the rider 'if you agree' was routinely added, no such parent was seen to dissent from the treatment plan).

Moreover, particularly when dealing with asymptomatic children with signs of cardiac disease, physicians would usually spend time emphasising the long-term clinical outlook with and without treatment. Although the clinical situation and outlook of DS children was clearly, indeed starkly, presented to parents, doctors seemed to prefer to dwell on the prospects of a happy family life which DS children could have *without* diagnostic tests and surgery. The outcome of this way of presenting the situation was that, almost without exception, the parents of DS children opted against the cardiac catheterisation that other children with the same clinical signs but without DS would routinely be given.

Discussions with a senior physician at the PCU revealed that this was in accord with an unwritten policy that major cardiac surgery was not the favoured option with DS children. This was supported by evidence about the greater risks of surgery on such children, some of which related to the chest infections to which they were prone. It must also be added, however, that a decision not to put them on a path towards surgery at any early stage meant that several DS children seen at the PCU already had developed severe lung damage that made surgery particularly dangerous.

The research thus discovered the mechanics whereby a particular medical policy was enacted. The availability of tape-recordings of large numbers of consultations, together with a research method that sought to develop hypotheses inductively, meant that we were able to discover a phenomenon for which we had not originally been looking.

The strengths of the research design paralleled those in the HC study in each of the four areas discussed above. No assumptions were made about the characteristics of doctor–parent talk. Instead, many hundreds of audio-tapes were examined in order to establish its 'normal form'. This consisted of a series of possible stages, some of which could be omitted although the order was relatively invariant (e.g. greeting exchange, agenda or grounds for consultation stated or established, history-taking, examination etc.; see Silverman, 1981: 256). In addition, variance in doctor–parent talk was identified according to the stage of treatment and the presence or absence of symptoms visible to the parents. So, for instance, where children were to be discharged with innocent murmurs, doctors routinely engaged in a 'search and destroy' operation in which parents were encouraged to voice any lingering doubts and fears in order for the doctor to show that these were groundless.

Alternatively, where surgery had not been totally successful or patients had terminal disease, the family were given decision-making rights which were much more than a formal 'if you agree' (see Silverman, 1987: chapters 2–3). In this way, the phenomenon of doctor–parent talk about the diagnosis and treatment of children's cardiac disease was made visible – just as counsellor–patient talk about sexuality had been identified in the HC study (albeit with better data from one centre where the videotapes gave access to body language).

Knowing what the 'normal form' of the phenomenon was meant that consultations with DS children stood out as a deviant case. The question that then arose was the quality of evidence that could be generated to test our assumptions about their different character. One of the weaknesses of much social research is that it asks the reader to trust its conclusions on the basis of either a few qualitative data-extracts or of statistical tabulations based on an 'operational' definition of variables with an unknown relation to how the phenomena they gloss actually present themselves in naturally occurring settings. In case study research, a favoured ploy is to offer a data-extract preceded by an observation such as 'One typical example of this was . . . '. Using the research design deployed here, it is at least possible (subject to limitations of space) to make available to the reader relatively large chunks of data sequenced in the order that it naturally arises. However, this still leaves open the possibility of using favoured examples to make a point and thus to tell a 'story' about the data that is rhetorically rather than scientifically convincing (see Silverman, 1989b). When asked by researchers who favour experimental designs and statistical packages where are the *numbers* to substantiate the claims, case-study workers can, however, reasonably reply that quantification can arbitrarily impose categories on complex, naturally occurring phenomena.

One way out of this impasse could be deployed here. Upon examining our tapes, we discovered that the format of the physicians' questions and the parents' answers seem to differ substantially in DS consultations from elsewhere. To test whether this was the case, I compared the DS consultations with which I had been working with a random sample of non-Down's cases. In Tables 15 and 16, I have set out the format of the initial 'elicitation' or history-taking question with each group.

On the surface, Table 15 provides apparently unexciting data. Notice, however, that reference to the child's 'wellness' is made, in two different forms, in a majority of cases (13 out of 22). Now look at the questions asked of the parents of DS children in Table 16.

Here the normal form of the elicitation question is reversed. Wellness is mentioned in only 1 out of 10 cases (and then only in an indirect form) compared to 13 out of 22 in the other sample. Conversely, 6 out of 10 times the question takes the form: 'How is she/he?', while this is true in only 4 out of 22 cases in the random sample. As I commented at the time, looked at in terms of the subsequent unfolding of the consultation and the treatment

*Table 15* Initial elicitation question (random sample)

| Question | Number |
|---|---|
| Is he/she well? | 11 |
| From your point of view, is he/she a well baby? | 2 |
| Do you notice anything wrong with her/him? | 1 |
| From the heart point of view, she/he's active? | 1 |
| How is he/she? | 4 |
| Question not asked | 3 |
| **TOTAL** | **22** |

*Source*: Silverman, 1981

*Table 16* Initial elicitation question (Down's Syndrome cases)

| Question | Number |
|---|---|
| Is he/she well? | 0 |
| From your point of view, is he/she a well baby? | 1 |
| Do you notice anything wrong with her/him? | 0 |
| As far as his/her heart is concerned, does he/she get breathless? | 1 |
| Does she/he get a few chest infections? | 1 |
| How is he/she (this little boy/girl) in himself/herself? | 6 |
| Question not asked | 3 |
| **TOTAL** | **12** |

*Source*: Silverman, 1981

decision eventually agreed, these minor variations might give an insight into the micro-dynamics of power because:

> in medical encounters, like meetings with the tax authorities, assessments lead to particular disposals of cases. To assess a child in terms of 'wellness' implies a medical obligation to try to restore the unwell child to a state of health. By avoiding the use of the parameters well/unwell, the doctor helps to prepare the way for an eventual decision not to intervene. An 'unwell' child has to be restored to its normal state of 'wellness'. Handicapped children, like these, cannot be said to have any such normal state. Born imperfect, they are imperfectible. Self-evidently, therefore, the restorative role of medical intervention becomes problematic.
>
> (Silverman, 1981: 258)

From the point of view of the field researcher's commitment to preserving naturally occurring data, the strength of these tabulations is that they go beyond a purely illustrative use of the data while *counting the natural-language terms used by subjects*. No researcher's categories are being imposed upon the data. Of course, this is not to say that research cannot categorise in ways which subjects do not, merely that our 'second-order' categories must be based on a proper understanding of subjects' 'first-order' categories and practices (see Schutz, 1964).

Such careful analysis of the local organisation of consultations can be generalised through the use of the comparative method. Although time constraints meant that no systematic data were gathered in relation to these practices at other PCUs, these findings turned out to be fully in accord with a study of the policies of surgeons towards handicapped children in a number of American hospitals. Using questionnaires which asked practitioners to give their opinion of the best treatment of a number of hypothetical cases, together with listings of the actual number of DS children put up for surgery, controlling for type of heart condition, Crane (1975) discovered that they were far less likely to receive catheterisation and surgery than other children. Furthermore, social variables, such as being an only child or a first-born, played a far more significant role in surgeons' decision-making with these children.

Clearly, this research has a direct bearing on analysing the effectiveness of health care in the terms defined in the introduction to this book: '. . . how well a procedure works in practice, whether it meets the criteria of humane care and whether the benefits are equitably distributed' (see p. 1). Obviously, one's ethical position will have a crucial bearing on how one responds to findings of this kind. I chose to argue that the real problem it highlighted was *not* that DS children were being treated differently from others. I could not argue with the clinical evidence about their survival rates, relative to other children. Nor, personally, would I want to condemn the parents who tend to oppose major surgery because it may kill their child or, even if successful, may condemn the child in adult years to a life in an institution. However, it seems to me that there *is* an injustice here. It arises in the routinised enactment of a particular clinical policy which is hidden from parents and inevitably stereotypes their varying circumstances and preferences. Unsuccessfully, I argued with the physician at the PCU we were studying to abandon the policy, while still deferring to the special needs of Down's Syndrome children and their families.

## CONCLUSION

As requested, I have, somewhat egotistically, focused largely on two of my own research studies, one of which is still continuing. I have offered them as examples of (what I prefer to call) 'field research'. I hope that they underline my contention that work that is not based on experimental or statistical methods need not be anecdotal, still less inelegant. Again, despite the preference of some of my colleagues for grand theory and redundant technical vocabulary, I hope to have shown how field research can have a practical, as well as an analytical, relevance.

The introduction to this book talks about the regrettable tendency in some quarters to distinguish 'strong' from 'weak' methods. In this chapter, in turn, I have criticised the distinction between 'quantitative' and 'qualitative' research. It is my hope that this publication can play a stimulating and worthwhile role in opening our eyes to the range of methods that can produce valuable research. Perhaps an initial way forward is to abandon the kind of boring polarities that stand in the way of the *sine qua non* of good research – namely lateral thinking.

## REFERENCES

Bryman, A., 1988, *Quantity and Quality in Social Research*, London: Unwin Hyman.

Byrne, P. and Long, B., 1976, *Doctors Talking to Patients*, London: Her Majesty's Stationery Office.

Chester, R.. 1987, *Advice, Support and Counselling for the HIV Positive*, London: Department of Health and Social Security.

Coxon, A., 1986, 'Pilot Study of Project on Sexual Lifestyles of Non-Heterosexual Males', unpublished report, Cardiff: Department of Sociology, University College.

Crane, D., 1975, *The Sanctity of Social Life: Physicians' Treatment of Critically Ill Patients*, New York: Russell Sage.

Denzin, N., 1970, *The Research Act in Sociology*, London: Butterworth.

Garfinkel, H., 1967, *Studies in Ethnomethodology*, Englewood Cliffs, N.J.: Prentice Hall.

Mehan, H., 1979, *Learning Lessons: Social Organization in the Classroom*, Cambridge, MA: Harvard University Press.

Miller, R. and Bor, R., 1988, *AIDS: A Guide to Clinical Counselling*, London: Science Press.

Sacks, H., Schegloff, E. and Jefferson, G., 1975, 'A Simplest Systematics for the Analysis of Turn-Talking in Conversation', *Language*, 50: 696–735.

Schutz, A., 1964, in Natanson, M. (ed.), *Collected Papers*, The Hague: Nijhof.

Silverman, D., 1981, 'The Child as a Social Object: Down's Syndrome Children in a Paediatric Cardiology Clinic', *Sociology of Health and Illness*, 3, 3: 254–74.

—— 1987, *Qualitative Methodology and Sociology*, Aldershot: Gower.

—— 1989a, 'Making Sense of a Precipice: Constituting Identity in an HIV Clinic', in Aggleton, P., Hart, G. and Davies, P. (eds), *AIDS: Social Representations, Social Practices*, Lewes: Falmer.

—— 1989b, 'Telling Convincing Stories: A Plea for Cautious Positivism in Case-Studies', in Glassner, B. and Moreno, J. (eds), *The Qualitative-Quantitative Distinction in the Social Sciences*, Dordrecht: Kluwer.

—— 1989c, 'Six Rules of Qualitative Research: A Post-Romantic Argument', *Symbolic Interaction*, 12, 2: 25–40.

—— 1990, 'The Social Organization of Counselling', in Aggleton, P., Davies, P. and Hart, G. (eds), *AIDS: Individual, cultural and policy dimensions*, Lewes: Falmer.

Silverman, D. and Perakyla, A., 1990, 'AIDS Counselling: The interactional organization of talk about "delicate issues"', *Sociology of Health and Illness*, 12, 3: 293–318.

Wellings, K., 1989, 'Talking About Sex', unpublished paper presented at conference on 'Communication Issues in HIV Infection and AIDS', Royal Society of Medicine, London, 24 May, 1989.

# 11   Why don't you ask them?

## A qualitative research framework for investigating the diagnosis of cardiac normality

*Jeanne Daly, Ian McDonald and Evan Willis*

In this chapter we set out the methodological background of a research project using qualitative methods. Our chapter concerns the interaction between medical technology and medical practice and takes the form of a case study of the use of echocardiography (cardiac ultrasound) in the diagnosis of cardiac normality, previously reported in Daly (1989a). Our aim is to outline the research process – how we identified the problem for investigation, how the research method was chosen and what it achieved. Our emphasis is on the methodological issues raised by the study.

### BACKGROUND TO THE STUDY

Echocardiography (cardiac ultrasound) is the most important non-invasive cardiac imaging test. It uses a reflected ultrasound beam to generate vivid videotaped images of 'slices' through the beating heart. While its use in the diagnosis of heart disease may seem self-evident, an earlier study showed that about one-fifth of patients undergoing echocardiography are found to be normal (McDonald, *et al.*, 1988).

Using a diagnostic test to establish normality is not unusual, especially when a test is used for screening purposes where the great majority of patients are expected to be normal. Its aim is preventive but there is doubt about whether treating subclinical abnormalities actually prolongs life (Sackett, *et al.*, 1985: 150). The real justification, argues Dollery (1978: 18–19), does not lie in the therapy itself but in the 'soft' outcome, the benefit of a negative test in reassuring anxious patients.

Patient reassurance is seen uncritically in medical textbooks as benefiting patients, but there is little analysis of what constitutes effective reassurance (Kessel, 1979). Clinical experience suggests that reassurance often inexplicably fails. Indeed, tests for the purpose of reassurance have been seen as inducing further anxiety and a vicious circle involving further testing (Warwick and Salkovskis, 1985). Despite this questioning of an important area of medical practice, there is a lack of empirical research into the notion of reassurance and none that we know of concerning the use of diagnostic tests for this purpose. We believe that the reason for this lack is in part that rigorous research methods for analysing 'soft' outcomes are not readily available within the medical field.

## THE SENSE OF PROBLEM

The present study arose as part of a research strategy developed in order to evaluate echocardiography. The first study in this strategy (McDonald, *et al.*, 1988) used a quasi-experimental design to study the impact of the test on the clinical care of a representative group of patients consecutively referred in the course of routine clinical practice. We used questionnaires to document the effect of the test result on the doctor's decision-making and to measure the effect of the test on patient anxiety, understanding and doubt.

The results of this study showed that echocardiography had a modest impact on clinical decisions and rarely contributed to the saving of life. One of the commonest uses of the test was referral of otherwise healthy people to rule out disease. This usually arose when a murmur, a heart sound heard with a stethoscope, was detected in primary practice or when patients presented with potential cardiac symptoms like chest pain. The patient was then referred to a cardiologist for assessment. A normal test result reduced anxiety about the heart but, after the test, patients claimed a lack of understanding and had doubt and anxiety about the heart too often to be clinically acceptable. Importantly, the limitations of the questionnaire method used did not allow us to understand how the patients came to be referred for a test with questionable patient benefit;nor could it tell us why some patients reacted unfavourably. In addition, the clinical experience of the cardiologists suggests that the use of tests to diagnose the patient as normal is not a simple issue. There might be a temptation towards excessive use of such tests to exclude unlikely disease 'just to be on the safe side' – the medico-legal complications of missing disease are well recognised. The benefit for patients is cast into doubt when the 'worried well' return to the medical system repeatedly for further reassurance. Even where patients do not return, cardiologists worry that the reassurance may not be sustained in the longer term.

The first, quantitative study thus focused our attention on problems which it could not answer. Importantly, the study had conceptualised the test as an isolated clinical *event* with objective benefit flowing from the test itself. An alternate was to see the test within its social context, as one aspect of an extended social *process* of diagnosis. The social context of the patient would have a bearing on the effect of the test, particularly in the longer term. Similarly, the cardiologists use the test in a professional context which might well attach professional value to the use of the test. What we needed to do was formulate a research design which would allow a more critical analysis of the experience of both cardiologist and patient when a test is used to diagnose normality.

## POSSIBLE RESEARCH METHODS

A randomised controlled trial (RCT) could have been used to measure reassurance (as a reduction in anxiety) with patients allocated randomly to an experimental group given the test and a control group given a clinical opinion only. However, when a patient is referred to a cardiologist with a specific or implied request for the test, random allocation to control and experimental groups would have upset the normative expectations of the referral relationship that a test be carried out. In addition, an experimental requirement of randomised allocation would mean that we could not study the way in which the test comes to be used in routine medical practice.

Next we considered doing a survey. The problem with the simple patient anxiety scale in the first study was that its validity was in question – patients could easily have under-reported their concerns about the heart as a result of the need to appear to be good patients. Thus a more extensive questionnaire was needed in order to measure state-trait anxiety and aspects of patient personality. This would have met the needs of the most prevalent medical explanation of recurrent anxiety after a normal test: that it originates in the personality of the patient (see Lantinga, 1988). The problem was that such a questionnaire reduces the problem to one of patient anxiety and we were not at all sure that the complexity of the patient experience could be addressed with as relatively blunt an instrument as an anxiety questionnaire. In addition, in extending the questionnaire we had made it much more intrusive; we feared that this extensive probing of the patient's psyche could so interfere with the patient experience of the test that the questionnaire could obscure the effect of the test itself. A shorter questionnaire was available but was insufficiently validated.

A major problem with both the RCT and the questionnaire is that we would use a measure of reassurance as the outcome, thus accepting the medical version of what the test is about. About this we were in doubt. Rather, we saw the process of testing as involving a variety of social and technical forces which we could not confidently identify in advance.

At this point then it became clear that the standard methodological approaches were inappropriate for studying the problem which we had identified. The researcher faced with such a problem has two options: to abandon the problem, putting it into the 'too hard' basket, or to modify the problem to fit in with methodological preconceptions about the need for quantitation. The medical tendency to choose one or the other of these could well explain the lack of analysis of mechanisms of reassurance. The alternative was to retain the problem and press on into the relatively uncharted waters of sociological analysis using qualitative research methods.

## THE RESEARCH METHOD CHOSEN

The next study in the strategy was therefore directed at the 'rule-out and reassure' category but designed to obtain more detailed empirical data on the role of the test in the social processes of medical care. Importantly, our aim was to interpret the use of the test directly from the accounts of the actors themselves and not from any preconceived rationale of the use of the test. An important reason why there has been a systematic neglect of these subjective accounts of the process of testing is the difficulty with both collecting and analysing the data in an objectively verifiable manner. This represents the major methodological problem which we faced.

Data collection involved as many 'slices of life' out of the long-term experience of patients and cardiologists as we were able to gather. Our first target was the consultation in which the patients were given the test result, the 'reassurance'. Tape-recording this interview gave us access to the interaction between doctor and patient during which reassurance was implemented.

The clinical and technical backgrounds to the way in which the cardi-ologist dealt with the patient were not necessarily evident from the consultation. These we analysed with a questionnaire including the reason for doing the test, a grading of the pre-test probability of cardiac normality, a record of any remaining uncertainty in the diagnosis after the test, decisions on treatment or follow-up, a grading of patient anxiety before and after the test result, and a prediction of the likelihood of recurrence of anxiety in the future.

The way in which the cardiologist deals with a particular patient is not determined only by the clinical circumstances of that patient but occurs in the cultural milieu of the practice of cardiology. Data on what constitutes this milieu we obtained from a number of relatively unstructured tape-recorded interviews with each cardiologist. These focused on experiences with patients in the series and with similar patients in routine practice. We discussed attitudes to diagnostic doubt, to dealing with the 'worried well', to echocardiography and to medical technology in general. During the interviews it became clear that cardiologists have a particular style of practice which they are able to describe and justify. As a result we extended the topics covered in the interview to include a discussion of where the style was learnt and how it came to be adopted.

The patients were interviewed at home soon after the test result and consultation and again nine to twelve months later, thus giving us data on the longer-term effect of the test. Interviews were largely unstructured, allowing patients to recount what they themselves saw as important. The interviewer did, however, have specific key topics on which information was sought – recall of what was said in the consultation, immediate and longer-term response to the test in terms of beliefs about heart and health. If a patient did not spontaneously raise these topics, they were introduced into the interview – how and when depended on what seemed most appropriate for that particular patient. As in the case of the cardiologists, the duration of interview was not fixed; rather the discussion continued until patients had finished talking about their experiences; most patient interviews lasted between one and two hours.

All interviews were tape-recorded and transcribed. In this way any potential bias introduced by the interviewer was accessible for analysis.

## THE SAMPLE

Each cardiologist was asked to enrol consecutive, otherwise healthy patients in whom the heart was considered likely to be normal but for whom an echocardiogram had been ordered. For a study such as this which does not use quantitative outcomes to formally test a hypothesis, a required sample size cannot be calculated in advance. Since the amount of data collected for each patient was large, some trade-off was necessary between the depth and breadth of data collection – that is, between detail and sample size. There were also obviously time constraints which imposed a practical limit on the number of patients and doctors who could participate in the study.

The approach which we adopted as most appropriate to our study was the concept of 'theoretical sampling' (Strauss, 1987). Thus we continued to recruit patients until adequate data was available for the analysis of the most important conceptual categories and until it was evident that the model was approaching saturation in the sense that new categories were no longer being generated. The study terminated after forty patients (P1 to P40) were enrolled by six cardiologists (D1 to D6).

## RESULTS

The two major medical justifications for doing the test are that it makes it easier for the cardiologist to decide on the correct treatment and that it helps to reassure the patient. These, the technical and the social aspects of the test, are separated here for conceptual purposes.

We found that the reasons for ordering the test were related to the confidence which the cardiologists felt in their clinical diagnosis of normality before the test. Table 17 shows that the need to rule out disease, thus clarifying treatment options, is an important reason for ordering the test, but so are satisfying the expectations of the referring doctor and, by far the least important, reassuring the anxious patient.

## THE TECHNICAL BENEFIT

The cardiologists are skilled in the accurate clinical diagnosis of minor heart disease. They classified fifteen of the forty patients as certainly normal on clinical examination alone. The test result itself was seen as doubtful and failed to resolve the cardiologist's uncertainty in three cases. Thus in nearly half the patients, the test had no clear diagnostic value.

In eighteen cases the cardiologists said that the test did increase their certainty that the patient was normal. Antibiotic prophylaxis against endocarditis was instituted as a result of the test in only two patients. On the other hand, a normal test result did not determine diagnosis. One patient with a normal result was scheduled for review; another echocardiogram performed six months later was also normal and the patient was then told that further review was unnecessary. Another patient had a repeat normal echocardiogram within six months, ordered by a different cardiologist although the result of the first test was available. One patient with a normal test result and a normal diagnosis by the cardiologist was nevertheless put onto antibiotic prophylaxis by his GP.

The cardiologists expressed concern about what they saw as a low technical benefit from the test. Not only do they trust their own clinical skill in diagnosis but they have doubts about the effectiveness of antibiotic

*Table 17* Cardiologists' reasons for ordering the test

| Normality | Total | Expectations of referral | Rule out disease | Reassurance of patient |
|---|---|---|---|---|
| Certain | 15 | 8 | 3 | 4 |
| Almost certain | 16 | 7 | 6 | 3 |
| Probably | 9 | 1 | 8 | 0 |
| **TOTAL** | **40** | **16** | **17** | **7** |

*Source*: Daly, 1989b: 138

prophylaxis for minor heart disease. Since the test carries a risk of false-positive diagnosis, any technical benefit must be offset against the iatrogenic potential of labelling patients with disease. This awareness coexisted with a clear understanding of factors built into the social structure of referral practice which favours a test rather than reliance on a clinical opinion. The benefit of the test lies in its social function within the medical system.

## THE SOCIAL BENEFIT TO THE MEDICAL SYSTEM

The cardiologists' primary reason for doing the test on the clinically normal patients was to comply with the expectations of the referring doctor. In more than half of all cases the referring doctor either requested the test or the request was implied in the circumstances of the referral (such as a superannuation examination). An additional contributory factor, not present in the table, is the use of the test done on the latest state-of-the-art machine as an 'objective' justification for reversing a diagnosis made by a colleague.

Professional reasons for doing tests, and the economic inducements which may be present, are recognised by doctors but are seen as less significant than pressure from patients to do the test. They are seen as raising difficult problems which the profession has not addressed adequately; in the following excerpt, one of the cardiologists discussed this vexing problem with a patient who is himself a surgeon:

| | |
|---|---|
| Cardiologist: | . . . we're trying to fight against this whole process. |
| Surgeon–patient: | But as doctors you realise we've also got other pressures from patients who sort of demand, 'Because the Prime Minister had a CAT scan, I've got to have a CAT scan!' |
| Cardiologist: | Right, it's built into the system, you know. |
| Surgeon–patient: | Yes, I know that. |
| Cardiologist: | It's nobody's fault. |
| Surgeon–patient: | And then the radiologists have got the CAT scan and commercially they've got to keep it rolling over too, so the pressures are there to do it. |
| Cardiologist: | And not only that: if someone's sent along to me for a test, I've got to be very discreet about not doing it and I don't do that often. [D1, P37] |

Despite what is said here, there was no evidence in the study that patients requested the test. Indeed, since very few of the patients could even remember the name of the test, it would have been difficult for them to recommend it to family or friends. On balance, it seems more likely that the major motivation for performing the test is the benefit, professional and financial, which accrues to the medical profession.

## THE SOCIAL BENEFIT TO THE PATIENT

The cardiologists saw twenty-seven patients as anxious about their hearts before the test. They believed that the test did reassure twenty-seven patients, three of whom they had classified as *not* anxious before the test. In two cases they saw the test as failing to reassure, and in one case the cardiologist did not know whether it had or not. While patient reassurance is seldom the primary reason why the cardiologists order the test, it constitutes a patient benefit which provides an important means of justifying the test. However, there are other considerations which contribute to the way in which the cardiologists go about reassuring patients.

## STYLES OF CARDIOLOGICAL PRACTICE

The cardiologists could be categorised on their reassurance styles (Daly, 1989a). The differences are particularly evident in those cases where the test result itself was uncertain. In such a case one approach used by cardiologists is to give the suspicious sign or symptom the benefit of the doubt and to try diligently not to miss any disease which might be present. In contrast, the second approach emphasises the relationship between potential cardiac symptoms (such as chest pain and palpitations) and neurosis. Here, giving the sign the benefit of the doubt is seen as having a potential for inducing cardiac neurosis, and consultations are aimed at removing the patient from the medical system by emphasising normality.

Cardiologists 1, 2 and 3 follow the second tradition. All three are keenly aware of the problem of patients focusing neurotic anxieties on their hearts (the 'cardiac crazies'). The test is used powerfully to reinforce the cardiologists' capacity to search out and destroy incipient or manifest cardiac neurosis. Despite reservations about the test, it is thus presented as definitive grounds for diagnosing normality. Cardiologist 2 does so in a particularly authoritative way, even, in one case, without seeing the test or receiving a report on it. The following is a complete consultation with a working-class, migrant woman whom he had judged as having 'pan-anxiety'. Her husband is present at the consultation and cardiologist 2 believes that the husband shares his perception that the woman is mad.

Doctor:   Aren't you a lucky girl!
Husband: That's right.

Doctor:   Proven normal heart! Proven! No question.
Husband: That's it.
Doctor:   All right?
Patient:  Very good.
Husband: She's better now.
Doctor:   I hope so.

[inaudible conversation as all talk and laugh together]

Doctor:   I think it's fantastic!
Patient:  That's good.
Husband: Well, maybe she's very bad.
Doctor:   No, you don't know; you haven't seen the test.

[husband talks to wife in rapid Italian in which the word 'dying' is audible]

Patient:  I worry too much.
Doctor:   I think that is the problem, you worry too much!
Patient:  Yes, I'm nervous, that's why.
Doctor:   Look, your heart's fine. All you've got to do is chop your head off and you'll be fine! [loud laughter]
Doctor:   Thanks, I'll see you later. O.K. then.
Patient:  Thank you.
Doctor:   Bye bye. [P31, D2]

It is worth noting here that, in the later home interview, the woman expressed her gratitude for what cardiologist 2 had said: he was the first of a long line of doctors who could confidently tell her she was normal and stop the expensive series of tests she had had. She repeated several times the cardiologist's phrase: 'A lucky girl!'. In contrast, a middle-class patient submitted to this dismissive technique phoned her general practitioner to complain.

Cardiologists 4, 5 and 6, in contrast, see the test more positively and see no reason to avoid doing it when it provides an easy means of 'making sure'. This raises the problem of what constitutes being 'sure'. Cardiologist 4, in particular, is remarkably tolerant of patients' 'functional' symptoms; he encourages them to return for review if they continue to feel anxious and he feels that cardiologists should:

. . . not just jump into that position where you just label everyone as neurotic . . . . I think it is our role not to dismiss them lightly, just like that, and say 'Go away; there's nothing wrong with you.'

He may even treat their chest pain with beta-blockers and, in persistent cases, may resort to the 'WHOLE BANG lot', including angiography.

In consultations normal diagnoses are qualified and uncertain, and patients are given a mixed message:

> Er, recall that, er, um, I was explaining to you about the two parts of the mitral valve . . . . Er, one of these, er, parts is just a LITTLE bit longer than the other, and, er, under some circumstances, it, er, it is responsible, I would think, for that er, sound or that murmur that he has. Er, but it is not quite prolapsing. In other words, it's er, . . . under resting conditions, under which the echocardiogram was performed, er, the findings are almost entirely normal . . . . [D4,P19]

Not surprisingly this uncertain strategy, applied even to clearly normal test results, left three out of ten patients uncertain about whether their hearts were normal. The remainder, it should be noted, were successfully reassured.

## THE CONSULTATION

The consultation is where the cardiologists put the test to use. From the consultation transcripts, we graded the information given to the patient and the manner in which it was communicated – in particular, any attempts made to interact with the patient. In almost all cases, the cardiologists did clearly inform patients that the heart was normal. They usually attempted some explanation of the murmur or symptoms in order to explain their conclusions. Very rarely did they encourage patient participation in the discussion so that they could identify and address the concerns of patients.

Neither the normalising nor the cautious approach predictably led to a resolution of patient doubt about the heart. Surprisingly, nor does the amount of information or the manner of its presentation. Most good outcomes for patients in terms of reducing anxiety about the heart followed consultations in which there was only a limited amount of interaction. Poor patient outcomes were equally common after consultations with a minimum of interaction and a consultation with extensive interaction. We therefore concluded that the explanatory interview was not a strong determinant of a good patient outcome.

What the cardiologists did in the consultation is explicable by the fact that they saw the test as an isolated event in which the outcome is determined by the powerfully persuasive evidence of the normal test result. Thus they underestimate the difficulty for patients in making sense of the diagnosis in the light of past experience or in the light of information from non-medical sources such as family, friends or the media. It is here that the lack of persuasion and interaction becomes of critical importance. As a result, in comparison with the patient account, the cardiologists overestimated the extent to which the patient had been effectively reassured and underestimated the likelihood of recurrence of anxiety about the heart.

## THE PATIENT CONTEXT

The personal circumstances and medical histories of the forty patients in the study varied widely. Aged between 3 and 74 years, they came from working-class families and from privileged sections of the middle class. Two of the patients had psychiatric histories.

How then did they fare and how predictable were their outcomes? The ten patients who went to the doctor with potential cardiac symptoms, worried about their hearts, were clearly most in need of reassurance, yet the effect of the test was to leave every one of these patients still worried about their hearts. The most common problem was that they felt that the original problem with which they had entered the medical system had not been addressed – instead of diagnosing the cause of the problem, the cardiologists substituted the problem of the murmur or other cardiac disease and diagnosed this as normal instead. One such consultation included the following exchange:

> Patient: Um, oh, sort of, kind of . . . . I've been noticing that, over the last week or so, I seem to be getting slight twinges every now and then.
> Doctor: Yes, yes . . .
> Patient: and . . .
> Doctor: So it really doesn't worry you?
> Patient: Not really, no.
> Patient: All right. Well that's really of no, er, great significance. Now you also had a heart murmur . . . . [D4, P13]

In fact this patient was so incapacitated by the chest pain that he had been taken to casualty by his parents. Dissatisfied by the cardiologist's response, he went back to his GP asking to be referred to another cardiologist. At the time of the follow-up interviews, three of these patients had returned to the medical system with cardiac symptoms.

The remaining patients all went to the doctor for some unrelated reason – in nine cases for an insurance examination – a murmur was found and this led to the referral. In only eight cases the patients did not start worrying about their hearts as a result of this initial diagnosis. They had varying experiences. The majority experienced some relief when told of the normal test result but retained residual concern which was not there before the test was ordered.

One of the problems concerns patients who were subject to serial review. One, a young sports teacher diagnosed with a murmur during pre-employment screening, had had heart disease diagnosed in childhood and had had serial reviews throughout childhood. She immediately recalled her childhood experience:

> I used to get very tired because I'm small anyway and I think that Mum used to watch me a little bit then because, I think, maybe the doctors said, 'She might get tired.' [P2]

After the initial diagnosis, she again connected feelings of tiredness with the heart query:

> And I can remember a month ago, and it really stands out, I did aerobics and I just couldn't get my breath and, I mean, I'm fit so that shouldn't have been a problem. And I can remember doubling over to get my breath so I was trying to convince myself that, ah, yeah, there must be something there if I had that problem that time ago. But . . . then when this heart murmur come up I thought, 'Mmmm. Maybe that's why!' [P2]

This raised for her the problem of whether she would be able to have children so she was keen to have the test. In the consultation she tried to raise her personal concerns. The way in which she did so was oblique and was rapidly brushed aside by the cardiologist who was busy 'normalising' her:

Patient:  . . . regularly I jog about three to six kilometres.
Doctor:  OK.
Patient:  I think it's about three. I find that the hardest, to jog in the morning.
Doctor:  So do I. Actually I find it hard at any time but particularly hard in the morning.
Patient:  You see, it's much harder to get my breath in, in the morning.
Doctor:  Yes, OK.
Patient:  . . . which probably is a lot.
Doctor:  All right, so you are a very fit person, swimming, jogging and so on. Any murmurs in the family? [D1, p2]

She remained worried about whether the murmur was a health problem.

In all, a quarter of the patients (ten) had had a previous query about the heart, three patients had had periodic reviews throughout childhood, three had been on cardiac medication and six had had previous echocardiograms. Living from childhood with a badly understood 'heart problem' readily translates into disease. But even when the patient has no past history there may be a family history of fear of heart disease. One patient knew that the cardiologist had said there was nothing wrong with her heart but when she got home she recalled that she has a niece who has a heart murmur and goes blue around the lips when she runs. Thus her own murmur worries her and she is not sure that her heart is normal:

> If you've got a murmur, it must be something to be looked at. I mean, not everybody has heart murmurs, do they? . . . I'm ignorant about it all. I don't know. I really don't know. If there was a murmur there I guess it would have to be watched. I mean, I'm overweight . . . . I don't know if you can just pick up a heart murmur overnight or whether it's something that just happens to you. [P 28]

Although she intended to resolve these doubts when she returned to the first hospital, she did not do so and the doubts remained.

## A PANDORA'S BOX

The results of the test seem so unpredictable that we liken the ordering of a test to the opening of Pandora's box. One example will be cited to illustrate the point.

P22 was a 52-year-old woman whose case demonstrated the instability of technological reassurance under the impact of social forces which the doctor could not predict and certainly could not control. When her GP referred her for the test he told her that she was probably normal and she did not become particularly concerned. After the test, she was readily per-suaded by the cardiologist that she was normal. However, a few days later she learnt that her sister had cancer. Recalling that her sister had had a number of normal diagnostic tests, she draws on her distrust of computers to reinterpret her own diagnosis as doubtful. The following extract is from the home interview at which her husband was present:

> Patient:   . . . she had every test under the sun, and now they've dis-
> covered it in the bowel and the bladder, and she'd had tests
> and it was clear. And she'd had an ultrasound, which is
> similar to what I had, so, since THEN, I've suddenly got
> doubts. I've thought, 'Well, that MARVELLOUS machine,
> perhaps it isn't right, and I'd have been better just stopping at
> [the family doctor] [laughs].
>
> Husband:  No, but she had a CAT scan, not an ultrasound.
>
> Patient:   Mmm. I thought that was a similar thing.
>
> Husband:  No. It's a CAT scan.
>
> Patient:   But that's a MACHINE of some sort, isn't it? But anyway, I
> just thought that the other day: you just don't really know, do
> you? They're all sophisticated and, when I saw it was a
> computer, I wasn't very impressed getting on it [laughs]. I'm
> not really . . . .

Husband: Because there was another [Davies] on it. You were worried
they'd got the right [Davies]! [laughs] . . .

Patient: And I mean, our first introduction to computers was at the
bank when it was always broken down and you had to queue
up, so I DO have rather a negative attitude towards computers. And when this woman [the technician] plugged everything in the other day, and started talking to it, and then said,
'Oops! That's not you; there's another [Davies] on this
machine,' I thought, 'Oh, that's it; they'll get me mixed up
with another [Davies]. What else would you expect!' Oh, I
wasn't that impressed. But I think I was pretty pleased when
the result came through that it was all right. And then, when
that happened to [my sister], I sort of said, 'Oh, these
machines, they don't really know.' So I'm really no better off
than if I hadn't've gone, I don't think. [P22]

At her sister's funeral, she had palpitations and made up her mind to retire
from teaching.


**THE PROBLEM**

A more comprehensive analysis of these problems is to be found in Daly
(1989a and 1989b), but these brief glimpses of the results of the longitudinal qualitative approach of the study will, we hope, indicate that the
problem lies in the way in which what is said in the consultations interacts
with the patients' own experience. Patients did not ask questions about the
diagnosis in any of the consultations; the doubts came later when they
thought about it at home or when they told their families about it. The most
common problem was difficulty in reconciling the existence of a murmur
with having a normal heart. After the test twenty-two patients had doubts
about whether the murmur was normal, twenty-three patients had doubts
about whether the heart was normal and for sixteen patients this translated
into doubt about their overall health. This indicates a state of considerable
confusion on the patients' part, a confusion which the cardiologist did not
elicit in the consultation and which could therefore not be resolved by the
test. These persistent doubts may present a serious problem in that they can
be reactivated if, as often happens, the murmur is queried again.

This is not to deny benefit from the test since the majority of patients
(twenty-six) were reassured and felt less worried about their hearts after the
test. However, we should also note that a measure designed to reassure and
not apparently controversial has been either ineffective or harmful in more
than one-third of all patients. More significantly, the wider perspective used

by our study also assessed the effect of the overall process of testing from the time when the patients entered the medical system; this paints a much bleaker picture. Most patients (thirty of forty) were unconcerned about their hearts when the query was raised, and anxiety about the heart is therefore induced by the process of referral. This anxiety is imperfectly resolved. As a result, only four patients were graded as having gained from this overall process of testing in being left better off. In the majority of patients (twenty-two) the query and testing process was judged as having harmed the patient, leaving them worse off than before.

Given the complexity of the social context of the test we have called into question the medical assumption that the test reassures anxious patients. This is not the major reason why the test is done and, moreover, the test fails consistently to reassure patients who are worried. We have shown that there are strong structural inducements for cardiologists to perform the test even when patient benefit is in doubt. The overall effect of the test is essentially unpredictable by either doctor or patient. A major problem is that the test is seen as a placebo substituting for interaction with worried patients over what the patient sees as a problem. Some patients respond to this better than others but all have to make sense of the experience of the test in terms of their own understanding which, in turn, relates closely to their social context; indeed the outcome of the test for an individual patient may change over time depending on changes in the social context, something over which the cardiologist clearly has no control.

We also concluded that a detailed understanding of the wide range of patient experience could not have been achieved in a study which measures an average response.

## PROBLEMS OF BIAS AND GENERALISABILITY

The kind of research which we have described is commonly seen as lacking the capacity to address questions of researcher bias. In addition, the small number of patient cases can be seen as contributing to problems with the generalisability of the study. In our study these questions were addressed as an integral part of the research method.

The data were analysed in two ways. First the transcripts were analysed by direct interpretation in order to make sense of the process of diagnosis. In this analysis it became clear that the experience of both patients and doctors could be categorised and used to make sense of their actions. This built up a detailed account of the social context of the test which could be substantiated from transcripts of what the actors themselves say. In most studies this should be sufficient, but we were working in a professional context where both cardiology and sociology might be seen as having a commitment, perhaps an opposing commitment, to the outcome of the study. The problem of researcher bias had to be confronted in more formal ways.

Developing the qualitative analysis meant that certain aspects of the consultations and interviews assumed more significance than others. We verified this analysis by developing specific criteria for judging an extensive set of data categories (variables), including them in a set of guidelines for grading so that a number of independent observers could generate their own assessment of the meaning of the data. The 107 gradings and supportive evidence from the transcripts were recorded on a computer database. Statistical analysis subsequently showed that inter-observer agreement between the independent gradings of the cardiologist and the sociologist researchers was good.

Later, still another researcher repeated the process and in cases of difference we turned to the data itself for supportive evidence until all three reached consensus. Those cardiologists who passed by in the corridor when we were 'reaching consensus' – a process which at times reached heights of discord as sociologist battled cardiologist over the interpretation of the practice of cardiology – know that the final analysis is not the subjective judgement of an individual researcher. Significantly, those areas where we failed to reach consensus did not go into the database. Instead they were retained for a later analysis of intra-professional differences of interpretation in a key area of medical practice.

The quantitative gradings deduced from the qualitative data form a carefully verified framework around which we have constructed the arguments of the study. This is not a necessary part of all qualitative studies but it has advantages in demonstrating lack of bias in the interpretation in areas where this is a prime concern. What it also does is to make evident what the deviant cases are. Thus if some of our 'athletic' young people do not fare as well as the others, it makes it necessary to explain how these differences arise.

One of the problems with presenting qualitative research is that it cannot be neatly encapsulated in tables and a minimum of discussion. Instead, it depends for its verifiability on the telling of a convincing story (Silverman, 1989), one which presents clearly how the data were obtained and shows how the interpretation was developed. Once this is done, it needs to be taken back to the participants to see if they see it as a reasonable exposition of their experience. A written analysis was presented to the cardiologists for comment. For patients, the follow-up interviews were used to check key points of interpretation. Once the problem of internal validity is assured, the problem of external validity remains.

The problem of generalisability is addressed in three ways. The first concerns the method of theoretical sampling which is used not to control but to extend the diversity of the sample. Thus we drew patients from private as well as public hospital practice and sought out cardiologists with divergent opinions about the use of tests. Patients came from working and professional classes. A comparison with the larger, earlier study showed that the categories of patients (for example, the 'worried' patients and those referred for insurance purposes) are represented in the same proportion as in routine clinical practice.

The second approach is to describe carefully the context of the study, who participated and the background of the cardiologists. This allows the reader to locate the study in a particular social context; extrapolation to other social contexts would depend upon how comparable they are.

Lastly, the study is not intended to stand alone but to form part of an ongoing process of analysis of reassurance from diagnostic tests. There will be other studies which will examine the same problem in different contexts, perhaps involving other diagnostic tests. But what brings all these studies together is that which we have not been able to address in this brief presentation: a theoretical understanding of the social structures within which these studies are located. Some of this has been done and we know a lot about the historical origins and present manifestations of the professional institutions of medical practice. Some of it, in particular the role of technology in medical practice, still requires further development.

## CONCLUSION

What we have addressed in this chapter is an example of how qualitative research methods can be used to address those problems in medical contexts which cannot be satisfactorily resolved by more conventional medical research techniques. The nature of the problem chosen for investigation led us to a research design based on the collection of extensive unstructured interview data and on qualitative analysis. This took us down a research path not often trodden by medical researchers. Nor, on account of the difficulties of arranging access to the clinical context, is it a path much worn by medical sociologists. The mix of technical and social issues which characterises the use of echocardiography in the diagnosis of cardiac normality meant that we were studying a complex problem which was best addressed by a multidisciplinary approach drawing on the understanding of both cardiologists and sociologists.

The study enabled us to assess the social context of the use of technical investigations in medical practice in a way which no other research design would have done.

## REFERENCES

Daly, J., 1989a, 'Innocent murmurs: echocardiography and the diagnosis of cardiac normality', *Sociology of Health and Illness*, 11, 2: 99–116.

—— 1989b, 'Innocent Murmurs: the social contruction of cardiac normality', PhD thesis, La Trobe University, Melbourne.

Dollery, C., 1978, *The End of an Age of Optimism: medical science in retrospect and prospect*, London: Nuffield Provincial Hospitals Trust.

Kessel, N., 1979, 'Reassurance', *The Lancet*, 26 May: 1128–33.

Lantinga, L.J., 1988, 'One year psychosocial follow-up of patients with chest pain and angiographically normal coronary arteries', *The American Jouranl of Cardiology*, 62, 1 August: 209–13.

McDonald, I.G, Guyatt, G.H., Gutman, J.M., Jelinek, U.M., Fox, P. and Daly, J., 1988, 'The contribution of a non-invasive test to clinical care. The impact of echocardiography on diagnosis, management and patient anxiety', *Journal of Clinical Epidemiology*, 41, 2: 151–62.

Sackett, D.L., Haynes, R.B. and Tugwell, P., 1985, *Clinical Epidemiology: a basic science for clinical medicine*, Boston: Little, Brown & Company.

Silverman, D., 1989, 'Telling convincing stories: a plea for cautions positivism in case studies', in Glaser, B. and Moreno, J. (eds), *the Qualitative–Quantitative Distinction in the Social Sciences*, Dordrecht: Kluwer.

Strauss, A.L., 1987, *Qualitative Analysis for Social Scientists*, Cambridge: Cambridge University Press.

Warwick, H.M.C. and Salkovskis, P.M., 1985, 'Reassurance', *British Medical Journal*, 290: 1028.

# Part V
# Conclusion

# 12 Research methods in health care – a summing up

*Ian McDonald and Jeanne Daly*

The many health care questions pressing for answers can be addressed only by drawing on a wide range of research methods. This was our contention in the introduction to this publication. The variety of methods presented, from the perspective of various disciplines, and the range of health problems addressed in the chapters, add weight to this claim. The study designs spanned a spectrum from the randomised trial, through quasi-experiment and survey, to qualitative method, yet each represented a logical and appropriate approach to the particular research problem. Indeed it would be difficult to avoid the conclusion that each of these methods has its legitimate place in health care research, and each its own particular difficulties which need to be overcome by the artful researcher.

Differences of viewpoint between participants there are, but none seems irreconcilable; nor does there seem to be disagreement with our perspective regarding the need for an eclectic choice of method. Yet the reason for convening the symposium, and for this publication, was our conviction that disagreement and confusion concerning appropriate research methods is a problem for both researchers and granting bodies and one which could blunt the effectiveness of health care research.

Despite the level of general agreement, over a period of time researchers, especially those from different disciplines, could still find themselves at odds over research method. This becomes most evident if we have to write or even review research proposals together. With goodwill, and a long period of discussion, differences over epistemological assumptions could perhaps be resolved. A broader theoretical framework within which such a rational interchange could take place would be useful. Unfortunately, constructive dialogue is all too often seriously hampered by fundamental differences of an ideological nature concerning the way science itself is perceived. This is likely to engage attitudes deeply rooted in our culture. Certainly to accuse a researcher of being unscientific is a powerful pejorative. We will therefore conclude with some thoughts about this difficult issue.

## CLASSIFICATION OF RESEARCH METHOD

It is not easy to classify research methods used in the field of health care in such a way as to preserve necessary distinctions, to take account of the different approaches of individual disciplines, yet remain understandable. This is particularly so since variations on the theme of a specific design are virtually unlimited, and, in the real world of research, methods often involve a mixture of designs. The purist might demand a more elaborate classification than that presented here but our objective is to introduce only as much complexity as is necessary to illustrate our argument.

We will also simplify the task by classifying only methods of data acquisition and exclude methods developed for the combining of results from different studies. The scholarly review article, books and the formal lecture may be used to synthesise information from a variety of sources. In an area of research such as health, in order to solve practical problems and generate policy, there is often the need for early application of the results of many studies. Hence there are a number of methods for formal data synthesis such as meta-analysis, consensus generation, and other modelling exercises such as cost-effectiveness and decision analysis, mathematical and computer modelling. We will not discuss these further.

Our primary axis of classification is whether or not the study objective is to observe a structure or process with the ultimate aim of modelling it, or to test a pre-specified hypothesis about outcome. In order to test a hypothesis concerning cause and effect, any other system variables have to be controlled. This is most efficiently achieved by comparing two groups which differ only with respect to one variable, say, the treatment under test. The ideal experiment of this kind is the randomised trial in which the intervention – drug, surgery or investigation – is randomly administered to the chosen groups. If randomisation is seen to be unethical or impractical, then allocation of patients may be non-random in the format of a quasi-experimental or cohort study.

If, on the other hand, the objective is to analyse some broader aspect of the processes of clinical care or health care delivery, then control is not the point. Where the researcher can identify and measure those variables which contribute to the phenomenon under study, a survey will usually be the means of observation. A limited number of factors are measured in the field in order to test hypotheses, using statistics to summarise and to explore the relationships between variables, and perhaps to generate further hypotheses.

If, however, our aim is to learn what is happening in a particular setting, we cannot start by pre-specifying the important variables, and we may not even want to place a limit on what is seen as relevant. More importantly, if we want to understand the structural nuances of a complex, changing system and the subtleties of interaction between its constituents over time, then we need a method which does not limit itself to one measurement of specified variables. What we need then is a method which allows direct observation, even participation, recording whatever data is relevant for understanding what is happening. Data is usually interpreted in the light of a particular theoretical framework. This is the field study analysed by the method of qualitative data analysis.

The papers in this collection illustrate the fact that a health care problem may require any one of these kinds of design, or some combination of designs in the form of a strategy, in order to deliver the answers to questions posed. When we have a good understanding of an area of study, we know whether or not it is possible and desirable to control variables in order to put an important specific question to the test of a randomised trial. This is the linchpin of the evaluation of drugs or of other clinical procedures, and it is used as the most definitive test. Jack Hirsh provided a summary of the structure of such trials and illustrated their value with examples in the clinical field. The randomised trial also has important applications in research into health care delivery, as illustrated by David Newell.

Because of its experimental structure and therefore high data reliability, the randomised trial has been presented as the ideal method for clinical investigation. While this is true for the testing of hypotheses, particularly for drug evaluation, the virtues of such trials must be kept in perspective. The randomised trial is designed to test a hypothesis about outcome. In clinical care and health care delivery, the problems which need to be solved are seldom so narrowly focused that we can address them in this way. The randomised trial is of limited use in studying clinical interventions more complex in their context of administration than drugs, such as surgery and particularly diagnostic tests. Not only is it more difficult to control clinical variables, but even successful control exacts its price; restriction of study population and control of variables in the name of data reliability can make it difficult to generalise results from controlled context to clinical circumstances. For this reason, as pointed out by Michael Jelinek, it can be difficult to interpret the results of a trial in the context of a particular patient. Trials are of very little relevance when addressing the broader questions concerning the processes of clinical care and health care delivery where a high priority might well be to identify those problems which can be studied with more narrowly focused methods of research.

In order to evaluate the results of trials, it is necessary to restore context by establishing the results' coherence with other research data and with clinical experience. To summarise, the randomised trial is without peer for testing a hypothesis, and the adaption of control measures originally developed in such trials for application to non-randomised studies has made an important contribution to research methodology. However, the random-ised trial has only a restricted application because control of variables is often problematic in complex health care contexts. In addition, there are problems with ethical constraints, high costs and duration of the study which makes it unsuitable for the study of 'moving target' technologies, those which continue to mature in their technical aspects and clinical application during the period of the trial.

Should a randomised trial prove to be unethical or otherwise impractical, as is often the case, the powerful technique of comparing outcome with and without intervention need not be abandoned. As Christel Woodward has shown, there exists a rich range of non-randomised comparative methods developed in the social sciences and epidemiology which have the virtue of greater flexibility, albeit at the cost of reduced control over error. Evidence for their wide applicability is provided by her examples. Thus there are the quasi-experimental studies such as those using non-randomised concurrent or historical controls or cohort analytical or case-control designs. The drawback of greater difficulty in controlling variables can be partially overcome by meticulous attention to counteracting specific 'threats to validity', utilising lessons learnt from the structure of randomised trials.

Of all the study designs the one most widely used is the survey. In many ways the survey is a compromise, lacking the control of the comparative study and the detail of the field study but being extremely flexible in gathering data from many everyday contexts in a structured form. Data on a large range of variables from large samples, analysed quantitatively, can be used for testing pre-specified hypotheses and for explanation and pre-diction. Woodward provides examples of cross-sectional and longitudinal studies generating important health care findings. As might be expected, such studies are an important source of further more detailed hypotheses. Such observational studies do have problems with regard to distinguishing cause-and-effect relationships from co-variation and association of vari-ables. They also have the problem that the investigator has to prejudge which are the important variables, and questionnaires may limit or pre-determine answers so that respondents may not understand or not be able to present their own experience.

The strength of surveys is obviously in their versatility, and this can be further enhanced by refinements such as skilful administration of a questionnaire by telephone; and their validity can be enhanced by attention to detail and careful training of interviewers. John McKinlay demonstrates how this can allow surveys' extensive use in the study of the elderly, and Jake Najman used survey techniques for a study of pregnancy.

When the objective is to study people in their everyday context, exercising only that degree of scientific control which is necessary to ensure valid observation, the obvious method to use is the field study using qualitative data analysis. The methods of observation are usually interview, direct observation and analysis of existing documentary evidence. Analysis is by the interpretation of what may be a wide variety of kinds of data collected in the field. The method is especially important where we know very little about a particular area and where the social contexts of people's lives is of critical significance. Examples are to be found in David Silverman's work on the study of problems encountered in talking about safe sex in the AIDS era, and in Jeanne Daly and co-workers' study on the notion of reassurance of anxious patients using diagnostic tests.

As data is collected, a reasoned argument is built up by a constant interplay, a dialectic, between concepts emerging from the data collected and pertinent theory. The process of analysis is simply inductive and deductive reasoning, using comparison as an important tactic, as stressed by Robert Dingwall; if appropriate, quantitation may be used as one form of data reduction. Precautions against error must be as stringent as possible, as in *all* study designs. David Silverman shows that, when considering the reliability of data and credibility of conclusions, in this case particular emphasis is placed on the convincing nature of the argument used to present the data and draw theoretical conclusions.

An important problem confronting the field study is that sample sizes are generally small, selected for theoretical reasons, and are thus not statistically representative of a larger population. This means that statistical notions of the generalisability of conclusions are not applicable. Instead, any qualitative research must present an argument concerning the degree of generalisability of conclusions. An important aspect of this argument, and of the argument concerning the reliability of findings, is coherence with the existing body of research in the field and with theory. Of course coherence of findings with existing evidence in the literature is the ultimate test of any scientific theory, as we have illustrated already in the case of the randomised trial.

An obvious fact, often overlooked in discussions of research method, is that a single piece of research commonly involves more than one study design. Jeanne Daly illustrates how quantitative and qualitative assessments could be used to mutually reinforce one another within the framework of a single study. David Newell describes how a strategy combining a randomised trial and qualitative method could be used so that the results mutually reinforce each other, with the trial structure providing a high degree of confidence in overall outcome evaluation and the qualitative data used to tease meaning out of its results and to answer questions about process.

## CHOICE OF STUDY DESIGN

A basic question is whether we really choose the most appropriate research method to address a problem, or is the method chosen for us by the specific questions to be answered, in combination with our commitment to maximum scientific rigour and the limitations of the context of research. We find the solution of algebraic simultaneous equations to be a useful analogy. In these equations, the constraints to the value of variables x, y and z are in the form of three equations relating them, and only one value for each will provide a valid solution. Similarly, when we are planning research, we are constrained by the specific questions, by the commitment to scientific rigour and by the inevitable limitations of a technical and social nature inherent in the context of the research. The optimal solution to these three simultaneous constraints is the optimal basic research design.

In the case of health care, when questions of importance have been prioritised by a funding body, we may have no degrees of freedom left in making our basic choice of study design. Should the questions be the effectiveness and safety of a drug, maximum scientific rigour would demand a randomised trial, on the assumption that this is ethically reasonable, that staff will co-operate and that finance is available. If the question concerns regional variation in the use of a surgical procedure, then a survey would be most appropriate. If the question concerns the subtleties of behaviour of AIDS patients, their attitudes and understanding of safe sex, then only a field study will be appropriate, assuming that the study is ethical and that the people most concerned are willing to involve themselves in the research.

## IDEOLOGY AS THE VILLAIN

If we accept the above argument as reasonable and logical, then we have to look elsewhere for most of the difficulty encountered in discussions of research study methods. As we foreshadowed, behind disagreements and misunderstandings is often something as fundamental as how science is to be defined. To some, such as Lord Rutherford, only physics was science and all else 'mere stamp collecting'. The dominant doctrine here is reductionism, which insists that all phenomena must be explained at the lowest possible level of interaction of variables. This thinking runs counter to the modern conception of the behaviour of complex systems and their emergent properties; to accept it would rule out the study of human beings or social phenomena. To Lord Kelvin, quantitation was the essential feature of science, a highly restrictive view in the case of research into clinical care in which so much of importance is of a qualitative nature. A softer version of these positions sees experimental control, preferably achieved in a laboratory, as a *sine qua non* of scientific research; the medical equivalent is the obsession with the randomised trial as the only way to evaluate anything in health care. Then there are those to whom only the testing of hypotheses is science, which would exclude the highly creative act of generating the most important questions and of observing with an open mind.

There is also the notion that there is something intrinsically inferior about research with no immediate application in view, a conceit refuted and placed in its historical context by Medawar. Finally there is the insistence on objectivity as a central plank of the positivist position. As an absolute requirement, this did not survive quantum theory. Although inter-subjective understanding is a worthy objective, in the social sciences, the rigid distinction between observer and observed which can be maintained for an inanimate object cannot be expected in the case of one human being observing another.

In contrast to these restrictive conceptions of the nature of science, to many great scientists and thinkers, among whom are included Einstein and Francis Bacon, the key is not to be found in procedure but in an attitude of mind – rigorous intellectual discipline as espoused by Bridgman: 'There is no scientific method as such but the vital feature of a scientist's procedure has been merely to do his damnedest with his mind, no holds barred' (quoted in Mills, 1959). Those who subscribe to this broader view of science will certainly have less difficulty accommodating epistemological views which are valid but different to their own.

## THE PENALTY FOR FAILURE

If our reasoning is accepted, then the characteristics of health care research will be an eclectic choice of research methods, joined together in the form of appropriate strategy for difficult problems. These requirements assume inter-disciplinary co-operation since few of us live long enough to become expert in more than a narrow range of research study designs. Failure to appreciate this will condemn health care research to irrelevant and often expensive studies and generally distort its direction. The same problems afflicting editorial policy will correspondingly distort the health care literature. Most researchers, free to pose questions of their own choice, are therefore able to apply their own well-developed methods to answer them, and apply for funding to a funding body known to be sympathetic. They may never be called upon to defend their epistemological assumptions and, at worst, may not even be aware of them. But if researchers at the coal face of health care research are to work together, they must learn at least to understand a smattering of each others' languages.

## REFERENCES

Mills, C.W., 1959, *The Sociological Imagination*, Harmondsworth: Penguin.

# Name index

# Subject index